THE GANG

THE GANG

A STUDY IN ADOLESCENT BEHAVIOR

HERBERT A. BLOCH
Professor of Sociology and Anthropology,
BROOKLYN COLLEGE

&

ARTHUR NIEDERHOFFER
Lieutenant,
POLICE DEPARTMENT, N. Y. C.

GREENWOOD PRESS, PUBLISHERS
WESTPORT, CONNECTICUT

Library of Congress Cataloging in Publication Data

Bloch, Herbert Aaron, 1904-1965.
　The gang.

　　Reprint of the ed. published by Philosophical Library, New York.
　　Bibliography: p.
　　1. Gangs. 2. Adolescence. 3. Juvenile delinquency.
I. Niederhoffer, Arthur, joint author. II. Title.
HQ796.B47　1976　　　301.43'15　　　76-6517
ISBN 0-8371-8865-2

Copyright 1958 by Philosophical Library

Originally published in 1958 by Philosophical Library, New York

Reprinted with the permission of Philosophical Library, Inc.

Reprinted in 1976 by Greenwood Press,
a division of Williamhouse-Regency Inc.

Library of Congress Catalog Card Number 76-6517

ISBN 0-8371-8865-2

Printed in the United States of America

CONTENTS

PREFACE   XI

PART I   ADOLESCENT GROUPS AND THE GANG: LIMITATIONS IN OUR UNDERSTANDING   XVII

CHAPTER I   1

Introduction   1

Some Preliminary Considerations of the Gang and the Adolescent Group   1

    Some Outworn Concepts Concerning the Gang   6

    The Gang Label as Applied to Economically Underprivileged Groups   7

    Delinquency as a Characteristic of All Adolescent Groups   8

    Organizational Structure of Adolescent Groups and the Boys' Gang   9

    Group Characteristics of Adolescence   10

    Adolescence as a Striving Towards Social Maturity   11

    The Essential Group Nature of Delinquent Acts   13

    An Hypothesis for the Study of Adolescent Group Behavior   15

CHAPTER II   19

Fundamental Shortcomings in Our Knowledge of Adolescence   19

  Anthropological Biases in the Study of Adolescence   22
  Puberty Rites and Gang Rituals   25

PART II   ADOLESCENT GROUPS IN CROSS CULTURAL PERSPECTIVE   33

CHAPTER III

Puberty Rites: Their Form and Meaning

  The Age and Sex Worlds in Which We Live   35
  Protective Subterfuges of Children   38
  Age-Level Conflicts   42
  Emotional Maturity   44
  The Psychological Components of the Child's and Adolescent's World   46
  The Inversion of Dependent Relationships   49

CHAPTER IV   53

Puberty Rites: Their Form and Meaning (Continued)   53

  Self Decoration   55
  Circumcision   60
  Acquisition of a New Name and Language   61
  Conditions Associated with Age Segregation and Breaking of the Household Tie   67
  Sexual Ambivalence and Homosexuality   74

The Myth of Rebirth of the Adolescent Novice	82
Classification and Description of Puberty Rites TABLE I	86

CHAPTER V — 95

The Contemporary "Rites" of Adolescence — 95

    I. Decoration by Adolescents in Our Society — 95

    II. Acquisition of a New Name and a New Language — 99

    III. Seclusion from Women, Bachelor Huts, Age Grades — 100

    IV. Break from the Home and Assimilation by the New Group — 101

    V. Sexual Ambivalence and Homosexuality — 103

    VI. Hazing and Ordeal to Prove Fitness to Become Members of the Group — 106

    VII. Element of Economic Profit for the Older Men — 106

    VIII. Education for New Roles and Incorporation into Men's Groups — 107

    IX. The Sex Fertility Theme in Puberty Rites — 110

    X. Death and Rebirth Myth — 111

Postscript — 113

CHAPTER VI — 115

The Universal Pattern of Adolescent Striving — 115

CHAPTER VII 133

  The Ganging Process As Symbolic Evidence of the Urge to Manhood 133

    Case 1: The Mundugumor 133
    Case 2: The Manus 134
    Case 3: The Kaffir 134
    Case 4: The Comanche and Plains Indians 135

CHAPTER VIII 138

  Summary: Society and Adolescence 138

PART III YOUTH AND THE SPIRIT OF OUR TIMES 141

CHAPTER IX 143

  Contemporary Adolescence and Delinquency: Some General Observations 143

    Adolescent Crime in New York City During 1955
    TABLE II 147

CHAPTER X 153

  Cultural Drifts: Anxiety and Conformity 153
    Anxiety and Conformity 153
    Alienation 155

CHAPTER XI 161

  The Gang Philosophy 161
    The Gang Definition of the Situation 161
    How the Gang Sees Life and People 167

CHAPTER XII	175
Theories of Delinquent Gangs: A Critique	175
CHAPTER XIII	183
The Automobile	183
CHAPTER XIV	186
Adolescence as a Social Movement	186
PART IV A STUDY OF A LOWER CLASS DELINQUENT GANG	191
CHAPTER XV	193
The Sociological Setting	193
CHAPTER XVI	201
Leadership and the Power Situation	201
1 Paulie	201
2 Lulu	202
3 Solly, the Diplomat	202
4 Blacky, Leader and Buffoon	204
Summary	205
Diagram of the Gang Power Structure TABLE III	206
Translation from Political Power to a Gang Power Situation	207
Postscript	215

CONCLUSIONS

    Decoration   218
    Age Grades   218
    Education of the Novices   217
    Profit for the Elders   218
    Sexual Ambivalence   218
    Quality and Extent of Crime   219
    Anxiety and Alienation   219

Selected Bibliography   221

PREFACE

Each age and each society tends to look upon its young with mingled and troubled feelings. Aside from the deep and powerful attachments with which the life-giving generation regards its successor, there are the equally profound feelings of concern, anxiety, and even resentment, towards the young who are said to represent our "best hopes" for the future. They are, in fact, our only hope.

The hopes we entertain towards our young, however, are frequently the result of our own exasperated frustrations. Without fully appreciating the great creative principle embodied in the emergence of each generation, we frequently fix upon such renascent groups our own outworn hopes and ambitions, our bitterness and sense of fury with life. The young, forever tractable and forever resistant, respond in varying degree to the sanctions of yesterday which our own aspirations impose upon them. For each age and time, the perennial question arises as to how much freedom and how much power should be accorded to our young in the search for their own future and their own destiny. Or, to frame the issue differently, the question becomes one of determining how much freedom should be allowed to the young in determining their own identity, both cultural and individual.

Youth, however, does not walk into the future with gaily tripping and eager footsteps. Youth, too, has its own fears, its own dark forebodings, and its own misgivings. As eager as the young people of our own age and culture seem to be to embrace the responsibilities of adulthood and maturity, their steps are often faltering and lagging, delayed and halting. It is possible perhaps, as we may have done, to draw out the childhood years into such a prolonged state of dependent care that the goal of adulthood may only be seen by the young in a kind of distorted and myopic haze. When this occurs, it is not uncommon to find that the emergent adult leaving the chrysalis of his adolescence and childhood behind him may regard his new state as a form of deserved patronage by the society which has reared him. The "impatient years," as we have more recently come to regard the adolescent period, frequently make their demand for adult fulfillment without adequate understanding of and preparation for the responsibilties which maturity betokens in any society, no matter how this maturity may be regarded. For, maturity is a social conception, far more than biological, and each youth represents a hostage to the future and to his own destiny. Each age and each society has to wrestle with this problem and how it resolves such a dilemma determines not only the careers of its young but the course of its own history.

During the past three decades, there seems to have been more than the usual concern for adolescence in our society, although the expression of this concern has deep roots in American society. Even prior to the period of the "roaring twenties," the Great Depression of 1929, the Second World War, and the Korean struggle, Americans have given evidence of their great concern for adolescence. There are many reasons for this, as this book tries to show. However, our concern has become far more acute, it appears, within the present and the recent past. Some of this concern, perhaps, stems from the fact that, in recognizing the deeply disturbing revolutionary period through which we are passing in world history, we place increasingly heavy demands upon our young in asking them to confront the recurrent and shattering crises of our day. It is upon our young that we place the heaviest responsibility of all—to give their lives, if necessary, in the preservation of "a world which they have never made." The uneasy legacy of conflict and cultural confusion which we pass on to our young provokes within ourselves a sense of misgiving as to whether we have given them an understanding and appreciation, as well as a sense of fitness and moral and psychological strength, for the burdens which will soon be theirs.

But these problems, as pressing and immediate as they

appear, are not alone true of our generation and our time. The great critical turning points in history have always raised these doubts in men's minds. What makes these considerations particularly pressing at this time is that the problems of adolescence appear unduly urgent and seem to have acquired a new social and psychological dimension. Proceeding through a period when the intransigence of our young appears particularly marked, as evidenced in the public concern over the so-called "delinquency problem," and when the psychological excesses of our adolescents appear somehow distinct from previous generations, we appear to press more eagerly for answers.

But is the problem of modern youth much different from the problems of previous generations? Is it much different from the problem of the "flaming youth" of F. Scott Fitzgerald's day, the "lost generation" of Ernest Hemingway, and the "flapper" of a scant generation ago who is now the mother of the present "rock and roll" addicted teen-ager? There probably are differences, as this book will try to show, neither as vast nor as small as popularly imagined, but differences which reflect the contemporary world in which we are living. If "mutiny in conformity" is a characteristic of modern adolescent youth, then it seems to echo strangely the kind of conformity which has become so much a part of all of our lives.

More important, perhaps, is the impressive similarity of adolescent crisis in all cultures and in all times. This, the present book tries to show in great detail by analyzing the adolescent period in a great variety, and in a large number of different societies. What particularly intrigued the imagination of the authors was the structure and power of the adolescent group in all cultures—the nature of the bonds which integrate the adolescent to his group with such fanatical loyalty and the characteristics of the peculiar adolescent group structure. Similarities were found in all societies and on all social levels, resulting not so much from the physiological changes of adolescence itself, but from the social necessity to confront the demands of the new adult status. In appraising the social and psychological characteristics which seemed on the one hand so similar, and on the other so distinct for each group, new light seemed to be shed upon the characteristics of the urban boys' gang. Indeed, the formation of such gangs, as distasteful as they may appear to families, civic bodies, and law enforcement agencies, appears to be almost inevitable, given certain conditions of social structure and cultural training.

In the first part of this book, the authors deal with some of our confused and contradictory outlooks concerning adolescent groups and gang behavior. Limitations in our understanding of adolescent group activity, and the reasons for such limitations, are explored. This lack appears particularly striking in view of the great strides forward made recently by the so-called behavioral sciences and the contemporary concern with the problems of the adolescent age-group. In the second part of this volume, a detailed and voluminous survey is made of adolescent behavior in a wide variety of primitive and modern cultures, with special reference made to the way in which these findings apply to the youth in our own culture. In the course of our investigations, incidental light is shed upon the function of other age-groups in our society, as well as adolescents. In the last section of this volume, pertinent conclusions are drawn, based upon contemporary findings in sociology, psychology, and psychiatry, in respect to modern gang and adolescent phenomena. Many of these processes are highlighted in the analysis of the structure and behavior of a typical predatory boys' gang which has been carefully studied and observed.

There are many debts which the authors of a volume such as this are free to acknowledge. Our principal obligation is extended to those pioneers in the social sciences, particularly in the field of anthropology, who have painstakingly and carefully compiled an impressive array of data describing the life of cultures completely alien to our own. We extend, as well, our debt to those few specialists who have devoted themselves, albeit for varying periods of time, to the study of the gang itself. In this respect, the pioneer work of Frederic Thrasher and the more recent work of Albert K. Cohen should be singled out for attention. In the field of anthropology, the work of Margaret Mead and Ruth Benedict has provided a rich source of information for which not only the authors, but social scientists in general, might well stand in continued debt. To Adeline S. Bloch, whose tireless efforts and unremitting assistance in this work as in so many others can never be adequately repaid, one of the authors make humble and profoundly grateful acknowledgment; while to Elaine Niederhoffer, whose stimulating and perceptive insight made a significant contribution to this enterprise, deep tribute is likewise paid. The authors likewise wish to acknowledge their gratitude to Miss Maureen Oshever for typing assistance rendered in completing the first portion of this manuscript.

In conclusion, it should be noted that the views expressed are solely the opinions of the authors and in no way should be construed as reflecting the policies of the New York City Police Department.

H. A. B.
A. N.

PART I

ADOLESCENT GROUPS AND THE GANG:
LIMITATIONS IN OUR UNDERSTANDING

CHAPTER I

INTRODUCTION

Some Preliminary Considerations of the Gang and the Adolescent Group

This book is the joint venture of a sociologist with considerable experience in the field of correction and penology, and a sociologically trained police officer. For somewhat different reasons, and from different vantage points, both authors became interested in a common problem—the observed similarities among adolescent groups within different contexts and on different social levels. What was particularly intriguing was the existence of such similarities where there was ample theoretical reason to question the existence of such facts and the marked tendency of society, despite such similarities, to label some of these groups as "good" and others as "bad." Upon investigating certain common impulses towards adolescent associations and gang behavior, it was found that police and academic specialists both, and for reasons which were not so dissimilar, entertained attitudes towards such groups which were inclined to be largely pragmatic and circumstantial.

The plain facts are that despite the frantic excursions and alarums being raised about teen-age crime, violence, and gang warfare, and the ofttimes pompous and learned words which have been said, there is actually so little known about the boys' gang and the adolescent group. Further, despite the relativistic conceptions of group behavior which infuse the entire modern sociological tradition, it was intellectually disconcerting to discover that adolescent groups widely separated in cultural orientation and geographic location maintained certain profound behavioral similarities. As the research unfolded, it was found that such similarities existed even in the absence of cultural contact and diffusion, and frequently, despite the development of widely different cultural traditions.

Prompted by a lively professional interest and a broad sociological background, the authors were impressed with the meagerness of information concerning the gang and the ease with which offhand judgments were delivered concerning the reasons for adolescent gang behavior and its several manifestations. In academic as well as in more practical circles, the frequent observations and generalizations about adolescent group behavior have rarely been subjected to penetrating empirical investigation nor adequately interpreted. Certainly, such observations have never been integrated into a comprehensive theory of group behavior.

The sociologically oriented police officer, youth patrolman and youth worker, despite occasional efforts towards sophistication, is apt to respond to adolescent gangs on the basis of familiar stereotypes, reflecting broad neighborhood, class, and ethnic characteristics. Much of the misunderstanding involved in handling such groups might be obviated if a clearcut comprehension of the natural processes involved in adolescent group behavior could be obtained. Many of the bitter outcries and loud denunciations of modern youth "going to the dogs" might be averted if we had a better understanding of how such social and psychological processes operated. Instead of acrimonious denunciation, we might be able to build constructively upon group processes which, now largely misunderstood, frequently produce or intensify deeply inlaid anti-social attitudes.

But there is a concern beyond such seemingly commendable objectives in the study of adolescent groups. There is a genuine need for a theoretical framework upon which adequate scientific understanding and analysis may be undertaken in relation to a problem which is of such vital urgency to modern society. For, without such a sound theoretical framework, the meaning of much adolescent behavior eludes us and falls beyond our ready understanding. During an age which cries for action and decries theoretical discussion, this lesson comes hard. It is sometimes difficult to perceive that a fundamental understanding of human behavior may only be gained through adequate theoretical insight. Theoretical analysis, in delineating the relationships between the individual and his group, and the place of such relationships in the entire social matrix, sheds light upon what would otherwise remain a set of isolated facts. For, facts do not speak for themselves, contrary to popular impression, but derive meaning only in relation to the attitudes and value-judgments which individuals bring to them. The true meaning of theoretical analysis, if it be sound, is to indicate clearly the function conveyed by one set of facts to a larger series of facts. Thus, only in the light of the function which adolescent group behavior serves in relation to the larger context of society can the true meaning of such behavior be portrayed. This type of insight, unfortunately, is sorely lacking in our understanding of adolescent behavior today.

Until last year, when Albert K. Cohen's *Delinquent Boys: The Culture of the Gang*[1] appeared on the scene, sociologists, with very few exceptions, either ignored the subject or simply repeated with tiresome monotony the tenuous observations derived from Thrasher's well-known work in the field.[2] Explanations as to the presence and concentration of boys' gangs, largely held to be anti-social, followed certain well-worn patterns. It might be well to examine some of these patterns.

Most of the explanations seeking to explore the critical aspects of gang behavior have either concentrated upon the descriptions of broad behavioral processes at work within the gang, or have attempted to show how they were related to certain aspects of urban life. In the case of the first approach, the explanations were largely on a broad descriptive level, relying principally upon reportorial accounts of what possibly transpired within the gang with a brief background glance at some of the most salient factors which may have contributed to such behavior patterns. In the case of the second view, geographically and ecologically oriented, gang behavior has been visualized as existing primarily in a spatial continuum. Within this ecological framework, gang behavior has been seen as resulting wholly or in part from the impact of certain phases of acute urban disintegration. This school, largely ecological in nature, has been aptly described as the "social disorganization" school of gang behavior. Although limitations of this type of study have been known for some time, not only in relation to studies of gang behavior but in relation to the examination of almost any phase of group behavior, studies of the gang have given little evidence of such awareness. Very recently, Herbert Blumer, for example, has shown how inadequate studies of this type are in attempting to establish relationships between two complex systems of variables (such as neighborhood conditions and gang behavior, for example), as if such related conditions were simply unitary and elementary forces operating in urban life.[3] The attempt to explain such a complex behavior pattern as gang activity, including as it does a variety of personal and social needs and producing a unique age-group structure of its own, can hardly be adequately described on the basis of the relationship between such broad concepts as "neighborhood" or "physical residence" and the equally complex conditions of age and puberty tendencies.

The view of neighborhood-determined gang behavior has been widely popular among sociologists and even now enjoys widespread currency. For example, until relatively recently, sociologists tended to subscribe, with certain reservations, to the concentric circle theory or gradient hypothesis, identified for many years with the ecological and "social disorganization" school of the University of Chicago. This well-nigh classical view attempted to show the existence of a progressively declining rate of delinquency from the center to the periphery of large urban areas and close correlations between areas of disorganization (referred to as "zones in transition") and delinquency.

Despite the popularity of this view since the 1920s, it has been consistently demonstrated that such concentrations of rates of delinquency and gang behavior do not apply to most American cities. This has been amply demonstrated by Maurice R. Davie, among others, who concluded on the basis of his research that there is no regular pattern of city growth.[4] More recently, Lander has shown by an impressive statistical analysis of Baltimore census tracts that these ecological theories, originally suggested by Professors Park and Burgess, are not applicable to this area.[5] Even when accurate, spatial or geographical theories of this type merely state the distribution of such phenomena as gang behavior and delinquency but offer little in the way of a searching explanation as to why such distributions take the form they do. Interpretations as to why variations in delinquency occur within the *same* zones or zones marked by the *same* social character are hardly ever explored. Auxiliary explanations are sometimes offered or secondary hypotheses may be suggested, but it is rare indeed to find efforts towards rational and comprehensive explanations based upon carefully controlled or related factual evidence.

Lander, for example, in illustrating the inadequacy of the conventional ecological explanation as applied to the city of Baltimore, suggests that the primary factor in controlling the volume of delinquency may be the cultural homogeneity or heterogeneity of a given area. In following a trend which appears to have become intellectually fashionable, he suggests as an explanation of varying rates the concept developed by the great French sociologist, Durkheim—the concept of *anomie,* i.e., normlessness, as the primary determinant of delinquent behavior. Although conditions of sociocultural diversity and heterogeneity are undoubtedly productive of various types of social disorder and dysfunction, the mere statement of such a condition tells us very little unless carefully articulated in terms of special relationships and how they operate to produce the problem specified. Actually, the assumption of such a condition as "*anomie,*" unless carefully delineated in terms of special conditions and specific effects, is meaningless as a causal explanation and is not even a very well informed guess.

Despite repeated criticisms of ecological and related views concerning gang behavior and delinquency, sociologists still tend to repeat the oft-cited corollary to such views, *viz.,* that gang behavior is a product of interstitial areas in which the conditions of poor housing, inadequate recreational facilities, poor schools, low economic status, deficient civic services, ethnic differences and a variety of other conditions combine to destroy a sense of communal solidarity. It is rare that one finds precise demarcation of factual evidence, with efforts to relate the precise effects of such variable conditions as types of resident populations, organizational networks in such areas, the impact of political machines, and a host of other factors which may function in such areas to produce the conditions observed. Still less are the effects of the complex interrelationships of such forces observed and interpreted.

Some Outworn Concepts Concerning The Gang

It might be well to consider what sociologists have traditionally held to be the meaning of a gang. Sociologists generally define an adolescent gang as a special type of age group, marked by a strong sense of solidarity and usually developing spontaneously from the play-group. It is generally considered a conflict group, often delinquent. Thrasher, frequently regarded as an outstanding authority on the sociology of the gang because of his previously mentioned pioneering work in this area, has added the idea of *movement* to the concept of the gang as an important associated characteristic. In this, he may have been influenced by the etymology of the term, since it is generally regarded as being derived from the Anglo-Saxon *gang*, signifying the process of moving or "going." The gang, as an integrated and highly *mobile* unit, has frequently been taken for granted. Whereas this may have been true of the gang in its original form, and is still largely characteristic of the gang in its present state as a group characterized by acute psychological restlessness, it certainly does not seem to apply to some of the more conspicuous manifestations of gang behavior as observed in many of our larger cities.

Observations of gang behavior in various neighborhoods of New York City, for example, seem to reveal just the opposite to be true. In fact, one of the outstanding characteristics of numerous gangs which have been observed appears to be their highly non-mobile and stationary nature, a fact to which many exasperated shopkeepers and building custodians, as well as the police, can amply testify. Gangs, thus, might just as well be characterized by an absence of movement since, for the most part, they frequent the same corner or candy store for hours on end, every day of the week.

The Gang Label as Applied to Economically Underprivileged Groups

It is rather striking that the gang as a descriptive concept has become rather peculiarly reserved for adolescent groups of low socioeconomic status. Upon close examination, in fact, it might well be said with considerable justice that the term, "gang," has an invidious coloration and has been applied by middle class sociologists to what they consider to be a uniquely lower class phenomenon. Rarely in sociological literature are middle class adolescent groups referred to as gangs, irrespective of their similarity to their lower economic-class counterparts. Such groups are more commonly referred to as peer groups, cliques, or clubs.

Actually, however, it becomes extremely difficult upon occasion to draw a clear line of distinction between such lower and middle class groups. If, for example, conflict or hostility to the out-group is one of the criteria of gang behavior, middle class groups are certainly not exempt from such a characterization. In respect to the perennial conflict between groups of adolescent youths and adult citizens, evidenced in the verbal and more direct "pushing and shoving" contests centering upon the aimless "milling around" in the vicinity of doorways, corner stores and other private premises, middle class youths are just as apt to be offenders as their slum-dwelling age mates. And, it should be noted, with considerably less justification—if justification must be sought—in view of the fact that there is not the same denial of access to playgrounds and recreational facilities as is more commonly believed to be true of their less fortunate contemporaries. Any evening, in our large cities, one can see storekeepers and residents of middle class neighborhoods arguing with these boys to remove them from the premises of a store or away from a street corner. Moreover, this applies to favorably advantaged youths who, ordinarily, do not lack the appointments of comfortable homes, playrooms, and well-equipped and established meeting places.

If we extend the concept of conflict over into the sexual sphere, middle class youths are marked by the same type of internal conflicts as their lower class brothers. In fact, the expression of these conflicts may even take more violent and disturbing form. The incidence of sexual conflict may be even more acute for middle class youths in view of the strain induced by the internalization of middle class values in a highly sex-conscious culture.

Thus, if conflict against the out-group in its various ramifications is seen as a ubiquitous characteristic of the gang, then all adolescent groups in contemporary American society may be said to reflect this process in varying degree. In fact, the study of adolescent groups on the American scene would seem to confirm and give added emphasis to the one-sided, classical views of the sociologist, Gumplowicz, that the process of conflict is fundamental to the development and survival of all groups.

Delinquency as a Characteristic of All Adolescent Groups

As far as the commission of delinquent acts is concerned, middle class adolescents, singly and in groups, participate in a variety of delinquent episodes, including such illegal activities as auto theft, operating a motor vehicle without a license, disorderly conduct, and a wide variety of other lawbreaking activities. The sociologist, Porterfield, as well as one of the writers, have shown the wide prevalence of delinquent activities among adolescent youths.[6] In fact, in the study made by Bloch college youths of considerably better than average economic circumstances, the vast majority (over 90 percent) of the young people studied of both sexes admitted to a variety of delinquent offenses ranging all the way from petty pilfering to manslaughter.

If precise legal technicalities were actually invoked in the case of the middle class, which they rarely are, middle class groups almost without exception would be found guilty of several sexual violations, as well as other grave infractions of the penal statutes. On the basis of direct experience, the writers have been impressed with the relatively high frequency of such crimes among middle class youths which, in the technical preciseness of the law, might be defined as carnal abuse, assault with intent to rape, impairing the morals of a minor, and seduction. Because of their prevalence in the youth culture of middle class America, it almost seems fitting to consider such practices as distorted phases of the normal behavior patterns of teen-age dating and courtship practice.

Organizational Structure of Adolescent Groups and The Boys' Gang

In respect to the type of organizational structure, there is little to distinguish, in one sense, between middle and lower class adolescent groups. Although middle class groups of teen-agers are not as apt to have the formal, almost military, structure characteristic of certain lower class "war gangs," like the present Chaplains and Gaylords in New York City, yet they do have similar and well-defined informal patterns of leadership and control. Even here, however, the distinctions become blurred and, upon occasion, almost indistinguishable when one recalls the ceremonial designations and ritualistic roles performed by college fraternity functionaries.

While the conditions of middle class life do not tend to accentuate in the same manner and degree the need for rigid structural associations, manifested in the form of honorific titles and clearly articulated rights and responsibilities of adolescent group members, the same ingredients and motivations may be found in middle class groups as among the economically unprivileged. Criteria for the assumption of leadership, the delegation of responsibilities, and the induction of new members follow strikingly similar patterns.

Group solidarity is just as strong on one class level as the other. Even as we move into the somewhat exalted atmosphere of the college fraternity, many of these characteristics are clearly in evidence, seemingly coming to light most clearly in the kinds of devoted loyalty which all adolescent groups seem to call forth, irrespective of class, ethnic and cultural level.

Group Characteristics of Adolescence

From the foregoing discussion, it would appear that many of the distinctive features which distinguish the gang from middle class cliques are primarily a matter of degree. Actually, what we are concerned with here are the general characteristics of the adolescent grouping process itself. May we assume that there are certain common features of this grouping process which appear to function irrespective of class, ethnic, and cultural level? Examination of the evidence of group behavior, characteristic of adolescents not only on different class levels within the same culture but even within widely divergent cultures, would seem to suggest that adolescence produces certain remarkable similarities in the group behavior of the young person striving for adulthood.

On the basis of the evidence which the authors have examined with painstaking detail, there is ample reason to justify the position that the best overall view for understanding the gang, as well as other adolescent groups, is to regard them as particular manifestations of the general grouping process upon a given age level. Observed differences among the several adolescent groups examined can be seen to be related to age, class, ethnic, and individual personality variations from group to group.

If we begin to discern clearly the underlying patterns which motivate most adolescents in their group associations, then we begin to recognize the role which adolescence itself plays within a given culture. In fact, we begin to obtain a far more clear picture as to what adolescence itself signifies and connotes within a wide variety of different cultures. Particularly impressive in the emergent picture is the fact that adolescence presents certain basic similarities in all cultures, irrespective of the differences between the cultures themselves. It should be helpful, therefore, to consider briefly how sociologists regard and define this critical stage in the social maturation of the individual.

Adolescence as a Striving Towards Social Maturity

Among sociologists, there is general agreement that adolescence is roughly that period of life that comes between biological and sociological maturity. Observations of many societies would appear to indicate rather clearly that the wider the disparity between these two levels of maturity, the greater the area of adolescent problems and the more acute the experience of adolescent strain. Actually, however, societies differ in the degree to which they will accord normal adult status to the young person in respect to the various conceptions of adult status. Fundamentally, as Frankwood Williams has put it, adolescence represents an effort of the young person to emancipate himself from the constricting bonds of his own family and to establish a basis for normal heterosexual relations.[7] If this is broken down into the fundamental categories of its full meaning, this signifies that adult status is ordinarily accorded when the individual is given the right to participate within the socially defined limits of normative adult behavior in respect to (a) sexual, (b) economic, and (c) civic and ritualistic responsibilities.

What confuses the picture of adolescence in most modern industrial societies is the ambiguity with which the adolescent role itself is defined. In societies where there exists a well defined conception of the adolescent role as part of the total social structure, and where the adolescent not only has an accepted status in respect to his social participation but recognizes the limitations imposed by this status, adolescent problems as we regard them are not likely to occur.

A serious problem which emerges in most societies, however, arises as a result of the variations with which many societies accord adult status for the several levels towards which the individual is striving in his quest for maturity. A society may permit considerable freedom in one sphere—sexual behavior, for example—but be highly restrictive in relation to the attainment of full economic status. Among other societies, serious restrictions may be imposed upon the young in respect to ceremonial participation, while granting considerable freedom of expression in the attainment of sexual and economic maturity. To further complicate the process, even when certain adult privileges are granted, the major sphere of adult activity may be denied to the young because of competitive reasons, with the result that the remaining privileges granted to adolescents may pale into insignificance or become vitally affected. In our own society for example, as Talcott Parsons, Kingsley Davis and others have pointed out, serious tensions may arise because the adult male may regard the rising young male adult as a serious competitor in the economic world.[8] This, in turn, may have certain serious repercussions in respect to the permissiveness given to such young adults in their sexual behavior.

In sociological terminology, the problems of adolescence resolve themselves into the capacity and willingness of a given culture to permit the growing youth to fulfill certain defined roles governing family life, work, and sexual behavior. For the individual adolescent, the problems may not necessarily occur as a result of obstacles placed by his elders towards the fulfillment of these roles. They may arise because of internal psychological strain occasioned by his own feelings of inadequacy, fear, and personal disability, themselves produced by a variety of social pressures.

In our own society, because of a complex of historic, economic and technological reasons, there is an added issue which appears to exacerbate the adolescent problem. This is the tendency towards continuing prolongation of the adolescent period itself. In view of the prolonged duration of the adolescent period, as contrasted with societies all over the world, it becomes rather dubious to refer to such a period as "interstitial," as certain sociologists are still prone to do. It certainly appears ironic to employ such a designation for a span of life that may extend for a period of from ten to twenty years.

Such, in very brief condensation, is the general social conception which underlies the manifestation of adolescence and its problems. It is expressed in the view of many sociologists in their current writing. A typical description of adolescence representing the view of many reputable sociologists is that of August Hollingshead, as presented in his study of *Elmtown's Youth*. He says:

> Sociologically, adolescence is the period in the life of a person when the society in which he functions ceases to regard him (male or female) as a child and does not accord him full adult status, roles and functions.
>
> In terms of behavior it is defined by the roles the person is expected to play, is allowed to play, is forced to play, or prohibited from playing, by virtue of his status in society.
>
> Sociologically, the important thing about the adolescent years is the way people regard the maturing individual.[9]

Herbert Bloch has pointed out that in America, adolescent tensions and problems are widespread due to confusions in definition of adult status and what he regards as latencies in our society. He emphasizes with the support of considerable evidence that such problems do not exist with the same intensity or scope in many other societies.[10]

The Essential Group Nature of Delinquent Acts

Age groups constitute their own subcultures within the broader patterns of social life. Although not so readily recognized, this is even more true of those groups for whom the processes of institutional life have not defined adequately the character of common interests, responsibilities, and accepted values. Among adolescent groups, therefore, a good deal of the common interests which tend to foster an intensive institutional life of their own, arises from what appears to be a rejection of and by adult society, which refuses to accord to the adolescent a recognized status. In a sense, this is a subculture of negation in which the positive values of the prevailing culture are distorted and inverted for uses best suited to a philosophy of youthful dissidence and protest.

Much, if not all, of the seething unrest and occasional violent protest towards organized society which appears to be characteristic of adolescence in our society is either precipitated or reinforced by the intimate group contacts of adolescents with their own peers. The adolescent group constitutes a cultural milieu of its own, with its own biases, predilections, attitudes, values, and jargon, from which adults, even those most closely concerned with the individual adolescent's upbringing, are sedulously excluded.

It is difficult, therefore, to consider such a disturbing modern phenomenon as delinquency when removed from its provocative and group-supported setting of the gang or other intimate adolescent group. Such subcultural groups, as Fritz Redl has pointed out, maintain their own psychological atmosphere, their own techniques for ego-reinforcement, and their own cultural sanctions.[11] Except for the occasional delinquent act committed by the lone offender, rare and symptomatic of a deeply disturbed youngster, most juvenile delinquency is committed by groups or gangs rather than by individuals. While it is true that a good deal of delinquency appears on the public record as that of an individual, the actual facts of such episodes reveal their essentially group or gang nature.

Often, thus, the solitary boy caught by police burglarizing a store is the unlucky victim, while his accomplices escape. Upon investigation it may develop that several others were physically present during the commission of a crime; some may have served as lookouts, others may have lowered the apprehended victim by rope from the skylight on the roof, and still others may have been waiting in the "getaway" car. Frequently, a group of boys driving in a car are stopped by the police. The car in which they were driving turns out to be stolen or "borrowed"; yet, as a matter of legal expediency, only the driver will be brought to trial while the equally guilty passengers are usually dismissed in court. This, too, in the peculiar method of compiling criminal statistics, would be recorded as an individual crime rather than the joint offense of a group.

But to associate such offenses wholly with lower class

groups is hardly warranted. As the sociologist, Porterfield, has shown, middle class youths commit their own very considerable share of delinquency.[12] However such youths frequently do not pay the same penalties for their derelictions as do lower class youths. Nevertheless, in recognizing the group nature of delinquent acts, it is significant to note that the lower class youth, exposed to powerful instigating forces of his own milieu and subcultural setting, does tend to develop a unique delinquent subculture of his own, as Cohen has recently shown.[13] Differences in the qualitative nature of delinquency, as well as the character of the psychological and sociological reinforcement of the delinquent act, would appear to follow as a result of such class and cultural differences. In this sense, therefore, *viz.* that delinquent acts in a lower class setting receive strong sanctioned support and approval, Cohen's recent view that the locus of much delinquency is in the lower class gang may not be seriously disputed.

An Hypothesis for the Study of Adolescent Group Behavior

We shall attempt, therefore, to examine the adolescent grouping process in a broad ranging perspective. In our examination, we shall note similarities and differences, attempting to discover how such differences arising from a common and seemingly universal process reflect cultural peculiarities in the adolescent's immediate environment.

In order to carry out this objective, we have relied upon three types of material which appeared to be directly germane to our object of inquiry. (1) In the first place, we have undertaken an intensive cross-cultural survey and analysis of a variety of different societies and cultures in order to determine, by direct comparison, whether similarities in adolescent behavior actually exist. In this connection, it is relatively easy for the person who falls outside of the culture to detect similarities when actually they may not be said to exist. As a means of avoiding this pitfall, we have attempted only to recognize such similarities when the evidence appeared quite conclusive and overwhelming, and when the resemblances between certain forms of adolescent behavior seemed so striking as to render it difficult to exclude this as a possibility. Further, as a means of theoretical implementation, we have attempted whenever possible to assess the meaning of the subjective nature of their experiences to the youths of different cultures.

(2) Secondly, we have brought to bear upon our observations and investigations recent salient data from the several behavioral sciences, notably sociology, anthropology, social psychology and psychiatry, which appear to lend substantial weight to the character of the conclusions we have drawn. What the untrained layman frequently misunderstands—and this probably applies to a degree to the highly overspecialized behavior scientist himself—is the fact that the various sciences of human relations are remarkably agreed in their interpretations of certain forms of human interaction and behavior. In another connection, Professor Bloch has demonstrated this rather striking consensus which exists in respect to certain phases of modern social scientific thinking despite the seeming contradictions in theoretical orientation.[14]

(3) A study such as we propose, however, could not be successful unless it was undergirded as much as possible by certain types of direct observations and other forms of empirical support. A good observer attempts to appraise the material coming before his field of investigation in terms of a highly disciplined and directed form of perception.

Indeed, all observations in the social and psychological sciences, if they are truly valid, are a form of *selective* perception. Through controlled and planned observation of the structure of groups and their behavior, the authors have attempted to see whether the far-flung character of adolescent cultural characteristics elsewhere have their counterpart in American adolescent society.

By a process which the American sociologist, Alfred R. Lindesmith, refers to as analytical induction, derived from the theorist, Znaniecki, and supported by observed and validly reported evidence, the outlines of a previously formulated hypothesis began to take on more sharply defined contours and features.[15] This hypothesis will emerge in our further discussion and will be more precisely articulated in the following chapters.

However, its major emphasis is that the adolescent period in all cultures, visualized as a phase of striving for the attainment of adult status, produces experiences which are much the same for all youths, and certain common dynamisms for expressing reaction to such subjectively held experiences. The intensity of the adolescent experience and the vehemence of external expression depend on a variety of factors, including the general societal attitudes towards adolescence, the duration of the adolescent period itself, and the degree with which the society tends to facilitate entrance into adulthood by virtue of institutionalized patterns, ceremonials, rites, and rituals, and socially supported emotional and intellectual preparation. When a society does not make adequate preparation, formal or otherwise, for the induction of its adolescents to the adult status, equivalent forms of behavior arise spontaneously among adolescents themselves, reinforced by their own group structure, which seemingly provides the same psychological content and function as the more formalized rituals found in other societies. This the gang structure appears to do in American society, apparently satisfying deep-seated needs experienced by adolescents in all cultures.

Such, very briefly, is our hypothesis. If it can be substantiated wholly or in part, it should have important implications not only for the pragmatic handling of gangs and adolescent groups in our own culture, but should shed considerable light upon the character of our theoretical thinking concerning groups and group psychology. Among other issues that such a viewpoint raises is the serious challenge to much of our relativistic thinking in the social sciences and social psychology, premised upon the view that group behavior reflects almost wholly the cultural and social context in which it is found. At the least, such an hypothesis would cause us to have serious doubts as to whether the present relativistic view would not have to be revised in part to accommodate consideration of certain limited but universal behavior patterns characteristic of all age and sex groups. Certainly, we do not propose this at the present as a definitive conclusion. We simply suggest that this is a possibility which may now have to be seriously examined.

The following chapter in Part I will be devoted to an analytical discussion of anthropological and cross-cultural data bearing on the subject of adolescent association, in which we have brought together the findings from a large number of widely dissimilar, as well as similar, cultures. In Part II, we will attempt to draw certain pertinent psychiatric and psychological inferences from the data we have gathered, supporting these inferences whenever possible from materials drawn from the behavioral sciences, but principally psychiatry and psychology. Part III will present a detailed study of an adolescent group drawn from actual observations and supported by selected observations of gang behavior elsewhere, as a means of illustrating certain phases of the hypothesis presented. Finally, certain conclusions will be offered based upon these observations which, hopefully, shall prove of some value both theoretically and pragmatically.

---

1. Albert K. Cohen, **Delinquent Boys: The Culture of the Gang** (Glencoe: The Free Press, 1955).
2. Frederic Thrasher, **The Gang** (Chicago: The University of Chicago Press, 1936).
3. Herbert Blumer, "Sociological Analysis and the Variable," **American Sociological Review**, 21 (December, 1956), 683-690.
4. Maurice R. Davie, "Pattern of Urban Growth," **Studies in the Science of Society**, ed. George R. Murdock (New Haven: Yale University Press, 1937), p. 161.
5. Bernard Lander, **Toward An Understanding of Juvenile Delinquency** (New York: Columbia University Press, 1954), pp. 24-27, 58-59, 84-85.
6. See, for example, Austin L. Porterfield, **Youth in Trouble** (The Leo Potishman Foundation, Austin, Texas, 1946), pp. 38 ff. and Herbert A. Bloch, **Disorganization: Personal and Social** (New York, 1952), p. 260.
7. Frankwood Williams, **Adolescence: Studies in Mental Hygiene** (New York, 1930), pp. 102 ff.
8. See, for example, Kingsley Davis, "Adolescence and Social Structure," **The Annals of the American Academy of Political and Social Science** (November, 1944), pp. 1944), pp. 8-15. Also, by the same author, "The Sociology of Parent-Youth Conflict," **American Sociological Review**, V (August, 1940), pp. 523-35.
9. August Hollingshead, **Elmtown's Youth** (New York: John Wiley & Sons, 1945), pp. 6-7.
10. Herbert Bloch, op. cit., pp. 140-45.
11. Fritz Redl, "The Psychology of Gang Formation and the Treatment of Juvenile Delinquents," in **The Psychoanalytic Study of the Child** (New York, 1945).
12. Porterfield, op. cit.
13. Cohen, op. cit., p. 39.
14. See, for example, among other writings making the same point, Bloch, **Disorganization: Personal and Social**, op. cit., pp. 583-602.
15. For an analysis of this method of research investigation, see Alfred R. Lindesmith, **Opiate Addiction** (Bloomington, Indiana, 1947), Chap. I, and Florian Znaniecki, **The Method of Sociology** (New York, 1934), pp. 232-33.

CHAPTER II

FUNDAMENTAL SHORTCOMINGS IN OUR KNOWLEDGE OF ADOLESCENCE

In surveying much of our leading anthropological literature, the point is immediately borne home that there is actually very little written on informal adolescent groups, as such, in primitive societies. Adolescent grouping patterns are largely treated as incidental by-products in the discussion of puberty rites, courtship practices, family structure, age-grading, and similar processes, or come to light briefly in sections culled from occasional life-histories gathered by anthropologists.

The absence of detailed descriptions of adolescence, particularly in their psychological and personality references, is not entirely an accident. However, it is even more striking when one considers the rather intense concern and preoccupation with this age group by the other behavioral sciences since the beginning of the present century. Americans, in particular, have shown a lively concern with this particular age group. This has been manifested not only by the spate of technical treatises devoted to the consideration of adolescence and its problems but by the wide variety of publications, popular and otherwise, which have been devoted to this topic. It has not appeared as at all anomalous to Americans that this parochial interest has found expression in some of the most distinguished writings by our native authors. Beginning with Mark Twain's *Tom Sawyer* and *Huckleberry Finn,* and followed in this century by Booth Tarkington's *Seventeen,* beloved by a previous generation as an endearing tale of adolescent foibles and idiosyncrasies, and by Eugene O'Neill's *Ah Wilderness,* the condition and plight of adolescent youth has engrossed the attention of generations of adults. In this way, perhaps, an older generation has regarded with some compassion and humor its own troubled past, now that the dangers have been surmounted.

That America's outstanding playwright should have achieved his greatest popular success in a plaintive story about adolescence is in itself a token of how deeply moved we are by a condition which appears to us inevitable and universal. More recently, the sustained success of a wide variety of Broadway plays, movies and TV dramas, ranging from yesterday's *Yes, My Darling Daughter* to the perennial series of the *Aldrich family* and the affairs of Corliss Archer, observed with amused resignation by hordes of parents identifying themselves with the agonizing torments of the parents depicted in such dramatic episodes, provides further testimony to the American concern with such problems. Considered inevitable and timeless, despite the occasional emphatic negations afforded by the anthropologists, the average American listens with incredulous skepticism to the accounts by anthropologists that such conditions need not be universal.

It is apparent, however, that a concern with a specific problem, whether it be the antics of teen-agers or the growing plight of the aged, reflects certain deep-seated impulses within the social structure itself. A growing cultural anxiety is manifested by the prolonged duration of this interest and the accustomed perceptions with which it orders the restricted universe within which it lives. In observing the problems of others, with which it identifies itself, a measure of reassurance is afforded that others have the same problems. One can laugh at such problems in the manner of guilty self-indulgence, if necessary, but the underlying conviction remains that here we have a basic problem which all of our social laughter and social incantations cannot readily dispel. This is the unease of a culture which ofttimes refuses to confront itself.

A pervasive and continuing cultural interest, however, engenders its own clinical dimensions and its own clinical perspectives. Americans, and Western Europeans to a lesser degree, have manifested this type of interest as well in the problems of growing youth since the last century. As a result of the vast dislocations in our social and economic structure brought about by the technological changes of the last century, bringing in their wake recurrent problems of mobility, migration, changing family structure, and the group process itself, the problems of adolescence have been thrown into sharp relief. So conspicuous did these appear to early students of American society and personality, that they tended to generalize from unique experiences found primarily in the Western World. G. Stanley Hall, for example, in his epochal three-volume work on *Adolescence,* published in 1904, regarded the pervasive youthful maladjustment which he saw around him as a universal condition and existing in some degree in all societies. In his hands, and likewise a reflection of his age and generation, adolescence became reified, not only as an inherent condition in the biological growth of man, but as a phase which distinguished entire societies in their slow crawl to occidentally conceived progress. This, of course, is rather typical of the common myopic view with which man is apt to regard himself. Under his distorted gaze, local and limited problems, because of their pressing immediacy, assume universal proportions and appear to be typical of mankind in general.

That the problem of adolescence has unquestionably presented and will continue to present a series of frustrating and harassing conditions to the American people for some time, there can be little doubt. That such problems are universal and inevitable, however, is a different matter. Indeed, as the facts of comparative societal research have disclosed, such problems need not present themselves in the same scope, form or intensity—or, in fact, present themselves at all—in cultures where the patterns of social living function differently and within different contexts of meaning and social value.

Unlike the peculiar attraction which the more bizarre and psychological aspects of adolescence exercised upon the other social sciences and psychology itself, the science of anthropology was a comparative latecomer upon this intriguing scene. There are a variety of reasons for this. The kinds of interest which a growing science acquires rest upon a number of limiting conditions largely determined by accident, precedent, the growth of a tradition and a way of selecting problems for study, as well as the practical opportunities for investigation and research. In short, this lack of emphasis in dealing specifically with adolescence in primitive societies stems to a considerable degree from the peculiar evolution of the study of anthropology itself.

Anthropological Biases in the Study of Adolescence

The science of anthropology, the comparative study of man in culture and society, has very likely proven the most invigorating and inseminating of all the social disciplines developed during the past three decades. Not a single behavioral science—and here we include not only its nearsister, sociology, but psychology, psychiatry and psychoanalysis as well—has remained untouched by the powerful new insights developed by this field of study. As in the case of psychiatric and psychological terminology, becoming a part of the idiom of everyday speech, many concepts of modern anthropology are now creeping into current vernacular. Although not an indisputable criterion of the public acceptance of a field of learning, such borrowing of concepts formerly reserved for the sacrosanct precincts of the specialist indicates a significant awareness of the existence of facts previously unknown or ignored.

Classical anthropology, from which the modern anthropologist has only recently tended to liberate himself—or, at any rate, to view in proper perspective—was a different breed of science. The forerunners to modern anthropology were primarily concerned with the structure of primitive society and devoted most of their enterprise to a discussion of the evolution of specific institutions, such as marriage, the family, kinship systems, and various technological usages. The great pioneers, Morgan, Tylor, and Westermarck, all illustrate this tendency. Within this older traditional context, people as individuals and the psychological complex of their multiple relationships, evidenced in how they feel, reason, react in moments of anger and joy, appear to have assumed a secondary importance.

With the advent of more recent developments in anthropology, an absorbing interest in studying the dynamics of human behavior, rather than exclusively their institutional expression, has come to the fore. Much of this vital interest in the individual's living relationships to the social matrix has come from the so-called "Culture and Personality" school of anthropology. This school represents an extremely significant development in our thinking concerning the relationship of the individual to his society and may, in the course of its already auspicious beginnings, contribute appreciably towards a completely new orientation in the fields of psychology and sociology.

The primary emphasis in this school is to ascertain precisely the ways in which the individual has become "socialized", i.e., how his unique personality characteristics as well as his social behavior have been fashioned by the *character* of his contacts with the social groups with which he has been in close and continuing contact. According to the perspective utilized by this school, the raw biological materials of the individual are structured by the constraints and permissive channels for action imposed by the limiting social situations, producing typological traits which are characteristic of his immediate groups and the larger social framework in which he functions. Further, this school is attempting to explore such problems as the meaning of "national" and "social" character, and is beginning to recognize the kinds of psychological configurations which lie at the basis of our institutional patterns of social living. The latter may be briefly explained by indicating that the kinds of social patterns or institutions a given society develops must prove congenial, in the long run, to the kinds of psychological characteristics possessed by the members of that society.

In the probing zeal to get at the fundamental psychosocial and psychocultural patterns basic to a given society, however, an undue stress has been placed upon early childhood to the exclusion of other age levels in the development of personality. Child-rearing practices, swaddling, and toilet training—giving rise to the satirical sobriquet of "diaper determinists"—seem to have taken precedence over the consideration of socializing tendencies in other periods of life. Perhaps this is due to the fact that women have figured largely in the development of this school of anthropology and seemingly were more adapted by interest and cultural role to pursue this line of inquiry. Among others, Inkeles has suggested this possibility in revealing the extreme emphasis upon child-rearing techniques utilized by students in this area. Indeed, there is serious reason to doubt the facile connections which are ofttimes established between such child-rearing techniques and adult manifestations of personality, as Inkeles has likewise shown. Certainly, such an overemphasis has tended to overshadow the significant role which economic, political, and other critical social institutions play in molding the personality of the mature individual.[1]

There is another factor which should be considered in recognizing the limitations of study upon adolescent youth in primitive societies, and that is the relatively short period of duration of adolescence in many societies. We tend primarily in our culture to consider adolescence a period of profound physiological change. As a matter of fact, this is largely an inversion of the true meaning of adolescence. Adolescence, as Ruth Benedict so wisely remarked, consists essentially of the way in which society *views* the young person during the period of sexual maturation and the way, consequently, in which he comes to regard himself. Physiological changes, as disturbing as they may appear to the child and to us, are simply an accompanying condition to the struggle for the attainment of adult social status. It is not at all uncommon, for example, to find in our culture children who are delayed in their physical maturation displaying far more of the excesses of turbulent adolescent adjustment than children who are in the midst of the physical growth process.[2]

In simple societies, unmarked by our overwhelming technological complexity, the attainment of such adult status is a relatively easy process. In such societies, boys seem to make the jump from childhood to adulthood with very little of the transitional and prolonged adolescent *weltschmerz* of our culture.

Puberty Rites and Gang Rituals

Of all aspects of primitive society, the well-nigh universal puberty rite complex appears to be the most relevant to our subject, since the study of such ritual behavior deals with the adolescent in a very specific institutional situation and setting. Most anthropological literature, however, gives very little attention to the actual attitudes of the adolescent and the psychological dimensions of the experiences he is undergoing, but describes mainly the formal ritual and institutional ideology basic to the rites themselves.

An institutional pattern, as the modern functional theorists are wont to point out, is designed to satisfy certain needs which the culture has come to regard as significant for its welfare or furtherance. To understand such needs properly, and the essential purpose of the institutional function itself, social patterns must be viewed in relation to the entire social structure. Relationships between institutional patterns, not only those extremely close in function and meaning but others which may be somewhat remote from the institutional pattern observed, must be carefully articulated and interpreted. Thus, a marital institution is closely related to institutions determining the place of residence, but the function of marriage must be likewise assessed in relation to a variety of institutional usages seemingly remote from the immediate concerns of propagation and economic support. Political, religious, and recreational patterns must also be observed in relation to how they converge in their own peculiar way and with their own transformed meaning upon the pattern of marriage, in order to understand completely the function which sexual union means in a given society.

In the case of puberty ceremonials, the obvious function is to prepare the young person emotionally, intellectually and socially for the imminent responsibility of adulthood which he faces. Each society conceives of the responsibilities of adulthood in its own peculiar way. For some societies, the primary function of adulthood may conform to a bare minimum, having simply as its obligation the responsibilities of propagation and the providing of certain forms of support for one's spouse and legitimate issue. However, in other societies, other significant functions may be added, and in time almost appear to overshadow the fundamental functions of reproduction and support. Functions of an aesthetic or religious nature may appear to constitute the ultimate purpose of adulthood after the necessary preliminaries have been attended to.

The purpose of an institution in its avowed and publicly recognized form is a "manifest function", in the terminology of the functional theorists. That is, the "official" function, generally speaking, the meaning of the institution in terms of common consensus, public recognition and accepted social definition, is objectively in evidence. However, there are a great many latent or "hidden" functions which an institution also serves. In fact, the latent functions, although not publicly acknowledged since they may appear to contradict the public ideology, may actually run counter to the accredited purpose which the institution serves.

Puberty rites, therefore, with all of their attendant ordeals and sacrifices for the young person, may be satisfying a variety of carefully concealed or only tacitly perceived needs which may be of extreme importance to the entire ritualistic structure. A ritual, thus, may satisfy a variety of well-established motivations, ranging all the way from imperious sadistic urges to "haze the young," the desire to intimidate and coerce, to impulses of the most profoundly ethical nature.

From the coarsest of motives, on the one hand, there may be the other extreme where the ritual satisfies a lofty, aesthetic impulse to view the regeneration of youth as a vital *mystique* in the religious panorama of social existence. It was in this sense that Freud regarded the ancient and recurrent mythologies of man as a reenactment in differing symbols of man's age-long struggle for psychological mastery.

What is important to us here is the fact that the recognition of such latent functions frequently brings to light the deeply-rooted psychological experiences of men and women during the exercise of their institutional responsibilities. The imposition of a puberty ritual upon a young adult and, even more, his willingness and eagerness to accept it, discloses some of the urgent psychological experiences and needs of his entire personality at this particular stage of his life. When the ritual to which the youth is exposed is frequently painful, ominous, darkly foreboding, and even dangerous, why does a youth expose himself so eagerly and so readily to a series of events which might prove completely shattering under normal circumstances? The need for positive adult identification is a powerful impulse and, of course, brings its own rewards and privileges. Nevertheless, there is also a more fundamental meaning. Prior to his social acceptance as a fully functioning adult member of his society, the individual experiences considerable self-doubt, anxiety, and insecurity concerning his status. But there is something which goes even far beyond the lurking fear that he may not be able to make it—the fact that he may not be worthy. This, apparently, is the completely exonerating need for absolute self-fulfillment. The need for self-fulfillment brings in its wake an entire process of conflicting doubts, resentments towards his elders, and a desire to understand (and hence to cope with) his world, which the childhood status precludes.

That these anxiety-states invade the personality of the youthful novice knocking on the threshold of social maturity, there can be little doubt. What is impressive, however, is the fact that in the absence of a well-conceived formal procedure for the induction of young people into the exalted state of adulthood, there should appear a spontaneous emergence of similar patterns of behavior among the young, grounded on the same feelings of youthful anxiety and self-doubt. It is impressive to note accordingly the presence of certain similarities between puberty rites in primitive societies and the informal practices of our gangs of today. It is almost as if the young person, in the absence of such rituals and ordeals, is moved to exclaim: "If you don't care to test us, then we will test ourselves!"

Thus, practices such as scarification, tattooing, age-grading, the institution of men's clubs, segregation in bachelor huts, indoctrination of young boys, trial by ordeal, and a host of other painful and weird practices which societies have laboriously contrived to discipline their young for the Great Adventure, not only constitute definite and important parts of primitive rites but appear to have almost their direct counterparts in contemporary gang ritual. We may well ask ourselves, therefore, what are the needs which both the primitive neophyte and the young gang tyro on the streets of a modern American city are trying to express by this behavior.

It is in this light that our hypothesis begins to take on significant form and added emphasis. Although a given social process may take on its essential meaning within the context of a given culture and in terms of the values of that culture, there are certain common psychological experiences which all individuals face in respect to the needs to preserve ego-identity and rapport with their fellows. As different as the meanings of social life may be to individuals all over the world, the basic distinctions of sex and aging will induce characteristic forms of strain in the effort to achieve the desired status which these unavoidable conditions of human existence establish. Irrespective of how a culture regards childhood, adulthood, and old age, the expectancies a society entertains concerning how people should behave in relation to their age-status will create a certain degree of ego strain and conflict for all individuals in their passage through life. The plaintive cry of "Be your age!" conveys more than the social contempt of others.

Because of the special responsibilities which adulthood imposes in all societies, the transition here is normally fraught with far more psychological peril than is true of the other chronological transitions in life. The need to pursue a desired self-image and to establish the necessary supportive props for the ego is a universal condition. The belief of modern social psychologists notwithstanding—that human psychological characteristics reflect by and large the value-structure within which the individual seeks his adjustments—the need to find some sort of equilibrium for the ego is universal. Fear and anxiety strain, irrespective of the conditions that produce them, are common to all men. The efforts the ego makes to fend off this strain are likewise universal, even though the form of self-reconciliation may acquire the unique value characteristics of a specialized environment.

Thus, it appears reasonable that puberty rites—so widespread, so institutionalized, so dramatic an event in the life history of the individual—must induce its own type of mental strain, with its own psychological impact and import for the young boy. Recognizing this, we may well ask the question: "Is there any similarity in psychological meaning to the boys of primitive and modern cultures in their subjection to the ordeal of masculine identification and initiation?"

We may now formulate in more specific terms the implications of the hypothetical view we are presenting: (1) From the primitive adolescent's point of view, puberty rites are the culture's institutionalized practices to help carry him over a crucial period of his life and to orient him to his adult responsibilities, as well as to assuage the deep-seated psychological malaise which this transitional stage induces; (2) informal rituals of contemporary adolescent gangs are very similar to puberty rites in primitive society and represent spontaneous attempts to **find** psychologically supportive devices to assist the maturing male to weather the crisis of adolescence; (3) when adolescent youths, as in our own society, find it difficult to enter the adult status, for reasons of delay, social or technical obstacles, or because of the lack of an orderly, facilitating process, they will attempt to embrace the symbolic equivalents of the adult behavior denied them. In this latter connection, we find that the youth denied the opportunities for full marital, economic, and civic activity may be apt to affect the superficial trappings of adult privilege. Thus, the adolescent drinking, sexual escapades, wild automobile rides, immature assertiveness, violent reactions to parental restraints, protests against authority, and the other forms of intransigence which, to the youth at any rate, appear to be the prerogatives of the mature adult. The investing of such privileges—if privileges they be—with the dignity of responsibility can only come later. Such responsibility can only arise from mature living and full social participation as a result of complete assurance of an accepted adult status. This fundamental lesson can never be adequately conveyed to the young people of a culture which has grown perhaps too rich and too complex.

Thus, we may conceive of much of gang practice and the spontaneous, informal rituals of gang behavior as arising because our culture has been unable, or has refused, to meet the adolescent's needs during a critical juncture in his life. That such a contingency has not arisen through design is apparent. In fact, the very problems of adolescent youth which we face have resulted in large part from our concerned efforts to protect our youth and to give them a better life than their forebears. This is the fundamental irony of the situation. In the process, however, we may have lost something of great value to the culture. In fact, although it is not our intention to strike dolorously the tocsin of public alarm, our contemporary culture despite its vast technological brilliance may have produced its own "lost generation". Only the future—and not the immediate future alone—can tell how great a price we may have exacted upon our youth and ourselves.

In posing the problem of similarities of adolescent behavior in different cultures, a number of pertinent questions and problems arise. These we propose to consider in due course. However, it will be helpful to examine the specific forms which puberty rites assume in a variety of cultures. After noting the characteristic forms of these practices, and the psychological and social implications which they suggest, we shall investigate some commonly observed manifestations of youthful gang behavior in our own culture. To the consideration of these widespread "rites of passage" we now turn.

---

1. Alex Inkeles, "Some Sociological Observations on Culture and Personality Studies," Personality in Nature, Society and Culture, ed. Clyde Kluckhohn, Henry A. Murray, and David Schneider (New York: Alfred A. Knopf, Inc., 1954), pp. 580-81.
2. See, for example, N. Bayley and N. C. Jones, "Some Personality Characteristics of Boys with Retarded Skeletal Maturity," **Psychological Bulletin,** 38 (1941), p. 603.

PART II

ADOLESCENT GROUPS IN CROSS CULTURAL PERSPECTIVE

CHAPTER III

PUBERTY RITES: THEIR FORM AND MEANING

The Age and Sex Worlds In Which We live

The kinds of bonds we develop towards others are the result of shared experiences in which the circumstances of our employment, place of residence, family life, marital status, and similar characteristics all intertwine. In all cultures, the conditions under which these crucial elements in the pattern of living occur are determined by a variety of institutional factors, including such strategic elements as the individual's cultural group and his family's economic and social position.

However, within the gradations of cultural contact and homogeneity emerging as a result of the separable institutional complexities in any social system, the social world in which the individual moves is significantly and primarily determined by his age and sex. The conditions which control the ways in which an individual of a given age or sex shall interact with others, providing thereby the basic experiences which convey a unique meaning to the individuals of a particular classification, result from the roles which the society deems appropriate for such age and sex groups.

The results, however, are that such groups develop their own sense of social kinship and their own feelings of intimacy. Despite the fact that there are numerous forms of relationships arising out of common interests which may bring people together, in virtually all societies the age and sex principle is fundamental. Thus, whereas individuals sharing a common employment or profession indicate their community of interest frequently through common points of view, the acceptance of many common values, and even a common jargon—what Robert Lynd has referred to as the effects of "the long arm of the job"—the age and sex differentials of society persist throughout life and through all of the changing vicissitudes of circumstance.

In any society, therefore, we may observe a variety of age groups through which members of both sexes pass, each with its own *esprit* and code, and each rigorously excluding those who don't belong there. Not only do we accept and take for granted separable pre-adolescent boys' and girls' worlds, as well as adolescent groupings which are also rigidly compartmentalized by the culture, but there are mutually exclusive "men's worlds" and "women's worlds" from which the outsider is carefully excluded.

The values which such groups share, whether they be age or sex groups, invariably reflect the conceptions and expectancies which society entertains towards such classifications. Thus, the character of the intimacies they share, what they say, do, and feel, is determined largely by the use, present or potential, which society makes of a given sex or age group at a given time in its development. Obviously, the social roles which given individuals are asked to assume provide the basis of a common experience which they can share with others. We frequently recognize this in our allusions, patronizing or envious, of "women's talk" and "men's talk," the prattle of children, and the chatter of adolescents.

Thus, a society in which it is customary for women to undertake the entire burden of homemaking and child-rearing produces a progressive series of self-enclosed feminine worlds, beginning with the young child who "plays house" and shares her imaginative housekeeping duties with other little girls who participate in the same experience, to the world of the adolescent girl revolving around the endless gossip of "who's dating whom," to the young matron's world of shopping for bargains, planning layettes, concern about the unmarried girl friend, and the annoyance of planning a varied menu that will please her husband.

The psychological nuances of these separable worlds are

endlessly complex. The semi-institutional patterns they develop are equally so. The pressing immediacy of day-to-day problems which members of the same age and sex experience constitutes a basic institutional framework, defining the actions and needs of such individuals, and which differ from group to group. The pressing needs of yesterday become the outworn memories of today and yet how real they were at the time we lived them and how important to the groups which shared them. It is difficult to recall the devices so painfully contrived which were essential to "save face" as an adolescent—the "running with the crowd" and the willingness to "take a chance"—while our present adult values seem so real and so sensible. The novelist, John Marquand, in his *Point of No Return*, portrays so graphically the separate age-levels in an individual life-history that his hero sees no continuity in his own life and no progressive growth from the youth he once was. Although a novelist's device, the divisions between age levels and sexes are frequently far more acute than we appreciate.

Age-level and sex groups, with their separate institutional frameworks, do not exist within a social vacuum but are continually oriented to each other and, in fact, reflect each other's vantage points and status in the social scale. Realistically seen, such groups live within a system of power-relations, competing with other age and sex groups for position and advantage. These competitive and frequently open-conflict processes are not always apparent to the naked gaze; nevertheless they always exist. The tacit agreement of a group of pre-adolescent boys not to tattle about one of their members to an adult becomes part of a stringent code comparable to the behavior of a group of teen-age girls who will ostracize the boy who dated a girl outside of the charmed circle.

The restraints which different age groups impose upon each other induce their own patterns of resentment and antipathies. The hostilities of children to parents may be repressed, but they find their own patterned levels of response and socialized behavior, reinforced by the age group. The psychological levels of aging, as Bloch, Cole and many others have indicated, establish limited horizons, bounded by their own feeling-states, attitudes, values, and perceptions. Such psychological limitations reflect the society's evaluation of the individual and the individual's reactions to the status to which he has been assigned.

Protective Subterfuges of Children

What we are saying, thus, is that each of the recognized age and sex groups in society engenders its own peculiar psychological atmosphere. The stability of the individual and, indeed, the judgment by others on both his own and different age and sex levels as to whether he is normal or not, depends to a considerable degree upon how well he has internalized these peculiar in-group values. In some way, each individual at the appropriate level of his growth and development must come to grips with these values since they provide the basis for his subsequent development within the given culture. In our own culture, as well as in others, we recognize this by the oft-declared assertion that "boys will be boys" and become alarmed if the youngster in question does not display his "age characteristics", as annoying and distasteful as they may be to us. We become even more alarmed perhaps if the ways of childhood are not displaced, at the proper time, with the characteristics, mannerisms, and emotional outlooks of adulthood. The scriptural admonition of St. Paul that there comes a time when we must "put away childish things" and array ourselves in the psychological habiliments of the adult role is a theme that runs through all societies.

In many cultures, as among the Omaha, until the individual attains and accepts the psychological characteristics deemed appropriate to his age group, he is, in fact, considered to be devoid of full human stature and identity. To insure the individual's place and his human identity, many societies confer such human status through a variety of ceremonials, simple or complex in form. In any event, the ceremonial constitutes a public recognition, supported by numerous religious and social sanctions and practices, of the status the individual presently enjoys and the behavior which may be expected of him as a result of this status. Prior to this conferral of status, the Omaha, for example, regarded the individual as lacking the most fundamental qualities of human existence.

When a child was born it was not regarded as a member of its gens or of the tribe but simply as a living being coming forth into the universe, whose advent must be ceremonially announced in order to assure it an accepted place among the already existing forms. This ceremonial announcement took the form of the expression of the Omaha belief in the oneness of the universe through the bond of a common life power that pervaded all things in nature animate and inanimate . . . .
(This first ceremony, introducing the child to the world, occurred on the fourth day after birth. The second ceremony was called "turning the child".) All children, both boys and girls, passed through this ceremony, which is a survival of that class of ceremonies belonging to the lowest, or oldest, stratum of tribal rites; it is directly related to the cosmic forces—the wind, the earth, and the fire. Through this ceremony all the children who had reached the period when they could move about unaided, could direct their own steps, were symbolically "sent into the midst of the winds"—that element essential to life and health; their feet were set upon the stone—emblem of long life upon the earth and of the wisdom derived from age; while the "flames", typical of the life-giving power, were invoked to give their aid toward insuring the capacity for a long, fruitful, and successful life within the tribe. Through this ceremony the child passed out of that stage in its life wherein it was hardly distinguished from all other living forms into its place as distinctively a human being, a member of its birth gens, and through this to a recognized place in the tribe. As it went forth its baby name was thrown away, its feet were clad in new moccasins made after the manner of the tribe,

and its (new) name was proclaimed to all nature and to the assembled people.[1]

Although we, in our culture, emphasize primarily the major stages of childhood, adolescence, adulthood, and old age, the age-grading procedures of certain societies become extremely complex, as among certain Australian groups, notably the Arunta. The self-enclosed worlds of human development may encompass a wide variety of differently recognized developments in the life of the human being, including such experiences as the period directly after birth, the time when the infant first shows recognition of an administering adult, the first smile or the first word, the period when he takes his first steps, the manifestation of early food preferences, and a host of other episodes too numerous to mention. In the conventional baby book of the modern parent, these too may be made a matter of record and occasional sentimental recollection, but such matters of record are quite different from the formal and declared public recognition of an individual child's change of status. Each one of these experiences may or may not provide the occasion for elaborate ceremonial observation but, at the least, they *do* signify for a great many societies an acknowledged recognition of the child's change in status.

Since the child's new status invariably involves new attitudes towards him and, frequently, the conferring of a new name or designation, his experiences begin to reflect rather acutely the psychological meaning which his social group has now accorded to his behavior. These meanings, as indicated previously, reflect the functions which society is now willing for him to play. Such functions are not static and will frequently change in the course of a society's development. In fact, with relatively rapid change (as in our own society), such functions may actually change rather precipitately within a given generation.

However, the basic attitudes which a society entertains towards its various age-levels will reflect some of the most basic values and orientations in the culture. Gregory Bateson, for example, has indicated that a culture may give evidence of what he refers to as "symmetrical" or "complementary" patterns which reflect themselves in the attitudes towards the child.[2] In the case of the symmetrical types, for example, the stress in relationships is essentially competitive, with the result that the culture may continually try to elicit from the child competitive impulses commensurate with his capacity. Because of his bodily and psychological limitations, however, such a child is apt to become extremely distrustful and hostile in view of the demands upon him to compete with adults in situations for which he is inadequate. The storehouse of repressed hostilities which such a child may develop—supported and reinforced by children of his own age level who have shared the same experience—may be considerable and constitute an explosive element in the child's own world. In the "complementary pattern," however, the relationships are essentially those of balance and dependence, with the result that the child fosters feelings of reliance and dependence upon adults while, at the same time, possibly expressing some hesitancy in moving towards maturational levels in which considerable self-sufficiency is demanded.

The orientations of our own society towards the behavior expected of children have changed drastically since our early history. The child of Colonial America, and even well into the period of the 19th Century, was expected to behave like a miniature adult with, however, none of the prerogatives of adulthood. The paintings of 18th and early 19th Century children reveal them in the same costumes of their elders and with the early assumed sober demeanor of their parents. The adolescent and post-adolescent periods during such eras included considerable deference to adult authority and the assumption of adult characteristics, with an attitude of resigned acceptance of the inevitable delays before the full mantle of adulthood could be worn. Children were expected to look and behave like little adults, where "to be seen but not to be heard" signalized their social presence under adult sufferance. The character of resentments and hostilities of young adolescents and children fostered in this type of family life can only be guessed at.

Their profound nature can be seen in an examination of the children's records of the period and in the dominance and repression of the young male adult, sometimes almost sadistic in his behavior, which appeared to emerge in the censorious moral tones of the later Victorian period. The philosophy of "spare the rod and spoil the child," despite the envy with which our present beleaguered generation of adults frequently regards an earlier age, tended to usher in the present period with which we are all too familiar—a period in which our attitudes towards children and adolescents are highly ambiguous and ambivalent.

Since our society has never developed the elaborate age-grading procedures of other parts of the world, we are apt to regard the four major periods of development—childhood, adolescence, adulthood, and old age—as being all-inclusive. Particular focus has been laid upon adolescence and the prelude to adulthood which this signifies. There are many reasons for this, although the principal factors seem to lie in the relative ease with which adolescence can be determined and in the previous historic need of our society for the enterprise and energy of the young. In the case of the girl, the advent of adolescence makes its own dramatic and unmistakable pronouncement, while in the case of the boy, although not as easily marked or precipitate, maturation reveals itself through its own startling patterns of growth. The transition from adulthood to old age, however, lacks the same clarity, particularly in a culture which accentuates youth and takes the most heroic efforts to fend off the visible signs of aging.

Age-Level Conflicts

It should be emphasized that the psychological characteristics which certain age groups manifest are not alone the results upon separate individuals of a common social attitude. These psychological characteristics are the result of powerful in-group sentiments of the group members themselves and the impact of their own generating tradition. For example, among teen-agers in a given community, their psychological identities and shared social interests are thrown into sharp focus by the attitudes of the community and its actual treatment of them. However, there is a further powerful force which plays an instrumental role in shaping the shared psychological orientations of such a peer-age group and that is the traditions which children pass on from generation to generation. These age-level traditions have a peculiar potency of their own. By indicating the kinds of heroic and model figures which previous generations of youth have venerated and by the kinds of prowess such groups have tended to admire, the children's and adolescents' worlds set up their own models of desired behavior.[3]

There are significant effects of these powerful socializing forces; for what the child or adolescent thinks may be important may have very little relevance to the values which society itself prizes. Defiance to adult authority (as one of innumerable examples), venerated as an important quality by the adolescent gang or play-group, may contradict sharply other values which the social system, through the family, may be more hopeful of cultivating. Aside from the common contradictions between the child's and the adolescent's world, as contrasted with the fond hopes and expectations of adults, is the frequently correlated problem of failing to provide psychological continuity in the cultural growth of the young. Thus, the kinds of social, cultural, and psychological characteristics fostered by a given age group may not equip the individual to assume his proper place in a succeeding age level. This, incidentally, may not only be found in the transition from youth to adulthood, but may be likewise encountered in the difficulties of aging adults to assume gracefully the requirements of old age. This problem of intergenerational continuity is an acute one and possibly one of the most serious of our modern age.[4]

Psychological traits may be deeply and powerfully ingrained on one age level, and powerfully reinforced by the group behavior of one's age peers, and yet have very little significance for the kinds of behavior expected on the next succeeding age level. The difficulty here is not alone one of inadequate preparation for the type of social role which an individual may be called upon to play, but even more significantly the fact that such psychological constellations of traits may produce deep strain upon the personality itself. The studies of different societies provide endless examples of such contradictions and the types of personal conflicts which such clashes in intergenerational continuity may produce for specific personalities. When the adult in a given society, for example, is expected to conform to a highly disciplined and cooperative form of life, willing at each juncture to subordinate himself wholly to the demands of some adult group, the previous in-group philosophy of the adolescent, in which individual competitiveness and concern for one's own special interests are paramount, produces its own disastrous results for the individual and the groups in which he must function. Or, as among the Crow Indians, where the adult male was expected to be a highly energetic extrovert, concerned with individual prowess on the warpath and in raiding parties, and given to loud boasting of his exploits, the acute conflict with the role of the aged person, where meekness, mildness, and docility were expected, becomes extremely marked.

Emotional Maturity

An examination of the conflicts produced by this lack of logical progression from one stage to another poses sharply the question as to the meaning of emotional maturity and growth in different cultures. All cultures recognize certain specific criteria of growth for the individual. Certain of these criteria are relatively easy to observe and recognize. Such evidences of maturing as the physical growth of the individual and his increasing competence in technical achievement in the skills of the group are readily acknowledged. In more complex societies such as our own, however, particularly with its extremely prolonged schooling, the character of the advance in technical proficiency sometimes presents its own problems. However, even among ourselves, by a series of devices—psychometric and performance tests—we can fairly well assess that period when we believe that the individual has become technically or, as we would more likely regard it, intellectually mature.

The matter of emotional growth, however, raises some very special problems. Among peoples less complex than ourselves, the criteria of acceptable emotional behavior can likewise be discerned without undue difficulty. An age-status brings with it certain expectancies as to how an individual may be likely to handle his emotions. By traditional social definition, the individual is expected to display certain types of recognizable emotions which are in keeping with the requirements of particular situations. Anger, fear, rage, and love have their own accompaniments of preferred social action and are to be expressed in relation to stipulated persons, conditions, and events. Among ourselves, for example, sorrow may be expressed by weeping, wailing, and a dramatic outward show of grief, while among the American Plains Indians, such an emotion might be more properly expressed through stoical demeanor, while among the Japanese, it might be expressed by a smiling countenance.[5]

Each culture, therefore, defines quite carefully not only how an emotion should be expressed, but indicates towards whom an emotional display should be directed and in respect to what special set of circumstances and places. In our own society, strong erotic displays are expected to be confined to the most private quarters, although some kissing and embracing in public may be permitted. Among the Japanese, on the other hand, kissing in public is regarded as a most flagrant violation of a most fundamental propriety in human relations.

Emotional maturity, therefore, is ordinarily attained in any culture when an individual utilizes his emotions to effect satisfactory social adjustments, and when the expression of his emotions occurs in keeping with the social expectancies of given situations. There is a further provision to be kept in mind here, however, although a provision which appears to apply with particular force to our own culture. This condition indicates that the expression of an emotion, while socially acceptable, must likewise be congruent with the needs of the individual's psychic economy. Thus, a truly mature state can never in itself be attained by simply conforming to the emotional demands of others; the emotional behavior must not, at the same time, produce undue strain for the individual incapacitating him for further adjustments. In well-integrated, simple societies, where the nature of choice is clear-cut, well-defined, and carrying powerful social mandates, the expression of emotions itself is unambiguous and devoid of emotional strain. In our own society, because of the complex personal loyalties of the individual, the opportunity to express emotional choices in this simple, relatively undiffuse way, becomes extremely difficult.

Age-level preparation for the handling of one's emotions becomes extremely important, therefore. The character of this preparation goes right back to early childhood. The adolescent period, however, is the great crucible, determining whether or not, in a great many cases, the individual will ever learn to handle his emotions properly. For many individuals, it becomes the final testing period in which the difficult problem of emotional control may be mastered. Although not definitive, it is likely that the individual who has not learned to grasp the significant rudiments of emotional self-mastery by the time he emerges from adolescence will never learn to do so.

The Psychological Components of the Child's and Adolescent's World

In the kind of world which children, and particularly adolescents, develop, there are powerful psychological forces in operation. These forces are usually of three types. (1) In the first place, there are powerful psychological urges and strivings on the part of the young person to emulate some desired adult role. There is a considerable play-element involved in this process, and for the very young, these psychological factors are almost entirely involved in the play activity of the child.

It is, of course, well known that disturbances in the emotional life of the child occur when he either lacks adequate adult roles with which he may readily identify himself, or is exposed to contradictory or mutually exclusive adult roles, rendering coherent identification difficult. Much of the emotional conflict which individuals experience as adults arises because of early failure in establishing adequate identification with a parent of the same sex or some other suitable adult figure. Concepts of masculinity and femininity, and the several dimensions of such concepts in the behavioral views of how adults should disport themselves in the innumerable social situations which comprise society, invariably reflect an entire series of such identifications which the child has made, beginning with the powerful initiatory prototype of the child's own parent.

However, this is merely part of the structure of the world which the child builds. To imitate, or to desire to be like something or somebody else, is one thing. To be limited in the exercise of one's imagination and activity, to be imposed upon and restricted, is another. Because of the restrictions which societies must inevitably impose upon their young, differing degrees of hostility towards adults (and the organized society which they embody), as well as socialized patterns of resentment, must inevitably arise.

(2) Thus, a second very important and powerful phase of the psychological structure of the child's world consists of the repressions and hostilities which are carefully nurtured as a result of adult authority. The degree of this hostility will, of course, vary. In certain societies, where considerable freedom is afforded the child, the degree of hostility may be negligible or even, as in certain exceptional cases, almost wholly absent. In most societies, a certain degree of this hostility is inevitable, while in others it may assume alarming proportions. The degree would depend upon the extent, character, and prolongation of the controls which the adult world imposes upon the young. A significant factor in determining the *form* which this hostility may take is the pattern of organization of children's groups and their relation to the social structure itself. Thus, in a society where the repression is severe and where the child is afforded little opportunity to consort freely with others, the form of his resentment may be largely covert and conspiratorial in character. In other societies, such as our own, where the culture encourages and facilitates the free play activity

of children, the pattern of resentment may be more direct and expressed through open defiance and hostility towards adult and social standards.

No society, however, permits complete open defiance of its young towards its standards. The result, therefore, is that in even the most permissive of societies, most of this hostility towards the adult world is expressed in covert form and through socially patterned artifice and subterfuge. This socialized resentment may range all the way from the derisive mimicry of the young child, to studied patterns of insult, the use of the most egregious vulgarity, obscenity and profanity, slovenly dress and attire, and the breach of what their elders may regard as the most elementary tenets of good taste and public decency. Such protests can be seen in such widely divergent practices as the graceless adornments and obscenities on the walls of public places to the violent protests of the editors of college humor and literary periodicals at adult efforts to cleanse such publications from uninspired and fatuous pornographic excess.

(3) There is, however, a third significant element which appears in the complex structure of the child's social world. The imposition of adult authority as, in truth, in the case of all authority, produces its own efforts towards countercontrol. In the power structure of any group of society, the individuals involved invariably attempt to set up their own techniques of avoidance and protection. Thus, in the children's world, a series of manipulative techniques are devised and passed down to ensuing generations of children. These are essentially techniques whereby the individual's integrity and that of his group may be safeguarded. We may observe accordingly a variety of manipulative techniques —some extremely subtle—whereby the child and his peers may feel themselves somewhat protected from what is conceived as the authoritarian whim of parents and elders.

An interesting phase of such protective devices is their reflection of the cultural standards of the group in which they are found. Thus, in a middle class group, where children are continually made to feel that they constitute an object of special concern to their parents, the feigning of illness or pain may be a highly strategic lever with which to control parents—a device, incidentally, which may be exceedingly well recognized by groups of children themselves. "Tell her you're sick" is an admonition frequently employed by such children to each other when protection is sought against parental displeasure. Or, among working class children, the ease with which a potentially punishing adult may be brought to your side is recognized in playing upon the cultural sensitivity to an insult upon the person's appearance, background, morality, or ancestry.

The interactive support which these three elements of *identification, repressed hostility,* and *manipulation* exercise upon each other provides a substantial underpinning to the social world in which the child lives.

The Inversion of Dependent Relationships

In all societies, there is a hierarchy of power broadly based upon age and sex. Age and sex groups develop a complicated series of superordinate and subordinate relationships in which the bonds of dependency and obligation assume a special character.

Although it is far too easy to refer to masculine or feminine dominance since the areas of control are so numerous, overlapping, and devious, nevertheless we can observe that in those areas which the given society regards as most crucial to its welfare, dominance usually goes to one group or the other. In a society whose ideology stresses equality in roles, there may be serious conflicts between the professed beliefs of the culture and the actual conditions of the power relations between the groups concerned. Thus, in American society, despite much high-flown oratory concerning the equality of the sexes in social behavior, the fact of male dominance in many crucial areas may not only create tension but also an inversion of the recognized principles of relationship. The tensions which this produces can be seen in a variety of typical "women's problems," such as the looming conflict in choices between marriage and a career, the claimed rights of women towards full participation in all cultural activities, and perennial protests against the double standard in sexual behavior. The inability to define adequately the full place and responsibility of women in American society is a topic which continues to concern the active interest of our public and our writers. Although the ardent feminist of the early century seems to have become a figure of the past, the former political focus of this problem seems to have given way to the more pressing contemporary problem of the psychological and cultural needs of modern women.

Allison Davis, in a recent statement, indicated that many American women entertain deep-seated, although largely covert, hostilities towards men which are only dissipated in the course of a successful marriage. Although suffering from the weakness of all generalizations, we can logically suspect that such hostilities do exist and manifest themselves in a variety of tension-states between the sexes. James Thurber's "war between the sexes" seems to derive added significance when we examine closely the judgments that women are prone to make in their public and published utterances, as well as in the more private judgments rendered in the analyst's consulting chamber. The very fact that such a "war" is presumed to exist constitutes an instructive commentary on the public temper of our culture.

In order to maintain a position of advantage, subordinate groups, irrespective of their character, attempt to place themselves in strategic positions. The meek can inherit the earth if they eventually learn how to utilize their meekness effectively. Russell Lynes, in his recent *A Surfeit of Honey*, although admittedly a non-scientific and satirical sketch, trenchantly reveals the kinds of controls which women may exercise over men in what is presumably a "male dominated" world.[6] Although an assessment of human relationships in this context becomes extremely complex and should be recognized in terms of the subtleties involved, the modern credit and property structure of our society might in itself provide an interesting illustration of the ways in which women can assume a superordinate position. One of many illustrations may suffice to make this point clear. The involvement in a heavy debt structure in suburban areas, augmented by a desire to have all the gadgets and appurtenances which go with suburban living, may place the married male in a subservient position from which he cannot readily extricate himself.

The inversion of dependent relationships, thus, refers to the ways in which an ordinarily subordinate group within a specific social context may find itself in a controlling position. In the case of teen-agers, for example, the manipulation techniques described in the previous section may actually place them in an ascendant position relative to their adult elders upon specific occasions. Our reluctance and outright unwillingness, upon occasion, to invoke the full penalty of the law against teen-age lawbreakers who may engage in extreme and ofttimes brutal activities, is a case in point. The lengths to which a middle class family may go to "save face" as a result of the behavior of a teen-age son or daughter is more than a tacit recognition of the power of the young to control their elders in the face of certain contingencies. The adolescent child may well know that he can virtually "get away with murder" with little probability of serious repercussion, so intent is the family to maintain its respectability. Aside from the abrogation of parental responsibility in such cases, the more lasting tragedy lies in the harm we do to the child and to the future society in which he must eventually take his place as a responsible adult. The "inversion" of such structured relationships is all the more painful since it so pointedly discloses a society which cannot make up its mind. Further, such indecision is a symptom of far-reaching doubt concerning other aspects of the social order and usually extends into many other vital segments of our social life The price of such indecision, especially when prolonged and epidemic, is frequently a prelude to eventual social disaster.

---

1. A. C. Fletcher and F. La Flesche, "The Omaha Tribe," **Bureau of American Ethnology, Annual Report,** No. 27, pp. 115-116.
2. Gregory Bateson, "Some Systematic Approaches to the Study of Culture and Personality," **Character and Personality,** 11 (1942), pp. 76-82.
3. One of the most fascinating aspects of this subject is the continuity of children's traditions themselves, with little or no assistance or intervention of adults. In some cases, children's games, pastimes, and group practices can be traced right back to ancient Rome. Aside from the lengthy history involved is the fact of the seeming crossing of cultural lines.

4. That many cases of senescent psychosis have been precipitated by the isolation of the aged person and his divorce from a previously active life has been cogently observed by recent students of geriatrics. See, for example, D. Rothschild, "Senile Psychoses and Cerebral Arteriosclerosis," in O. J. Kaplan, ed., **Mental Disorders in Later Life** (Stanford University, 1945).
5. See, for example, Weston La Barre, "The Cultural Basis of Emotions and Gestures," in Douglas A. Haring, ed., **Personal Character and Cultural Milieu** (Syracuse, 1948), pp. 487-506.
6. See Russell Lynes, **A Surfeit of Honey** (New York: Harper and Bros., 1957).

CHAPTER IV

PUBERTY RITES: THEIR FORM AND MEANING
(Continued)

As we begin to recognize the remarkable psychological solidarity of the several age and sex groups which exist in any society, we become increasingly conscious of the factors of opposition and reconciliation which tend to bring all such groups together into a coalescent unit. The tensions which may exist between such groups in what may appear as an uneasy social partnership are largely overridden by the compelling necessity of the society as a whole to function efficiently as a unit. Consequently, many of the barriers that exist between such groups are merely a reflection of social tensions which must be substantially overcome if the group is to exist, no less to advance or to progress.

At the dramatic moment when the youth feels himself able or eligible to join the ranks of adults, or when the society feels that this recognition is essential for its own purposes, the transition becomes marked by a series of social and psychological episodes, many of them highly projective in form. For, in recognizing the attainment of a new adult status, the fact of this recognition inevitably manifests itself in changes of attitude and social concern. Even if the climactic denouement of recognized adulthood is not accompanied by the dramatic enactments which are characteristic of so many cultures, or even if the ceremonials become somewhat attenuated as in our own society, there are nevertheless a number of revealing acts, signs, and tokens by which we show our acknowledgment of the new status. Such acts and episodes serve as reminders and landmarks to the perceptive adult.

For example, in our own culture, where the advent of

young adulthood may be extremely gradual despite the fact that we have minimal religious confirmation and graduation ceremonials, such recognition becomes clearly manifest through certain significant events. Such events appear to center around such episodes as the departure for college, presenting the youth with his own personal house key, the willingness to exchange confidences with the adolescent child, heretofore not indulged in, the tacit acknowledgment by parents (frequently through the exchange of glances) of the physical maturity revealed by a new dress or garment, the "first date," and a wide-ranging series of other emblematic reminders.

It is truly remarkable, however, to discover the variety of customs and ceremonials which are found all over the world and which are common to a variety of different peoples. Although each general category of ceremonial behavior marking the transition to adulthood appears similar, it should be emphasized that such ceremonials must be viewed in the peculiar light of each culture itself. Nevertheless, it is still remarkable that such striking similarities exist.

Generally speaking, puberty ceremonials seem to fall into the following broad classifications: self decoration; the acquisition of a new name or language; leaving one's residence to live with one's own age and sex mates; separation from the mother and her household ties; the manifestation of sexual ambivalence and homosexuality; exposure to an ordeal or "hazing" to prove fitness; economic exploitation; educational procedures for the recognized novice; use of sex and fertility symbols; and the myth of death and rebirth of the adolescent novitiate.

In our discussion of these several ceremonials, we are primarily concerned with their use in respect to the coming of age of boys, although many of these practices apply to young girls as well in certain societies. It should be recognized that these *rites de passage* are not all equally applicable in all societies and that their use, separately or in conjunction, will differ in meaning and context for different societies. Nevertheless, to a certain degree and even when not emphasized, latent aspects of such rituals may be found in the majority of cultures. In the absence of a specific practice or ritual, its non-institutionalized psychological equivalent is frequently found.

Self-Decoration

Self-adornment of the body usually assumes one or more of the following forms: (a) tattooing; (b) painting the body and face; (c) scarification; and (d) circumcision. In examining these several procedures, a number of considerations must be kept in mind.

(1) In the first place, it must be recognized that the youth undergoing the transition to adulthood becomes extremely conscious of his body, engaging in a form of adolescent narcissism. This appears to be universal among youth in all societies. If one has any doubt about this, we may recall to our minds briefly the excessive concern with appearance and the tendency to exaggerate the factors of sexual difference among young people in our own society. One's maleness and femaleness are at a premium at this particular stage of development. The almost ludicrous efforts upon occasion of the young person to reveal, within the limitations of propriety and public censure, the bold lineaments of his sexual character is ofttimes revealed. This is frequently accomplished through the costume worn and the artificial contrivances and embellishments of undergarments and clothing to enhance the sexual features.

(2) It should be noted, thus, that much of this preoccupation with the body revolves around the concern to emphasize the fact of anatomical difference. The emphasis upon the hips and breasts of the young girl is matched by the symbolic and candidly displayed interest of the boy in his own genitals. A particularly revealing aspect of this interest within the present can be seen in the scant and tight-fitting bathing trunks affected by many of our teen-agers on the beaches during the summer months.

(3) A third aspect which must be considered in the analysis of ritualistic devices of self-adornment is the fact as to whether or not the decoration is self-imposed or applied under duress and pain by selected members of the society.

(4) Finally, it need be ascertained as to whether or not the ritualistic practice is part of a more elaborate religious or magical ceremony.

We may consider each of these aspects briefly in further detail. Tattooing and scarification may be a continuing process, initiated by the young person during the adolescent period, or confined largely to the period of adolescent transition itself. In the case of the latter, it is ordinarily imposed by others and frequently under great pain and hardship, and even danger. The willingness of individuals to develop and maintain a form of bodily beauty, frequently emphasizing those features of the body of greatest erotic interest to the group, reaches extreme form in many societies. Among the African *Bagesu,* for example, women carry their instruments of beautification with them constantly and devote themselves sedulously to the improvement of their appearance. This is strangely reminiscent of the "cult of the vanity case and lipstick" in our own culture.

> Women scarify their bodies freely, from the breasts to the pit of the stomach and also on the forehead, thus forming rows of small almond-shaped swellings. These are produced before initiation and their production is a painful and often prolonged operation. Those on the stomach a girl usually makes herself, while those on the forehead are made for her. The instrument used for making scarifications is an iron hook some four inches long, a quarter of an inch thick and bent to a crescent. One end is beaten fine to a needle point, the other end has a ring to slip on the finger to carry it on the back of the hand when not in use. The flesh is pinched up between the thumb and finger and the hook run through it. This is done in several places at a time and fine wood ashes are rubbed over to stop the bleeding; the wounds heal, leaving raised flesh.[7]

That this process can be extremely painful is apparent. However, if we are inclined to think of such excesses as simply the distorted behavior of a primitive people, we have but to think of the endless ordeals to which American women will expose themselves in order to attain a cultural standard of beauty. We have but to think of the eyebrow plucking, the painful (and frequently dangerous) regimen of dieting, the endless massaging, anointing and rolling of the skin, the use of rigid beauty masks, the lengthy hours spent under hair-driers and sun lamps, and the more effete contrivances of what we choose to regard as a more civilized society, to realize that the cultivation of beauty is a formidable, time-consuming, serious, and painful process.

Scarification (or *cicatrization*) may be an unusually painful process and, as in the case of tattooing, may be self-inflicted or imposed by others. The pride with which the young person bears his wounds, as in the dueling scars of the German student *mensuren*, finds its psychological counterpart in the satisfaction experienced by the young boy who can display his own hard-won scars. Recklessness among young boys is frequently practised as a deliberate attempt to acquire a serious wound so that the scarred tissue can be conspicuously displayed later on. As a prelude to such a "mark of distinction", it is interesting to note the pride with which the young child displays his bandages and wound-wrappings.

There is a peculiar masochistic-sadistic element involved in the imposition of wounds upon the body. The willingness of the youth to endure pain, particularly if it can be borne stoically, may in part be motivated by the sense of danger and misgiving which the youthful novice experiences in contemplating his entrance into a new world, mysterious and strange, and one in which he regards himself as an interloper. The sadistic element finds ample expression in the behavior of those who operate upon the boy, and in the presence of the "elect" who are privilged to view the mutilation proceeding or ceremony. Such onlookers may be of both sexes in accordance with the selective tradition of the culture. Much of this sadism may stem from a desire to indicate authority through fear and pain, and to provide a respected institutional pattern for the expression of resentment towards the new rival. For, in effect, the attainment of adulthood actually constitutes an acknowledgment that the new arrival is a legitimate (and, hence, potentially dangerous) competitor in the social, economic, and sexual fields. What appears to be almost an intense and morbid ferocity in some of these mutilation ceremonies can be seen in the practice of the *Neuer,* an African Nilotic tribe.

> A depression is made in the ground to hold the boy and a hoop of grass is placed under his head.... The operator squats on the right side of the head. He places the knife in the middle of the forehead and draws it above the eyebrow to well toward the middle of the right ear. Blood vessels and all are cut down to the bone. This is the principal cut and the most painful. About a centimeter higher comes the second, and then the others, in all six. (The left side is cut in the same way.) When the skin is thus completely severed from the forehead it frequently drops down somewhat and a broad skinless space appears.
>
> The loss of blood in the operation is frightful, often dangerous to life. On that account great care is exercised with the patients. After the operation the boys are carried, often unconscious, by men into a neighboring hut, care being taken that the head shall be moved as little as possible.... The patient must lie on his back for several days and keep the head immovable to prevent the recurrence of bleeding.... When the candidate is obliged to sit up or rise, the head must not be inclined forward or sidewise but bent backwards. The first twenty-four hours are the most critical. Not infrequently an old man who watches during the night or comes early in the morning finds a boy unconscious or even in the throes of death.
>
> Care is exercised in the selection of the boy for the first operation of the series. Sometimes an older and larger boy applies for the honor. If he shows fortitude the others will follow his example and will not have to be held forcibly. Usually the feeling of honor prevails over the frightful pain, especially when the boys are older, and they remain quiet and silent under the knife.[8]

It should be recognized that in many mutilation ceremonies, the prevailing concept is that the resultant scars and wounds have been caused by a totemic monster or animal. When the operation itself is performed secretly and privately —upon occasions when only the youth's own sponsors are present—the general effect is to augment the impression of fear and mystery to the outsider, and to enhance the prestige of the initiate. Aside from the mechanism of psychological identification which the young mutilated novice may make with some mythological figure, and even when he learns the painful truth, the cohesion of a separate adult world is more firmly established by such a proceeding. Further, the sadistic impulses of the operators upon the boy find a respectable and traditional rationale through such thaumaturgy, frequently imbued with deep religious significance.

The cheerful acceptance by the boy of the frightening ordeal to which such mysterious rites may expose him is reiterated as frequently in our own culture with the desire of the college freshman or fraternity neophyte to be hazed. We have recent evidence in several reports by the press during the past few years of college freshmen demanding to be hazed as a traditional right and resenting the enlightened policies of certain college administrators who have attempted to do away with the hazards of such practices, conceived as anachronistic. The sadism unleashed upon such occasions can readily be attested to by anyone who has either witnessed a college fraternity "hell week" (a significant designation) or the induction of a slum youth into a neighborhood gang. The elaborate paddle carried about by the college youth during such a period has both a symbolic and realistic significance.

Mutilation follows many other patterns, however. Prominent among some groups is the removal, chipping, or filing of the teeth. Here again, differences must be noted as to whether the act of mutilation is self-imposed or inflicted from without. Among the *Bakitara,* as other groups, the young male is not deemed fit to marry until the six front teeth in the lower jaw are knocked out. Although in our own culture, gleaming and even dentures are considered a criterion of attractive appearance, we need not look too far in our own history to recall the genuine pride with which newly arrived immigrants to our shores displayed mouthfuls of gold-capped teeth.

The cultural conception of physical beauty is a highly variable condition and very likely reflects a peculiar organic adaption in the past to the social environment. Thus, beauty fits into a variety of molds, ranging from the prized extreme slenderness in our own culture to extreme obesity in others, and a constriction, distention or enlargement of virtually any segment of the anatomy. Although originally conceived, very likely, as a necessary condition of physical survival, the character of bodily distortion and mutilation has lost much, if not all, functional value. Nevertheless, we may very well examine with some suspicion the sublimated satisfaction which many individuals in our own society derive from surgical operations whose necessity may often be disputed.

Circumcision

Circumcision, regarded by us today as a modern hygienic safeguard, is nevertheless to be viewed in many cultures as a beautification procedure. Its counterpart for girls in many societies are various forms of subincision, excision, and self-amplification. Among boys, such operations upon the sex organ may consist of a single incision of the upper or lower surface of the prepuce, circumcision or removal of the prepuce, subincision in which the whole length of the glans is split to the middle on the lower surface, and, in rare instances, castration or ablation of the sex organs. The extremes to which such operations may proceed can be seen in certain instances where the male organ is pierced for the purpose of inserting a small ring or cylinder.

Among the Australian *Arunta,* Spencer and Gillen report that there is occasional public rivalry among men for a repetition of the operation of subincision, as painful as the ordeal may be. Among the *Tonga,* supercision "was regarded as a sign of manhood and any youth who declined to be operated upon would be forbidden to eat with the other members of the household, must not touch another's food, and would be spurned by the girls. An uncircumcised person is called *kou* or *tartefe*." [9]

In certain societies, the willingness to submit to such operations where they assume excruciatingly painful proportions becomes a token of the youth's manly qualities and seems to provide a mass sadistic spectacle for the male and female adult onlookers. Among the East African *Nandi*, the boy is not supposed to flinch during some of the most painful aspects of the ordeal, although during parts of the operation the boy may collapse from pain. During the second part of this elaborate operation performed by the *Nandi*, the assembled friends and relatives engage in merry-making and festivities. To flinch or withdraw earns for the boy the opprobrious sobriquet of *kipite,* or coward.

W. I. Thomas states that "the unique concentration of the Jews on circumcision as a political symbol is explicable as a feature of the struggle of a desert group, with a Canaan complex, seeking a place in the fertile crescent of Mesopotamia and at war with Egyptians, Hittites, Babylonians on their borders and with the Philistines and other groups within the borders. The early books of the Old Testament have various passages which may be viewed as propaganda of the rite, always associated with the promotion of the worship of Yahweh. In the covenant between Yahweh and Abraham (Genesis 17) circumcision is made the condition of tribal fertility, increase, and conquest. In Joshua 5:2-9 a whole army is circumcised."[10]

Acquisition of a New Name and Language

The physical changes of the adolescent child are marked by modifications in tonal inflection, intonation, appearance, and size. The previous affectation of a diminutive nickname can hardly be applied to the gangling youth who is forever, it seems, growing out of his clothes. We become confused as adults as to whether to treat this towering youth before us as a child or as a man.

The change in voice, sometimes extremely sudden in the case of boys and more gradual in the case of girls, discloses to us what appears to be a new personality. And actually, in a very profound sense, this *is* a "new" personality being revealed to us, with new interests, new perceptions, new orientations and values, and suddenly, seemingly inflexible and deeply-rooted attachments to his friends and cronies.

The previous salutation of "Billy Boy" seems singularly inappropriate somehow and gives way, admittedly with begrudging reluctance on the part of the fond parent, to the more dignified "William" or "Son". But this seeming rebirth of the personality finds expression in myriad other ways as well. The adolescent boy and girl, in their own groups and in respect to each other, have new secrets to share, new information to impart, new ideas to bandy about, in which the prying ears and eyes of the adult world have little place and, in fact, are cordially resented.

Thus, the estranged and astounded parent learns that his or her beloved William (the erstwhile "Billy Boy") is now addressed fondly by his companions as "Toughie", "Pal", the "Rock", and by as many other cognomens as the fertile imagination of the adolescent world can conjure up in relation to attainments, real or imagined. Further, the teen-ager husbands with fierce pride and pleasure the attainments which his new name betokens and resents any intrusion by parents and elders into this private domain as an infringement upon its own inalienable rights. Thus, although "Stinky" may hardly be an honorific title to one's beloved offspring in the opinion of the outraged parents of "Billy Boy", it may become a guerdon to be cherished and fought for by the beleaguered child.

The prized confidences of this youthful world are conveyed in the form of pleasantries which defy, and frequently shock, the understanding of the suddenly bewildered parent. This is not only exemplified through the use of a new array of vernacular usages, idioms, cliches, and jargon for each generation of emerging adults, as in the case of the contemporary "hep talk" or "jive" which is already being supplanted by its successor, but by the elaborate development of what constitutes a "private language" for adolescents. Further, girls' talk becomes different in degree and kind from boys' talk, and the use of a complicated system of suffixes and prefixes to ordinary terms of speech renders the language largely unintelligible except to the *cognoscenti*.

The emergent status of a "new" personality, with its own language, terms of reference, and personal names, becomes formally accepted and institutionalized among primitive peoples and many other cultures. This is usually sharply emphasized in the form of the separate social functions which various segments of the social system tend to illustrate. Thus, for example, among the *Arapesh* where a sharp distinction is made between the reproductive functions of the woman and the food-getting responsibilities of the male, the character of the ceremonial and the several designations employed point rather clearly to the widespread social understanding of the fundamental nature of this distinction. Where the responsibilities of the male and the world he is about to enter are clearly and generally understood, the sounds and sights to which he is exposed during the puberty ceremonials are intended to insure a rightful understanding of his responsibility and to exclude those who can never assume such a function.

Thus, the use of a special language and magically potent terms may become zealously guarded as the cult-secret of one sex and age group as compared to another. The ceremonial occasion or situation when such new knowledge can be given is itself widely variable, irrespective of the universality of its occurrence. It may, in fact, be part of a formal phase of the induction ceremony, in which the lad's elders or sponsors systematically attempt to indoctrinate him in the language and practices of the mysteries being unfolded before him. It may, however, be almost entirely devoid of elaborate ritualistic trappings and become part of the individual's solitary and lonely quest for self-fulfillment and identity, as among the Plains Indians. The mystic experience to which the young *Pawnee* voluntarily exposed himself, through a self-imposed regimen of fasting, isolation, and pain, induced the deeply moving trance-like visions which frequently laid the basis of the individual's entire subsequent career. Under such solitary conditions of experience, voluntarily undertaken, the sacred quality of the vision was considered far too deeply personal and significant to be revealed to anyone.

The rebirth of the personality during this process of adult

emergence, which can vary in duration anywhere from days to months and even years, stresses the new world in which the voyaging spirit of the youth ventures and in which the symbols and realities of everyday experience become transmuted. Among the *Bakongo* in Africa, a separate *vela* stockade was erected outside the village to which a group of youths might retire for a period ranging from three months to three years. In the *vela,* a deliberate effort was made to teach a new and secret language. Common objects were referred to by impressive titles—the eye as the "possessor of sight," for example—and ordinary words were obscured by the use of special prefixes. (This appears to strike a respondent chord among many of us who have become singularly impressed by the unexpected and awkward euphuisms occasionally interlarding the vernacular of our own teen-agers.) The entire effect of such devices, apparently, is to convince the outsider that the experience has actually produced a new revelation and outlook, an experience which signifies the emergence of a renascent individual.

The application of a new name in itself constitutes a remarkably interesting psychological fact. The name of an individual becomes a deeply rooted part of his personality. Aside from the cultural significance to the parents who confer a name upon a child, reflecting a variety of social values and prestige-bearing preferences, the name in itself becomes a symbolic referent embodying distinctive traits in the mind of the individual. Thus, the child's family or parents may search diligently for a suitable name which will signify pride in ancestry or the need to establish status in terms of a current, fashionable trend. Since, traditionally, names have seemed to suggest cultural class, position, or historical background, we frequently are amused at the juxtaposition of names which appear to have little relevance to the individual's background and social mobility. We reflect this very often in our annoyance at names which seem to be pretentious and which, in our minds, bear little relationship to the child's unique tradition. It is not uncommon to direct humorously critical barbs towards individuals bearing such names.

During childhood and adolescence, however, the young person may show distinct evidences of protest against the name arbitrarily conferred upon him. The name given him was an arbitrary decision, irrespective of the ardent soul-searching which parents may have exercised in choosing exactly the right cognomen pleasing to one's position, place of residence, expectations, friends, and relatives. Now, however, the child is free to make his own choice. Moreover, the new name is associated with a profound experience or series of episodes in which the individual has attempted to express his own powers and his own capabilities. Further, the name expresses what his own peers have learned to expect of him under certain conditions and thus contributes to his own understanding of his identity.[11]

The formalizing of this process of adolescent name-giving is well established in other cultures and, in a sense, provides a highly rational basis in the acceptance of the natural stages of each individual's growth. Among the *Pawnee*, thus, each individual's life is a continuing quest for new levels of growth and, consequently, a recognition of the emergent personality designated by a new name.

> A man's life is an onward movement. If one has within him a determined purpose and seeks the help of the powers his life will "climb up".... (As) a man is climbing up he does something that makes a place in his life where the powers have given him the opportunity to express in acts his peculiar endowments, so that this place, this act, forms a stage in his career, and he takes a new name to indicate that he is on a level different from that which he occupied previously.[12]

Indeed, in many cultures, the identification of name and personality is so intimate that the individual is virtually nameless until he is able to show in certain experiences of culturally-determined growth evidences of his talents and propensities. As many names may be utilized in a lifetime as there are significant age-level experiences to which the individual exposes himself and in which he has displayed his peculiar talents.

It appears thus, on the basis of what has been said, that the conferring of a name constitutes a symbolic landmark in the individual's quest for self-identity. The quaint conceits of teen-age boys and girls in our own culture brings this rather clearly to light. Aside from the nickname cherished by a boy, we may observe the curious and meaningful artifices of young girls who go through a stage where they give their names a peculiarly elegant twist. This may be seen specifically in the affectation of an oddity in spelling and in the vehement insistence upon a desired pronunciation as well as in the caressing flourish with which a name may be written.

If we apprehend with some care the significance of such devices on the part of teen-agers, we can frequently gain an insight into the problems, peculiar and generic, which may be actuating their behavior. For example, a nickname conferred upon a youth may not necessarily be honorific or laudatory in character but may express the peer-age group's scathing contempt and denunciation. The child who suffers from such an unpleasantly invidious cognomen has, in the opinion of the group as well as of himself, failed somehow to measure up to the standards of his clique. The mark of such failure, whether rightly bestowed or not, is not assuaged by the appellations of endearment by a fond parent. Indeed, the hostility which such a child may experience is directed towards the self as an attitude of self-disparagement; this hostile self-attitude is frequently heightened, and not relieved, by the protective attitude and nomenclature of the parent.

For, in a sense, this conferring of a derogatory name to the person signifies that one has failed in the only area of social activity which is significant at the time, no matter how meaningless it may appear later on. A cruel nickname which persists can leave a lasting scar upon the growing child. When the process of name-conferring becomes institutionalized, the chances for such ignominy are considerably lessened —although such tokens of poor esteem may also arise upon occasion—since the positive, self-fulfilling aspects of the individual's personal growth are stressed. The new name, thus, becomes a public accolade attesting to the individual's promise rather than a condemnation of the individual's present shortcomings and failures.

Conditions Associated With Age Segregation and Breaking of the Household Tie

As age-segregation may occur on virtually any level during the course of the individual's development, its meaning takes form in relation to the social values and attitudes which a society places on a given age category. Thus, in our society, the child from five to seven, still an object of extreme protective concern to the parent and consequently entirely dependent, views his playmates in terms of what he considers the proprietary functions of the parent. The child's helplessness and dependence, accentuated among ourselves, finds expression in the need "to tell all to mama" and in the haphazard, shifting pattern of loyalties to companions characteristic of such a young children's group. In the child's eyes, the parent is identified almost wholly as an appendage of the playmate—as the source of that unknown and unexplained adult power which may be swift, capricious or orderly, but always unremitting and authoritarian, the parent being addressed as "Jimmy's daddy" or "Susan's mommy." The stress of this adult care provides a framework within which the child may only view himself in highly egotistic and dependent terms.

If we examine another chronological level in our industrial society where the accent is so relentlessly upon youth, the conception which the aged person entertains towards himself and those of his own age category is infused with a sense of isolation and frequently unconcealed rancor towards more youthful segments of society. The well-nigh tragic and desperate efforts of the aged to "cling to their youth" by the exercise of ingenious devices of beauty care constitutes a bitter struggle to fend off this isolation which society fastens upon them. Such attitudes of isolation and resentment are engendered by the growing recognition of the essential social disutility of the old in our society, although this may be artfully concealed by lofty statements and a guilt-laden sense of obligation. The in-group loyalties binding together the aged in specific groups, such as the currently popular "Golden Age Clubs" so-called, are frequently framed in a bond of common commiseration at their rejection by society. Topics of conversation frequently revolve around carping criticism of the seeming callousness of their young or veer in the opposite direction in boasting about the achievements of a son or daughter from whose exploits reflected glory may be derived. Status within the old-age group itself is largely *derivative* rather than as the result of one's own accomplishments.

For the teen-ager, however, the problem is quite different. For the adolescent youth, the conditions governing his associations are derived almost wholly from his attitude of protest and dissent towards recognized adult authority. As a necessary prelude to adulthood, this ironically appears to be universal in all societies—even in those societies where the protest is neither acknowledged or accepted.

The period of puberty represents the first powerful forward thrust into the previously barred world of adulthood, for which all else has been preparation. This seems to be well established in all societies irrespective of the age-level when adolescence is officially recognized and whether the age-level coincides naturally with the physiological changes of puberty. In accordance with the severity with which restraints are imposed upon the recognizable and socially acceptable drives of adolescence, powerful protests of varying degree and form will emerge. To apprehend this fact properly, this should be viewed in relation to other categorical age statuses, such as those of early childhood and old age. As previously described, the early childhood state is generally conceived as a period of dependence, and the sporadic protests of children which arise because of restraints imposed upon them, even when capricious, are due to the needs of self-protection and *not* because the child conceives himself as entitled to adult privilege. In the case of the aged, the protest is borne out of an ignoring by society of the personal insistence of the aged person that he be recognized as a full adult. In paraphrase of Arthur Miller's play, *Death of a Salesman,* the aged are insistent that "attention be paid."

None of these conditions apply to the young adolescent whose protest is actuated by the fact that he is impatient to arrive at a state which is actually awaiting him. In the rebuffs he may experience, or the indignities from which he imagines he is suffering, his protests are apt to assume diametric form—with protests highly positive and ideal in nature, or just the opposite, strongly rejective and negative reactions to those very values he will eventually rightfully assume. As an illustration of the former, we have but to think of the impassioned and idealistic defenses of our youth in the past to what the cynical adult regards as "lost causes", unrealistic and futile perhaps, but vivid, clear, and alive in the progressive growth of mankind. Our own history, as well as that of others, is replete with those occasions where the young person has felt that he must lend himself to great religious, political, or moral causes.

But in accordance with the character and structure of society, and the channelled opportunities it presents for protest, the opposite may also be true. In fact, for the average young person in any period, heroic as well as inglorious ages, the two forms of protest in differing degree are usually interwoven. One of the ominous aspects of the present period is the fact that whereas the protest is very much in evidence—powerful, vigorous, and self-assertive—it does not seem to become harnessed to the "great causes" which typified so many generations of youth in the past. Although in the past the storming of youth upon the barricades of some forgotten and lofty cause may have produced mortification, annoyance, counter-protests, and even mild amusement among adults (who remembered their own youth), such movements were frequently construed as signs of youthful ebullience, vigor, growth, and promise of future achievement. As annoyed as adults may have been with such protests, there was a recognized and even hopeful feeling that such dissidence was worthwhile and gave an edge to the youth's discovery of recalcitrant realities. Today, however, as Robert Lindner has pointed out, this youthful protest appears diffuse, disordered, and anarchic. It assumes no recognizable or concrete form. It finds no barricades to storm. Rather, it becomes, in Lindner's excellent phrase, a "rebellion without cause." a kind of "mutiny within conformity." And this conformity, seemingly so aimless and sterile, finding expression primarily in the similarities of a common accent, jargon, insignia, and apparel, appears to be almost a frightening foretaste of the dry-rot of mechanized, uniform monotony. This psychological character appears to reflect a form of social living in which the clarion call to the latest affectation of the Madison Avenue hucksters has achieved the ultimate triumph and in which the invidious comparisons of popular consumption have become the principal arbiters of good taste and social success. The landscape in which such a psychological and cultural atmosphere flourishes is the dreary expanse of suburban-urban developments where the outlook is not upon the limitless horizons of man's soaring spirit but upon the picture-window which faces monotonously upon one's neighbor's. To the former youth of the slums, the hope may have been for eventual escape from his sordid surroundings and this may have been a prime motive for adult identification. In fact, for the youth of today still living in slum-ridden quarters, this may still be the way out. For the more fortunate and middle class youth, however, the question becomes "Escape to Where?" Even for the parents of such chidren, the "better life" frequently means removal from heavily mortgaged "junior executive" homes to increasingly mortgaged "miniature estates" with double garages. The picture window view, however, remains largely unchanged.

The protest of youth, whether positive or negative in form, stems to a considerable degree from the omnipresent compulsion to shatter the household ties and to assert one's independence as a self-initiating personality. Even in those cultures where the youth's transition to adulthood is eased, a certain degree of inner turmoil and protest is inescapably present in view of the necessary psychological and cultural conditions involved in this seeking for emancipation. To win one's spurs as an adult involves not only the freeing of one's own profound emotional ties to parents and family, but the psychic strain and tension, the "fears and trembling", induced by the novelty which such a severance of deeply-laid emotional ties presupposes. Thus, although the outward path may appear smooth and unruffled, as in some idyllic South Pacific atoll (actually non-existent today), the signs of protest, self-doubt, and resentment are present here too if one examines the signs deeply enough.[13] Further, some tension is invariably provoked by lurking intransigent attitudes of adults themselves, irrespective of how artfully concealed and self-sacrificingly subordinated, in view of the fact that one must step aside and make room for the newcomer. Also, as a final factor, the admission of young people into the ranks of adulthood may foster a number of difficult practical problems, themselves productive of increased tension, in the form of expensive and elaborate preparations for the induction of new adults. It is not uncommon for a society to accept with the greatest reluctance this advent of "coming of age" and to be forced to husband its limited resources for a number of years in order to conduct the appropriate ceremonial of admission. A comparable modern analogue may be found in the strain upon the modern middle class American family which places itself under severe economic strain in order to send a child through college. Thus, even among a relatively relaxed group such as the *Arapesh*, described by Margaret Mead, the preparation of the young male adult for his initiation produces reverberations throughout his entire social orbit.

> The large initiations are held only every six or seven years, when repeated gibes between communities at big feasts have finally goaded some community into undertaking the huge work of organization and preparation that is necessary if some twelve or fifteen boys and their sponsoring relatives are to be fed for several months in one place. Such a feast takes several years to prepare, and has its echoes throughout the lives of the group of novices, who years later, as middle-aged men, will be finding pigs to take back to that village to be distributed in final long-deferred repayment for the initiation. Meanwhile, in the six-year period between initiations, boys who were too small when the last initiation was

held have grown very tall, embarrassingly so. They have gradually learned most of the secrets.[14]

All of these conditions conspire to bring the young person closer to his own age and sex peers. The youth, therefore, may repair with his fellows to a selected spot for differing periods of time and under widely varying conditions. His associations with his own peers assume a highly intimate character. Into this closely circumscribed orbit, his adult sponsors may likewise be drawn to share certain aspects of this newly found intimacy. Food may be left for him or he may have to forage for himself and, in certain societies, he may be free to engage in various forms of sexual dalliance, either of a furtive nature or with openly approved sanction. The idiosyncrasies of behavior typifying himself and his fellow novices during this period tend to assume an expected pattern which may be tolerated under sufferance or encouraged by the adult members of his society during this period.

Thus, among the *Arapesh,* as Mead points out, the comradeship between all of the boys is stressed as well as the special care that is taken of them by their fathers and elder brothers, and by the designated sponsors. Whether simple or elaborate, "the essentials of the initiation remain the same: there is ritual segregation from the company of women, during which time the novice observes certain special food taboos, is incised, eats a sacrificial meal of the blood of the older men, and is shown various marvelous things." [15] The "marvelous things" consist largely of the symbolic objects which tend to emphasize the fact of his newly gained responsibility and the various revelations which portray graphically the peculiar role which the adult male must exercise, particularly in relation to women. The content of the information imparted reflects those values which the society has come to regard as most important for its survival and the special role which men must play in upholding this value-structure. The physiological facts of adolescence, as has been so frequently shown, are secondary; the social implications for honorable adult behavior are paramount.[16] The theme of the educational content of the adolescent ceremony, therefore, becomes endlessly variable, even though the forms appear so similar. The themes reflect those values which are most highly prized and which the young person may hopefully emulate and strive for.

Adulthood in central North America means warfare. Honour in it is the great goal of all men. The constantly recurring theme of the youth's coming-of-age, as also of preparation for the warpath at any age, is a magic ritual for success in war. They torture not one another, but themselves; they cut strips of skin from their arms and legs, they strike off their fingers, they drag heavy weights pinned to their chest or leg muscles. Their reward is enhanced prowess in deeds or warfare.

In Australia, on the other hand, adulthood means participation in an exclusively male cult whose fundamental trait is the exclusion of women. Any woman is put to death if she so much as hears the sound of the bull-roarer at the ceremonies, and she must never know of the rites. Puberty ceremonies are elaborate and symbolic repudiations of the bonds with the female sex; the men are symbolically made self-sufficient and the wholly responsible element of the community. To attain this end they use drastic sexual rites and bestow supernatural guarantees.[17]

That the values bestowed upon the youthful male novice are designed to leave an indelible imprint upon his imagination can be seen in the secrecy with which the proceedings are conducted. The separation from women is clearly established and despite his eventual close association with his wife and other female members of kinship and other groups, the preservation of this separation is made inviolable. The free and easy-going sexless existence of the child, if it ever truly existed, can no longer be envisaged or tolerated. The recognition of this basic dichotomy insures the continuance of the life and labor of the group in its manifold ramifications. "To be a man" signifies more than an elementary recognition of physiological difference and function; the enlivened awakening brought about by the rites of passage implies a knowledge of the full social meaning of life, how one must live with and yet protect one's self from the opposite sex, and the paths one must take towards honorable self-fulfillment.

In New Guinea, the *tamberan* cult has been developed as a means of accentuating the differences between men and women. When the *tamberan*, the supernatural patron of the men, enters the *Arapesh* village, the women all flee and remain out of sight until he is safely housed in the ceremonial hut reserved for his presence. The sounds and flute-playing which emanate from this hut, which only initiated males and prospective initiates may enter, are disregarded by the women as matters pertaining only to the men. The mysteries which take place there had better not be pried into, according to the women's viewpoint, and—we may well imagine some smugness here—if men have their mysteries, women have theirs too. While the *Arapesh* women do not readily show the same fright of the *tamberan* which is frequently disclosed among the women of neighboring peoples, the function of the cult is to establish and sustain irrevocably the separation of male and female responsibilities.

In a recent study by Eisenstadt of different age groups in a variety of cultures, the point is made that age groupings provide the basis for "the transmission of the social heritage and maintenance of social continuity". [18] The form which such age groups take, according to the same writer, and the character of their interaction and peculiar ideology, result from the need to establish proper identification and supportive group solidarity. An examination of the puberty rites in a large number of societies would tend to confirm this supposition.[19]

Sexual Ambivalence and Homosexuality

On the basis of what has already been said, it must not be assumed that the relationships between men and women in all societies are necessarily hostile or that their social functions are contradictory and exclusive. Although hostility between the sex groups of a culture may actually be quite acute and the corresponding social functions of the sexes sharply disparate, there are ample evidences of common goals of achievement and values shared by both sexes in many cultures, even those in which sex conflict appears quite prominent. Nevertheless, in all cultures, the coming of age of the young male tends to induce a state of heightened self-consciousness concerning his sexual role and function.

In a great many cultures, such as our own, the distinctions in the social character of the sexes have become vital—basic to the entire conception as to how the social order must function. A recent popular song "It's a Woman's World," provides a satirical commentary of our general acceptance of the fact that socially ordered sexual differences are somehow at the very basis of our *Weltanschauung*. Further, as the doggerel wryly suggests, it is the "weaker" traits of women which seem to dominate in the end. The fact remains that in many cultures a wide variety of temperamental qualities, as well as social and cultural traits, are associated with one sex or the other, and it is further assumed that such sex-linkages are "natural".

One of the most significant disclosures of anthropologists during the past three decades has been the clear and concise demonstration that there is no definite linkage between specific temperamental and social traits and membership in a given sex. Where, because of historic reasons, the culture has come to emphasize such distinctions sharply, it appears almost self-evident to members of such a culture that these differences are part of the immutable and natural order of things. There is, of course, no actual proof of what appears to be an incontrovertible fact to the members of such a sex-divided culture. Indeed, as the anthropologists have shown, the evidence appears to point significantly to the contrary. As Margaret Mead has suggested, to ascribe to one sex or the other certain specific traits is largely a matter of historic social classification and is no more valid biologically than the arbitrary classification of traits on the basis of eye color. Some conception of the difficulties which arise in any culture which focuses so largely upon such a distinction may be gained if one imagines the type of psychological and social strain which might be induced if the culture was equally insistent that blue-eyed and brown-eyed individuals adopt only certain approved behavioral characteristics.

Thus, in our culture, we tend to place an inordinate stress upon the child to fit into the proper classification. From the very outset of his career, the child is enjoined, wheedled, cajoled, and coerced to behave in the appropriate manner of his sex, irrespective of whether he is temperamentally or socially suited for such behavior. As a boy, he learns that he must be a "good loser", aggressive, ready to defend himself with his fists, able to control his tears, not to hang on to his mother's apron strings, use certain graceless profanities, prefer baseball to music, not to admit when he's tired, and to "be a man like his daddy". The girl soon learns, despite any congenital or acquired temperamental disability to the contrary, that anger must be displayed differently from boys, certain forms of petulance and sulking may be allowed, tears are permissible where they may not be for boys, quiet games are better than noisy ones, strenuous exercise should be limited, dolls are to be preferred to bats and balls, certain forms of language are not to be used, and, in a myriad of other ways, that "she must act like a little lady." The innumerable facets of social control we exercise in imposing such classificatory procedures upon our young manifest themselves in countless small details which often escape notice. The girl is told how to sit, how to walk, how to wear her clothes, when not to cross her knees, and a thousand other minor instructions which begin to seep into the personality and which eventually will make it self-evident that she is properly classified. The same is true in countless ways of the endless mannerisms we almost unconsciously impose upon boys. One throws a ball hard to boys and not to girls; girls are expected to tire more easily than boys, and the young male is soon taught that special consideration must be made for these seeming inevitable and natural limitations.

The result of such extreme pressures in those cultures where sexual lines are so sharply drawn is to impose an enormous burden upon individuals who cannot, by reason of temperament or acquired trait, fit into the accepted patterns of sexual difference. In our culture, very likely, there is no more serious handicap than to be unable to measure up to the temperamental and social expectancies of one's associates of both sexes. Lest there be any misunderstanding, it should be noted that failure to meet a required social standard may have very little to do, if anything, with the individual's sexual potency. A mild unaggressive male may suffer from no physical disability other than the psychological strain induced by his embarrassment, chagrin, resentment, or hostility at not being able to meet an arbitrarily imposed social standard. An aggressive, dominating female may likewise have no inherent limitation concerning her sexual capacity but may nevertheless be at a serious disadvantage because of her seemingly masculine characteristics.

The type of psychological strain induced by the continual reminder that we must never deviate in the slightest from the prescribed standards is likely to be excessively severe for *all* individuals, not alone those who may resemble in some habit, practice, or affectation one sex or the other. This is something which is frequently overlooked. In this type of culture, all individuals suffer from the strain to make one's sex-identity translucently clear. Nevertheless, the natural preferences in social, aesthetic, and athletic behavior which an individual displays may have very little to do with his sex. The individual may develop strong emotional attachments within the family, laying the basis for powerful psychodynamic drives, which repudiate rather strongly expected oedipal ties. Within the family situation, for example, a physically normal child can identify himself very closely with a parent of his own sex, not because of any sinister, pathological disorder, but simply because of temperamental affinity. The young girl who likes to scramble among the rocky crags of some hillside with her geologist father may be motivated by intellectual and outdoor interests which the mother neither shares or appreciates. A deeply sex-conscious culture may accordingly become unduly alarmed at what it may regard as a sinister fixation.

Many individuals may find the greatest scope for the expression of their talents and abilities among members of the opposite sex. In a rigidly sex-dichotomous culture, this immediately limits and handicaps them. In fact, as we know all too tragically, the end-result of such continued association may be disastrous for the individual and a loss in creative value for the society. What we are doing, in effect, by this arbitrary linkage of sex and certain socially defined traits is to deny the fundamental creativity resident in the individual differences of the organism and personality *irrespective of sex*. The little boy who likes to sew, for example, is not necessarily doomed to a life of inversion (although we may help to make it so), purely on the basis of his indicating such an early preference. Such an artistic bent expressed in childhood may be an available channel—the only one possibly open to him—in which he can express a need for creative digital exercise. This may, in turn, lay the basis not necessarily for sexual inversion but for the skillful handling of a surgeon's tools or intricate laboratory equipment—if we permit him to exercise this bent unmolested. However, the fact that we constrict the individual's traits in accordance with a sex-defined pattern of psychological and cultural difference makes the adjustments of certain children extremely harsh and virtually forces them into a pattern of inversion, whether we will or not.

In a culture marked by such sharply defined sexual differences, the individual is apt to struggle valiantly to achieve the characteristics which are considered natural to his sex. But there is considerably more to this than the mere outer conformity to a socially imposed pattern. It means, as was previously stated, that the individual is forever on his guard not to betray by the slightest misstep that he may not be entirely male or, in the case of the girl, that she is not entirely female. Such individuals are continuously in a state of self-jeopardy in which any questionable behavior may asperse the individual's sexual character. Such behavior may not only cause suspicion on the part of others but, even more ominously, may cast doubt in one's own mind concerning the ever present issue of sexual validity. Mistakes, even innocent and casual mistakes, can mean the ruin of one's career and, more serious, even the ruin of one's life and its conceived purpose.

This contrast of sexual difference is carried to an extreme during the age of puberty. The individual must continually assure others, his peers, especially, as well as himself, that he is unmistakably a male. The bizarre and extreme male antics and buffoonery characteristic of this age are, in essence, efforts to demonstrate one's sexual authenticity. But the lurking fear always persists, and with the lurking fear is strong resentment towards persons and occasions which, in any way, may tend to disparage the official sexual attitude and role. The deeper the suspicion that one may not be entirely male or female, the greater tendency towards excessive compensation in order to receive complete vindication and confirmation. The adolescent male gang, therefore, is forever on guard concerning any threat, real or imagined, which may challenge its sexual position.

If a culture, therefore, makes this stress the ultimate condition of honorable admission to adulthood, strongly ambivalent attitudes towards women are inevitable. The young male learns to distrust and dislike—even hate—any trait of the opposite sex which he must learn to deny for himself. In fact, he may become terribly afraid and morbidly anxiety-ridden in the presence of such traits. For this reason, it is no surprise that among preliterate societies an elaborate mythology and demonology is developed concerning the malevolence and malignant danger of women to men. This frequently becomes ceremonialized in the culminating episode which indisputably sets women apart from men—the menstrual cycle. The powerful and evil danger to men at this period is manifested in the rigidly prescribed taboos which separate women from men at this time and in the careful precautionary safeguards by which their return to normal society can only be accomplished by an elaborate purification ritual. How much of this fear still remains in the peculiar sexual attitudes of men and women of modern times during the period of the menstrual flow is largely undetermined. It would appear, however, that much of the attitude of women towards themselves during this period of traditional "uncleanliness," and the popular reference to this physiological function by women themselves as "the curse", has deeply-rooted and irrational historic sources. The effect of such attitudes upon the various psychosomatic complaints of women during this period, to which men have become inured, may stem in large part from this traditionally-rooted complex of fear and hostility. This may also be the basis for those occasional ritual acts among certain aborigines where the penis is slit at recurrent monthly intervals as a means of simulating the mentrual cycle of women.

Despite his fear and hostility, the young male is powerfully drawn through his awakened sexual impulses towards those very creatures whose traits he has learned to reject for himself. This partially explains the intense dislike on the part of many men towards women who in any way display masculine characteristics. Such women are not only invading territory which is not theirs but create disquieting doubts as to one's own true identity.

Because of its very preparatory nature towards sex fulfillment, such ambivalent attitudes are brought to their sharpest focus during the adolescent period. To a degree, we assume that this would have to be true of all cultures, even those in which the cleavage between the sexes is not extreme and pervasive. Despite his urgent physical needs and his gravitation towards women, the young male must disparage and denigrate those women and girls about him whose very presence constitutes a challenge to his manhood. In their very traits, he unconsciously looks for characteristics which may be revealing of himself, and hence dangerous and traumatic. Barred by powerful cultural barriers in having free access to the opposite sex, by means of which he can discover and affirm his difference, he is apt to resort to powerful imagery, largely of a negative sort. Only later, as Willard Waller has shown, when he is genuinely seeking a wife does the imagery assume an idealistic and positive character.[20] For some individuals, the imagery always remains on a negative or deprecatory level, however, as we so well know.

During the turbulent adolescent search for identity, however, he must prove by word and deed that he is different and worthy of acceptance in terms of his difference. Confronted with what appears to be a continual goad, his curiosity concerning the opposite sex becomes extreme and obsessive. Prominent in the questions running through his mind is the issue of what does it actually mean to be a girl, a woman. Even with opportunities for sexual gratification, this essential and dynamic curiosity is not necessarily appeased or diminished. The exploration of a woman's body, mind, and personal characteristics is a never-ending source of wonder. When the sexual taboos are very strong, as in our own culture and despite ample opportunity for their transgression, the mystery of woman's presence and personality becomes even more powerful.

Much of this ambivalent yearning, thus, finds expression in forms of behavior which either resemble patterns of inversion or which appear to the non-discerning eye as outright manifestations of homosexuality. That the genuine adolescent homosexual can find sanctuary in these peculiarly deceptive forms of inversion appears quite likely. That some do so without recognizing that their behavior is actually homosexual, there can be little doubt. However, for most adolescent groups, the preoccupation with the opposite sex, and their intense desire to identify themselves with sexual opposites as a means of self-discovery, manifests itself in a variety of subtle forms of mimicry, imitation, modified transvesticism, and fetishism.

Among Australian groups, such mimicry and imitation is sometimes carried to an extreme. Certain male members of the initiation party may actually invest themselves with female ornaments and dress, and engage in artful simulation before the young novices of feminine mannerisms and characteristics. In certain instances, this may even proceed to the point where simulated amorous advances are made. Among adolescent groups in our own culture, priding themselves on their manliness, ribald imitations of girls and women are commonly practised and playfully coy advances made to each other. By mimicry, the use of falsetto tones, and suggestive movements, much of the random and aimless play of adolescent gang boys employs such outwardly homosexual features.

Among the American Plains Indians, transvesticism assumes an institutional pattern for those young men who deliberately choose this path at the time of puberty, without any special stigma being attached to that status. A modified form of transvesticism is found among many peoples, however, and is not necessarily associated with genuine pathological deviation. The fetishism among adolescent American groups seems to provide a similar outlet and pattern. The wearing of feminine undergarments or carrying an article of feminine wearing apparel upon the person frequently appears to be more than a symbolic evidence of profound sexual interest. The recent wave of "panty raids" in women's dormitories on several college campuses by middle class adolescent youths, the retention among one's possessions of some intimate feminine object, and the exchange of garments between boys and girls, as well as related practices, may be adduced as limited tendencies resembling certain phases of inversion.

Aside from the incorporation of such feminine elements into a strictly pretentious masculine world, certain practices may be found among adolescents in many cultures which suggest strongly latent and active homosexual impulses. Such evidence may be found in a wide variety of assaultive adolescent pranks. One such prank commonly found in our own culture consists in the hazing of a frequently unsuspecting and helpless victim of one's own group by pouncing on him, stripping him wholly or partially, and abusing or playing with his genitals.

The Myth of Rebirth of the Adolescent Novice

The function of a myth is to reinforce a social attitude. When the myth is well established and deeply implanted, it suggests that the need to accept the attitude as it has been traditionally developed is no longer open to serious question. In many cultures, therefore, in keeping with the belief that the adolescent represents a new emergent personality, ceremonials and rituals have been developed to indicate the death or passing away of the previous personality and the emergence or rebirth of the new adult form.

It is relatively easy to see why the surrounding group

regards the rapidly changing and growing adolescent as a new personality. The changes which appear are, in a considerable sense, quite dramatic; the little boy or little girl seems to disappear before one's eyes and a young man or woman seems to materialize in their place. Not only are such changes dramatic and frequently quite sudden, but they are reinforced by modifications of voice, tone, and attitude, all of which seem to betoken a newly arrived stranger in our midst. This gangling and deep-voiced youth standing before you—what relationship does he bear to the little awkward boy tugging at your hand a few yesterdays ago? This lovely young maiden with the soft curves of burgeoning womanhood can no longer be casually fondled as the seemingly sexless member of the household of a few scant months ago.

It is understandable that, in the face of such dramatic changes, a society is inclined to regard such a metamorphosis in religious or magical terms. It is for this reason that in many societies these profound changes of personality become ceremonially reenacted in the form of a drama of dying and coming to life again as a new personality. It is almost as if the changes are too profound for the ordinary adult to accept unless he can convince himself through the employment of some artfully contrived dramaturgy that these events are actually taking place. Such rites, therefore, may be highly variable, ranging from a brief, formal, and perfunctory ceremony, in which the rebirth is publicly acknowledged, to elaborate procedures in which the young person may absent himself and then reemerge in his new form days, weeks, or months later. So important may the ceremonial become that all of the other phases of the rites of passage are in some way linked up with it. Thus, the scarification and mutilation of the body may be considered as the marks of a mythological monster, patron, or deity who swallows the young person and then disgorges him in the new form. When the ceremonial calls for the young person to absent himself for a lengthy period of time, the deception of rebirth is even more convincing because of the actual changes in the appearance of the young person which only a few weeks or months may produce.

This conception of adolescent rebirth is particularly well illustrated in the custom of *ndembo* among the African *Bakongo*. So vividly is the death and birth drama reenacted here that the individual is actually conceived as dying, disintegrating, and coming to life once more with all of the strangeness and unfamiliarity which the newly emergent personality would be expected to display in confronting a new environment.

(When it is time for the young adolescent to become a member of the *ndembo* society, those who are eligible) are instructed by the doctor to feign sudden death at a sign from him. Accordingly, in some public place the novice falls down as though dead. Funeral cloth or a blanket is laid upon him; the doctor beats the ground round the 'dead' person with plantain stalks, and after singing, and gun firing, and dancing, he is borne away to the *vela* stockade outside the town. He is said to have "died ndembo".

In the *vela* they are supposed to decompose and decay, until but one bone of each novice is left in charge of the doctor. They remain in the *vela* for a term varying from three months to three years. No clothes are worn, for "there is no shame in *ndembo*;" the bodies of the novices are rubbed with red ochre, arnatto red, or powdered camwood.

When the term appointed is at an end, preparations are made for the 'resurrection' of those who have "died ndembo". Parents and relatives have to make certain payments to the doctor, and the news is spread that, on a certain market day, there will be a grand resurrection at the market. All the countryside collects to the fete.

The initiates, now called *nganga*, "knowing ones", are clothed in fine cloths, sent by their friends, and are led with reddened skins in solemn procession to the market, and file two or three times round the crowd assembled. All have a tassel of palm fibre on their arms. After the march round, the mystery is complete, and mothers and friends hug the long-lost *nganga*. The *nganga* are instructed to pretend to know nobody and nothing. They appear dazed, and cannot talk. They want whatever they see, seize whatever takes their fancy; no one is allowed to resist, because "they do not know any better." They behave like lunatics, and pretend not to know how to eat; even food has to be masticated for them, so well do they act their part. After a few days the excitement and interest of the deception wears off, and they gradually resume intelligence. If anyone asks curious questions as to the land of the dead whence they have come, they stick a piece of grass behind their ears, and pretend to be perfectly unconscious of being addressed.[21]

The magico-mystical belief of rebirth may be seen in many cultures, including our own, as the biblical drama of Jonah and the whale would suggest. Even without the elaborate ceremonial trappings of the past, and even in such highly attenuated religious ceremonies as confirmation, the psychological impact upon modern parents and adults in the Western world of the "new stranger" is vivid and clear.

A Summarized Classification of Selected Puberty Rites

As an indication of the variety of customs concerning adolescent transition which have been partially discussed, the following chart attempts to articulate in greater detail the major patterns within which such variegated customs fall. The chart illustrates the wide variety of such practices, the sources from which this material is taken, and in the last column offers certain interpretive comments indicating the meaning of the customs to the society in which it is found. (In order to facilitate identification, the source for each reference is indicated in the third column rather than in a series of special footnotes.)

TABLE 1
CLASSIFICATION AND DESCRIPTION OF PUBERTY RITES

Puberty Initiatory Practices	Some of the Societies in Which These are Found	Sources	Comments
I Self Decoration A. Tattooing	Solomon Islanders[1] Fijians[1]	1 Hutton Webster, *Primitive Secret Societies* (New York: Macmillan Co., 1932), p. 201.	Webster says: "Until tattooed a Samoan Boy could not think of marriage and was taunted and ridiculed as of no account."[2]
	New Zealanders[2] Tahitians[2] Marquesans[2] Samoans[2]	2 *Ibid.*, p. 205.	"In the Marquesas tattooing is the principal initiatory rite."[2]
B. Painting the Body and Face	Tchambuli[3]	3 Margaret Mead, *From the South Seas*, Vol. iII, *Sex and Temperament in Three Primitive Societies* (New York: William Morrow and Co., 1939), p. 250.	"The Arunta boys while being painted—the first initiatory ceremony—are informed that this will promote their growth to manhood."[5]
	Masai[4]	4 Bruno Bettelheim, *Symbolic Wounds* (Glencoe: The Free Press, 1954), p. 84.	
	Arunta[5]	5 Webster, *op. cit.*, p. 22.	

C. Scarification	Tchambuli[6]	[6] Mead, *op. cit.*, p. 249.	
	Mundugumor[7]	[7] *Ibid.*, p. 183.	
	Andaman Islanders[8]	[8] Eliot Dinsmore Chapple and Carleton Stevens Coon, *Principles of Anthropology* (New York: Henry Holt and Co., 1942), p. 491.	"No one may hold office until after initiation. The visible symbol of such initiation consists of deep scarification from the back of the neck downward."[9]
	Vey of Liberia[9]	[9] Webster, *op. cit.*, p. 26.	
D. Circumcision	Sulka[10]	[10] Webster, *op. cit.*, p. 5.	Lowie includes circumcision under the category of decoration, stating that, "Circumcision is best treated under the heading of decoration."[15]
	Masai[11]	[11] *Ibid.*, p. 13.	
	Madagascar[12]	[12] *Ibid.*, p. 56.	
	Fijians[13]	[13] *Ibid.*, p. 79.	
	Tribes of Northern New Guinea[14]	[14] Sir James G. Frazer, *The Golden Bough* (New York: The Macmillan Co., 1947), p. 694.	Bettelheim argues that circumcision can be considered a type of decoration since many tribes feel that it adds beauty and desirability to the sexual organ. He quotes a young African Sebeyi male who reported that every boy desires to be circumcised because it is beautiful and because the women reject uncircumcised men as sexual partners.[16]
		[15] Robert H. Lowie, *An Introduction to Cultural Anthropology* (New York: Farrar and Rinehart, Inc., 1941); p. 82.	
		[16] Bettelheim, *op. cit.*, p. 163.	

II	Acquisition of New Name or Language	Arunta[17] Dukduk[17] Maidu Indians[17]	The elements upon which this practice is based, appear to be the symbolic rebirth as a new person after undergoing the rites and the increased solidarity of the men's group resulting from this special knowledge.	[17] Webster, *op. cit.*, pp. 42, 43.
III	Leaving Home to Live with Male Age Mates and Period of Seclusion from Women	Amoxosa[18] Susu[18] Mandingoes[18] Bondei[18] Bechuana[19] Kaffir[19]	Many primitive tribes have established formal institutional provisions for the facilitation of this practice. For example: The Kiva of the Pueblo Indians, The Sweat House of the Navaho Indians, The Men's House of the Eskimo and Arapesh Societies. For the related practice of age grading the Canella Indians of Brazil have six or more distinct competing age groups with definite territorial areas in their central plaza.[20] Chapple and Coon have an interesting description of the complex system of Age Grading in Australian tribes. So prominent is this complex classificatory system, that an individual can truly be said to enjoy his social status only in relation to the age group with which he is identified.[21]	[18] *Ibid.*, pp. 44-45. [19] *Ibid.*, p. 81. [20] Lowie, *op. cit.*, pp. 431-33. [21] Chapple and Coon, *op. cit.*, pp. 323-27.

IV Separation from Mother and Home. Incorporation into the Older Men's Group	Numerous Societies[22]	Almost all puberty rites involve this transition, so that numerous examples need not be given. A typical ceremony of the Yaroinga of Queensland wherein the families and the young novices cry bitterly and smear themselves with ashes is depicted by Webster as a formal expression of grief because of this separation.[22]	[22] Webster, op. cit., p.21.
V Sexual Ambivalence and Homosexuality	Omaha Indians[23]	In the Nozhizho rites of the Omaha Indians the boy's vision may cause him to become a transvestite.[23]	[23] Bettelheim, op. cit., p. 109.
	African Chaga[24]	In certain East African tribes the young initiates after circumcision wear female clothing and are addressed as girls.[24]	[24] Ibid., p. 213.
	Iatmul[25]	The Naven ceremonies of the Iatmul which often celebrate puberty initiations contain definite features of transvestism and other sexually ambivalent conduct. An outstanding part of the ceremony is the dressing of men in women's clothing.[25]	[25] Gregory Bateson, Naven (London: Cambridge University Press, 1936), p. 12.
		Their kinship system stresses the close relation between the mother's brother (wau) and the sister's child (laua). During Naven, "The elder rubs his buttocks down the length of his laua's leg, a sort of sexual salute."[26]	[26] Ibid., p. 13.

Arunta[27]
Ilpirra[27]

While the emphasis is on the older man, yet there are homosexual overtones for both of the main participants.

Australian tribes use subincision as a major operation in puberty ceremonials.[27]

This may be interpreted as an attempt of men to imitate the woman's sexual organ by slitting the penis open. The bleeding caused would correspond to menstruation.[28] In fact, the Banaro repeat this performance every month to make the analogy even more striking.

The Death and Resurrection theme is a very common occurrence in many puberty ceremonies. It is usually interpreted as the symbolic death of the boy and his rebirth as a man.

Bettelheim[29], and Mead[30] as well, suggest that if this is examined from the point of view of a more Freudian position, it could be interpreted under the heading of sexual ambivalence in that by the elder men's group symbolically creating a new life, they really may be attempting to imitate the fertility of women.

27 Webster, *op. cit.*, p. 84.

28 Bettelheim, *op. cit.*, p. 177.

29 *Ibid.*, p. 109.

30 Margaret Mead, *Male and Female* (New York: William Morrow and Co., 1949), p. 103.

VI	Ordeal or Hazing to Prove Fitness to Become a Man	Macquarrie[31] Euahlayi[31] Torres Straits[31] Ona[32] Tuscarora Indians[33] Iatmul[34] Indians of North America	In the Husquenaugh Ordeal of the Tuscarora Indians of North Carolina, the youths being initiated are beaten and starved. Many die, but the elders justify it on the grounds of eugenics. They say that in this way their society is assured that only the best physical specimens will survive to procreate.[33]	31 Webster, *op. cit.*, p. 34. 32 *Ibid.*, p. 70. 33 *Ibid.*, pp. 32-33. 34 Bateson, *op. cit.*, pp. 130-31.
VII	Economic Motive, Profit for the Elders	Kurnai[35] Jabim[36] Fijians[36]	For example, in the Barlum rites of the Jab Jabim tribe of Kaiser Wilhelm Land, the elders make a substantial profit from the gifts of food they receive.[35] In many puberty rites the choicest morsels are taken from the novices and reserved only for the elders.[36]	35 Webster, *op. cit.*, p. 59. 36 *Ibid.*, pp. 68-69.
VIII	Education of the Novices	Poro[37] North American Indians[38] Omeo[39] Koombanggary[39]	The Poro Bush schools teach the young initiates specialized trades for several years.[37] Initiation very often serves to indoctrinate the youth of the society with the necessary skills and the culture's chief values. For example, the Apache Indians,[39] and the Hopi.[39]	37 Chapple and Coon, *op. cit.*, p. 501. 38 Ralph L. Beals and Harry Hoijer, *An Introduction to Anthropology* (New York: The Macmillan Co., 1953), pp. 588, 596. 39 Webster, *op. cit.*, p. 51.

IX Sex and Fertility	Arunta[40] Murngin[40] Urrabuna[40]	[40] Bettelheim, *op. cit.*, pp. 106, 177-180. Sex and fertility are often associated with puberty ceremonies. Bettelheim conjectures that because initiation rites occur around the time of puberty, the developmental period of life when procreation just becomes possible, it may well be that the attainment of the age of procreation is the most important factor in the ceremonies. "Human fertility, thus appears to be the most important, large concept underlying them." Frequently, initiation is a subform of more generalized fertility rites.
	Iatmul[42] New South Wales[43] Lower Murray Tribe[43] Murrumbidgee[43] Coast Murring	[41] *Ibid.*, pp. 177-180. [42] Margaret Mead, *Male and Female* (New York: William Morrow and Co.) pp. 103-104. [43] Webster, *op. cit.*, pp. 71-72. Circumcision and subincision are connected to the sexual symbolism surrounding the procreative organ. In fact, subincision may be considered a result of womb envy according to Bettelheim.[41] Mead indicates that man's envy of woman's sexuality colors a large part of the ritual connected with adolescent initiation.[42] She refers more specifically to the Death and Resurrection myth often associated with the rites. The adolescents are often forced into a ritualized period of separation from women and abstinence from sexual activities. In return, after the ceremonies are over, there may follow a greatly increased heterosexual activity.[43]

X Myth of Death and Rebirth of the Adolescent Novice	Yabim[44] Bukaya[44] Kai[44] Tami[44] Kakian[45] Kwakiutl[45] Poro[46]	The Death and Rebirth Myth is probably the principal motif in these widespread rites. The usual variation is that of the boy being swallowed by a mythical monster, often the totem ancestor in disguise. When the boy is disgorged, the teeth of the monster cause the scarification on his body.[45] The Poro Bush Society goes through a very realistic ceremony. The neophytes are supposedly swallowed by a crocodile, a favorite mythical monster of primitive tribes, the counterpart of which is our own biblical whale. Realistic effects are simulated by discharging a pierced bladder full of blood over the boys who are forced to scream horribly. Some boys are actually killed to reinforce the lesson to the other initiates.[46]

[44] Frazer, *op. cit.*, p. 694.

[45] Webster, *op. cit.*, pp. 39-40.

[46] Chapple and Coon, *op. cit.*, pp. 501-504.

7. J. Roscoe, **The Northern Mantu** (Cambridge University Press, 1915), p. 165.
8. Cited in William I. Thomas, **Primitive Behavior** (New York, 1937), p. 341. Crazzolaro, P., "Die Gar-Ceremonie bei den Neuer," **Africa**, 5: 28-33 **(resume)**.
9. E. W. Gifford, "Tongan Society," **Bernice P. Bishop Mus. Bull.**, 61 (1924), p. 187.
10. W. I. Thomas, **Primitive Behavior** (McGraw-Hill Book Company, Inc., New York, 1937) pp. 347-8. A good deal of the previous material on bodily mutilation may be found in the same book, Chapter XII.
11. The way in which certain names have become traditionally associated with disliked traits and individuals regarded with ill-concealed contempt and suspicion can be seen in the attitude towards such a name as Percy or Percival among ourselves. Irrespective of the noble lineage of the name, which indicates something quite diametric to the popular conception, our veneration of "red-blooded" masculinity finds the name effete and particularly distasteful. The bases for such irrational opinions are due to historic and cultural accidents.
12. A. C. Fletcher, "The Hako: A Pawnee Ceremony," **Bur. Amer. Ethnol., Ann Rep.**, 22 (1900-01), p. 365.
13. For an interesting picture of what was previously regarded by the non-sophisticated Westerner as such idyllic conditions under the impact of change, see Margaret Mead, **New Lives for Old: Cultural Transformation Manus, 1928-1953** (New York: William Morrrow & Company, 1956).
14. Margaret Mead, **Sex and Temperament in Three Primitive Societies** (New York, 1935), pp. 60-61.
15. **Ibid.**, p. 61.
16. See, for example, Ruth Benedict, **Patterns of Culture** (New York, 1934), pp. 22-29, for a classic statement of this point of view. Also Bloch, **Disorganization: Personal and Social** (New York, 1952), pp. 137-41.
17. Benedict, **op. cit.**, p. 23.
18. S. N. Eisenstadt, **From Generation to Generation: Age Groups and Social Structure** (Glencoe: The Free Press, 1956), p. 321.
19. Although awkward in exposition and cumbersome in its approach, Eisenstadt's scholarly work seems to support many of the points of view raised in this and the preceding chapter.
20. Willard Waller, **The Family: A Dynamic Interpretation** (Dryden Press, New York; 1938). pp. 103 et passim.
21. W. H. Bentley, **Pioneering on the Congo** (New York: Fleming H. Revell and Company), 1, pp. 285-87 cited in W. I. Thomas, **Primitive Behavior** (New York, 1937), pp. 346-347.

CHAPTER V

THE CONTEMPORARY "RITES" OF ADOLESCENCE

Attempting to place this material in proper sociological perspective, it becomes apparent that the practices described are not necessarily the remains of a dead past or the peculiar thaumaturgy of certain exotic cultures. In observing the behavior of boys' gangs, partially based upon the experience of fifteen years of police work in the streets of New York City by one of the authors, it is evident that there are patterns of action and behavior among contemporary gangs that resemble with startling similarity certain primitive puberty rite practices. This may be more easily seen by grouping these practices under categories used in the previous tabulation.

I. Decoration by Adolescents in Our Society

A. Tattooing is often observed among modern gang boys. On summer nights in Coney Island, adolescents line up in front of the Tattoo Artists waiting their turn to have their arms and chests decorated. On the East Side of New York City a group of boys fifteen to seventeen years old proudly display the name of their gang tattooed neatly across their wrists. By an interesting coincidence they call themselves "Corner Boys." It might be added that they had never read William Whyte's well known and widely read sociological account of a gang, entitled *Street Corner Society*.[1] They are proud of this label, displaying it at every opportunity as a mark of status and membership in the gang, as well as for its decorative value.[2]

In California, adolescent Mexican-American gangs calling themselves Pachucos, also use tattoo marks as an important symbol of group membership. Those desirous of joining the gang must undergo some ordeal, usually the performance of an act of bravado or some reckless escapade in defiance of the law. Only then are they admitted to full gang membership and allowed to wear the coveted tattoo of a cross and stars on the skin between the thumb and forefinger.

B. In a culture where the body is ordinarily carefully concealed and where the display of the body is a source of embarrassment and shame, the decorative theme is frequently found in distinctive articles of apparel. The distinguishing clothes and uniforms of gang members—for example, zoot suits, motor cycle jackets, blue jeans, pastel-colored pants and shirts, and similar raiment—are all decorative schemes whose analogues may be found in preliterate societies. Likewise, the recently popular practice of gang boys bleaching a streak of color in their hair seems to belong in the same category. In this respect, these practices may bear some relationship to the ambivalence of the adolescent toward his sexual role. In extreme form, a visit to Greenwich Village or to many East Side bars in New York City will reveal groups of adolescent homosexuals, their cheeks rouged, eyes and lips exhibiting feminine makeup.

C. In respect to scarification, although the evidence at first glance seems more difficult to find, careful investigation brings up repeated examples of self-inflicted mutilation among boys and girls. If we go back to the well-known *Bruederschaften* of the German Universities, where duelling scars were eagerly sought as a mark of manhood and social status, we may find an interesting parallel. In Negro and Puerto Rican gangs, many a boy will proudly wear a knife scar for the same reasons, although it may have been acquired involuntarily in a gang fight. In later years, scars due to gang battles are often exhibited with pride by mature men to prove how tough they used to be. Although such scars do not necessarily lend themselves to a highly formalized decorative pattern, the expectancy and hope that acts of recklessness will produce a conspicuous scar in a highly visible part of the face or forehead is a compelling motivation for many gang boys. The scar, as a symbolic equivalent of military decorations in organized warfare, becomes a token of one's willingness to have performed "far beyond the ordinary call of duty" in the cause of gang loyalty.

But scarification even among our own youth may assume a far more formalized pattern. An interesting experience during the past year has thrown further light upon this matter, when two fourteen year old girls were found to be engaged in a fight as champions of opposing gangs. Having been separated, one of the girls, in displaying her injuries, rolled up her sleeve to show finger nail scratches. The name, George, was indelibly scarred into her upper arm. She explained it by saying that most of the girls in her set branded themselves in this fashion. They produced the scars by pricking their flesh with bobby pins until blood appeared, thereby forming a permanent scar. Her opponent in the fight, upon being questioned, proudly exhibited a scar clearly spelling out the name, Paul, on the upper thigh in the vicinity of the genital region. Both girls asserted that their boys friends had scarred themselves in the same manner as a sign of solidarity. Further investigation has indicated the wide prevalence of this specific type of practice which, incidentally, is not confined to working class children or to gang members of either sex. Similar practices have been widely found among middle class boys and girls far removed from the atmosphere of the socially condemned and predatory neighborhood gang.

D. Since circumcision has come to have entirely different connotations in our culture, the practice is not directly comparable to circumcision among non-literate societies. The Hebraic religious code requires circumcision of the male soon after birth; the custom has recently spread with considerable rapidity to other groups largely because of hygienic reasons. With our attitudes toward sex and the genitals, it is difficult to obtain valid information on such a "highly charged" subject. However, the evidence of certain psychiatrists would strongly suggest that the fact of circumcision creates an attitude of prideful distinction among adolescent boys, irrespective of the reasons, sacred or secular, which have been responsible for the operation. Although the operation occurred during the individual's long-forgotten infancy, the adolescent period fosters an enlivened interest, satisfaction, and curiosity in this highly distinctive characteristic of the individual's maleness.

There is some evidence that in primitive societies circumcision is regarded as an operation which makes the male organ more attractive to the opposite sex, either for aesthetic or functional reasons.[3] Bettelheim reports that his clinical observations of neurotic children lead him to believe that circumcision arouses in them a phallic pride which corresponds to the feelings of primitive neophytes.[4] In any case, circumcision sets the boy apart and makes him a member of a special group. In this sense, it performs the same function for the Jewish child as it does for the primitive adolescent.

Certainly, it would not be straining our comparison too far to say that the numerous decorative features of puberty rites, and their modern counterparts in adolescent gangs, serve the following purposes: (1) to show membership in a particular men's club or gang, and to show arrival at a highly meaningful and status-laden period of life;[5] (2) to confer social status as an accepted member of the group; (3) to conform to societal expectations regarding the role played by the adolescent boy, even though society may disapprove of the gang boy's activities; and (4) to increase one's attractiveness to the opposite sex.

Adolescent gang members manifest these impulses through a variety of distinctive decorative media, frequently to the despair of their elders, and ranging from the wearing of brightly colored clothes, the drab monotony of blue jeans and garrison jackets, moccasin shoes, sagging heavy woolen socks, to unusual forms of hairdress such as the currently popular sideburns of a reigning adolescent entertainer.

It should be noted that whereas uniform garb may be characteristic of other age-groups as well and for members of both sexes— unavoidable in a mass production society— the adolescent motif strikes a highly distinctive accent. Adolescent costume tends to emphasize the bizarre and unusual —is "off-beat" in the adolescent's jargon—and tends to exaggerate in open contrast verging on rebellion the conventional clothing of one's social class and milieu. More recently, the military type of motorcycle jacket, garrison belt, and army boots have become popular. Possibly, this is a reflection of the military emphasis in contemporary culture and an expression of the yearning to show authentic masculinity. This recent militaristic vogue seems to reflect as well the well-nigh impassioned desire for uniformity and the need to experience a sense of "disciplined belonging".

II. Acquisition of a New Name and a New Language

In puberty rites, after symbolic death and resurrection, the novice theoretically emerges as a new person with a new name and a new language. In many gangs we can find the same features. Nicknames, as is well known, are popular in all gangs. In Harlem, especially, a new name descriptive of some heroic deed is a badge of honor. A gang informant relates that among Harlem gangs there is serious competition and much recognition given to those who can make up new words. Although the contriving of new words as a means of gaining status and prestige seems to represent a subcultural trait of certain Negro groups as well, the coining of new phrases is a marked characteristic of many adolescent groups in our culture. In observation of many widely scattered adolescent groups, both rural and urban, in the effort to determine increase of vocabulary and the addition of unique terminology, it was found that such additions to vocabulary are common and are frequently associated with the prestige of the individual who initiates the given usage.

The jive talk of adolescent groups, whose jargon is frequently incomprehensible to anyone but a "hep" initiate, has become all too familiar during the present period. In the attempt to determine the source of new nicknames and terminology employed by different sociocultural groups, interviews with several adolescent cliques revealed that the nickname, for example, frequently reflected value distinctions with which the group was intimately concerned. In one case, the nickname applied to a member of a middle class adolescent group in the Kings Highway section of Brooklyn—a better than average middle class neighborhood largely inhabited by Jewish families—was "C.P.C." Upon investigation, it was divulged that the initials stood for "class", "polish", and "culture". This youth had a wealthy father, and he had just returned from a well-known Southern university, driving a new car, and accompanied by a good-looking girl. It appeared quite obvious in the course of discussion that he seems to have represented the secret aspirations of many members of a middle class gang.

At first glance, it may appear that such episodes are unique and should not be applied in a broader interpretation which would include the general dynamics of group interaction. Actually, this is not so, as a later discussion in this volume will illustrate. The use of special names and terms, as a direct reflection of value-aspirations of special groups and *as a means of symbolizing preferred social processes,* appears to be well established. In fact, the distinctiveness of *any* group within the social structure, not alone adolescent age groups, is frequently marked by the degree with which it develops its own specialized vernacular.

III. Seclusion from Women, Bachelor Huts, Age Grades.

The adolescent gang is preeminently a male sanctuary and throws into sharp focus the typical ambivalent attitudes towards the opposite sex so characteristic of adolescents. What is significant, however, is the reinforcement of such attitudes held by the individual adolescent by the solidarity of the group structure.

The gang "hangs out" on a corner at a candy store, or pool room. At these gang locations one rarely sees gang members with a girl. Even when he has a steady girl, the gang member keeps her far away from the gang. One teen-ager in a middle class group explained that he never brought his girl around to the corner "hangout" because "she's a good girl." It was apparent that he had internalized the traditional American middle class attitude that distinguishes between "good" girls and the other kind. Thus, he continued, "I wouldn't take a chance bringing her around these wolves. We do a lot of things that I wouldn't want her to see."

Night after night the gang collects on the same street corner at a regular time, moves *en masse* to the pool room, ends up at the bar for a couple of beers, then back to the corner for a final bull session. There is virtually no contact at all with girls during these purely masculine activities. Thrasher says:

> On the whole it is safe to say that sex represents a decidedly secondary activity in the gang. In the adolescent group in particular, it is subordinated to the primary interests of conflict and adventure.[6]

Gangs also have their institutional "bachelor huts" not very different from the Trobriand Islanders' bachelor house —the "Bukumatula"—which figured so prominently in Malinowski's study of that Melanesian society.[7] The pool room and the cellar club, which latter is frequently used for sexual purposes, provide a corresponding analogue to the far-ranging bachelor hut found so often in primitive life.

Age grading is a common element in gang life, with sharp divisions conferring particular roles and status upon members of these distinct groups. It is not unusual to find that:

> Each club was divided into several divisions usually on the basis of age. These divisions were called 'Tiny Tims,' 'Kids', 'Cubs', 'Midgets', 'Juniors,' 'Seniors'. These divisions regarded themselves as autonomous groups, at the same time they had strong feelings of kinship with each other. As the boys grew older, they graduated from one division to another—a feeding process which insured the continued life of each club.[8]

This could almost be a paraphrase of an anthropologist's conclusions based on observations of age societies in some preliterate groups.[9]

IV. Break from the Home and Assimilation by the New Group.

Van Gennep, who originated the term "rites of passage," believed that these ceremonies always involved three consecutive processes: (1) separation; (2) transition; and (3) incorporation.[10] Chapple and Coon have used these processes as a framework in analyzing the various rites of the Andaman Islanders in terms of their own theory which makes use of such concepts as "interaction," "equilibrium," "sets," and "originators."[11] Translating these concepts to a modern setting, we find a similar process expressed in Thrasher's view that the gang is an interstitial phenomenon that helps the gang boy bridge the transition from childhood, through adolescence, and finally to maturity. In analyzing the details of this social process, we find similar stages of development. The boy separates from the family, as the oft-repeated drama of poignant conflict between harassed parent and shrilly assertive children so trenchantly reveals. So prominent is this process in the life of American society that the psychiatrist, Frankwood Williams, in his study of adolescence, asserts that "emancipation from the home" constitutes a primary function of what he regards as an inevitable adolescent conflict.[12] There is likewise a transitory phase in which the individual is tested and observed by his peers before he at last is incorporated into the gang as a fully functioning member. In another sense, the gang period can be looked upon as the transition before he is incorporated into the adult group of the larger society.

Actually, there are important differences in the rationale underlying this comparison. Puberty rites usually have as their ultimate aim the full acceptance of the novice by the whole society, and therefore, it is proper to characterize the rites as transitional. However, the situation in contemporary society is different in many respects. The point of view advanced here holds that, because of the extreme prolongation of adolescence in our urban society, it would be incorrect to go on labeling this important and extended period as transitional or interstitial. Albert K. Cohen's concept of the adolescent as a member of a definite subculture, enduring for varying periods of time and having specific functional relationships to the entire social order, appears more in keeping with present conditions in American society.[13] This view is further supported by Talcott Parsons' portrayal of the existence of a distinctive "youth culture" in American society, transcending any specific class orientation.[14] From this position, gang ceremonies and practices do not result in their acceptance by *all* of society—a meaningless term in our complex and heterogeneous urban society—but really aim at incorporation with the next stage of development, which is the world of the adolescent gang itself. This alteration in function does not necessarily invalidate the point of view originally suggested since, from a long range perspective, the Thrasher "interstitial" concept may still be applied. We may assume this to be valid since ultimately most gang members do pass on to become more or less typical representatives of those segments of society in which they have been socialized and with which they have been identified.

V. Sexual Ambivalence and Homosexuality.

The investigation of this topic appears to provide a fertile source of inspiration for the psychoanalytically sophisticated. That our adolescents identify themselves with varying degrees of closeness with their mothers has virtually become a cliche among many perceptive and informed observers of the American scene. Philip Wylie has established "Momism" as a by-word among intellectuals and pseudo-intellectuals.[15] To Wylie, the American adolescent and even the adult male has been caricatured as "Mom's boy" with all that this implies in the loss of culturally conceived manhood and independence.

Parsons[16] as well as Margaret Mead[17] entertain views some what similar in nature to those suggested by Wylie, basing their observations partially on the father's prolonged absence from the home, and the consequently important role that the mother plays in the typical American urban family. The Kinsey Report appears to give statistical support to the prevalence of homosexuality among American males. Analyzing homosexuality among single males, Kinsey reports, "The figures rise to nearly one in three in the later teens."[18]

Aside from any overt evidence of actual homosexuality, American adolescent behavior is replete with more subtle and devious expressions of a homosexual nature. It may be seen during hazings and initiations into high school and college fraternities where the initiates parade through the streets dressed as girls, painted with rouge, and speaking in feminine voices.

In the recent proliferation of homosexual groups which finally have broken out of the segregated confines of Greenwich Village, one can see a significant number of adolescents who, while previously perhaps concealing their feminine characteristics, now openly assume a female role.[19]

There is an element of homosexuality in the common gang pastime of suddenly pouncing on a boy and exposing his genitals, or in gang sessions of group masturbation. Other interesting indications of possible homosexual ambivalence in modern gangs is the increasing use by "toughs" of pastel-colored silk shirts, and trousers of red, lavender, and green, sartorial touches of color previously reserved for the feminine sex. An anomalous note in an otherwise highly masculine emphasis may be seen in the spectacle of a young hoodlum, known to be a terror in gang fights, an expert burglar, and an accomplished ladies' man, to boot, who suddenly stops to use a store window for a mirror, takes out a comb, and carefully pats a wave in his beautifully set pompadour. Not long ago, one such gang member even exceeded this bit of effeminacy by bleaching a blonde streak in a coal black head of hair, a form of tonsorial elegance which seems to have set off a pattern for other gang members to follow.

A striking trend during the present period is the well marked tendency for the two sexes during adolescence to dress like each other more and more. On the girls' part, this is increasingly found in the current trend of wearing blue jeans, men's shirts, and jackets. While this may not be exclusively a gang phenomenon among adolescents, it seems to have found ample and extensive expression among city gangs.

In reference to a phenomenon already noted, there is sexual ambivalence in the gang's exclusion of girls from its activities and then suddenly forcing some luckless girl to submit to the gang "shag," or "lineup," where each member of the gang waits his turn for sexual relations with the female victim, a characteristic gang practice. It should be noted here that girls are rigorously excluded from gang activity and participation. The only function of the young girl is to relieve the periodic physical needs of gang members. Their advice, help, counsel, and interest is not sought; in fact, it is rigorously rejected. Some slight modification of this may be seen in the recent tendency to use girls as decoys or to carry weapons. Bettelheim, in discussing American anxiety over sex, says: "The prime purpose of gangs of children of one sex is often mutual protection against forming relationships with the other sex."[20]

In our sophisticated Western world, it is difficult to find practices directly comparable to primitive subincision or circumcision but there are numerous recorded cases wherein emotionally disturbed boys expressed the desire to possess a vagina and envied the girls' ability to menstruate.[21] In high school locker rooms, adolescent boys are often seen to conceal the male organ by pressing it between their thighs; this appears very much like the manifestation of an unconscious urge to imitate female characteristics. Bettelheim has adduced an impressive array of evidence to support his theory that subincision, and possibly circumcision, are attempts by the men of preliterate societies to imitate the sexual organs of women. The view he presents seems to suggest that the "penis envy" of women, so frequently portrayed in psychoanalytical literature, finds its counterpart in an equivalent "womb envy" on the part of many men.[22]

The death and resurrection theme may be seen not as a rite primarily for the edification of the novice, but intended as a symbolic attempt to prove that the older men, as well as the women, can create life in the form of the reborn initiate. The monster that swallows and disgorges the boys thus becomes a symbol of the womb. Psychoanalytic accounts describe primitive tribes who conceive of the womb as a sucking and biting organ, the expression for womb itself having this connotation. Although the psychoanalytical view may be seriously questioned, the same idea is put forward by Margaret Mead who analyzes this death and rebirth myth as a manifestation of the male womb-envying pattern.[23]

Certainly, among the psychoanalytically oriented, there is substantial agreement that primitive men, and specifically the adolescent initiate, utilize ceremonies in which an attempt is made to assume symbolically the female role. Similarly, evidence points to the existence of the same phenomenon among American adolescents.

VI. *Hazing and Ordeal to Prove Fitness to Become Members of the Group.*

In high school and college fraternities, hazing has become such a dangerous practice that administrative regulations against such practices (which have frequently in the past resulted in maiming and even death) have been invoked to stop practices that are considered dangerous, anachronistic, and barbaric. College authorities have had to bar hazing because of the serious injuries which were often inflicted upon the initiates as a prerequisite for membership. Pachuco boys are reputed to perform outstanding deeds in violation of the law in order to gain admission to the gang. A gang operating in East Harlem uses as a test for membership an ordeal which they call "cramping." The youth applying for membership is held by two of the older boys while the rest of the gang pummels him in the abdominal region as hard as they can. If he "chickens out," he cannot become a member of the gang. In their investigation of gang behavior, the authors have found the use of such ordeals to be virtually universal, even though the form which the ordeal assumes may not be readily acknowledged as a "fitness" test.

A sexually related phenomenon is the oft-cited newspaper account of sex clubs among high school youth where proof of loss of virginity is required before admission. In both primitive and modern society, the rationale of this proof by hazing and ordeal is essentially the same. It is a means of proving the novitiate's fitness to leave the ranks of women and children and to join the men's club or gang. It indicates that he is strong enough and "man enough" to measure up to the standards required.

VII. *Element of Economic Profit for the Older Men.*

Some investigators consider the economic gain accruing to the older men in many societies to be a major reason for institutionalized rites imposed upon adolescents.[24] In this way the older men force the novices to supply them with food and choice dishes by imposing food taboos on the boys. At the same time, the young and more desirable women are kept for themselves. The elders of a tribe upon occasion even engage in deceit and chicanery in the attempt to use puberty ceremonies for their own advantage, especially among Melanesian and African tribes.[25]

In modern gang lore we are familiar with the stereotype of a Fagin, the arch-criminal who preys on the young boys and profits from their lawbreaking. Consider also the "fence," the racketeer, the dope peddler, the "bookie," and the crooked ward politician who derive profit from the gang, each watching out for likely young prospects to serve his own illegitimate purposes. In primitive society, the formal initiatory institution may be frequently viewed as a form of subversion for producing private gain for those older men who are in a position of power. Nowadays, in the informal patterns of interaction between the lower class gang and the underworld, we find a similar situation, where older men may act as mentors in leading the gang into a life of crime and who may also reap a substantial gain from these gang activities.[26]

VIII. *Education for New Roles and Incorporation into Men's Groups.*

In our society there are very few institutions which dramatize the "coming of age" of our adolescents. High school graduation exercises might be considered such an occasion, but in middle class society it is frequently just one more step on the road to still another educational level, the college. Very few middle class high school graduates are at this point actually treated like adult males. For the girls, the "Sweet Sixteen Party" or debutante's "coming out" ball may be thought of as representing a very tepid and mild analogue of the primitive girl's puberty rites. For boys, however, there is nothing quite so apposite. Religious confirmation and Bar Mitzvah ceremonies among Jews occur very often around the age of thirteen and do retain the religious quality, although not the intensity, of some puberty rites. But too often these modern ceremonies have become mere empty rituals because they contradict reality. The Jewish boy says, "Today, I am a man," but the meaninglessness of this ritualistic and traditional phrase is demonstrated by the humorous allusions showing him returning to his childish practices after the Bar Mitzvah ceremony. In other words, at adolescence, when the boy in our society is expected to stop being a child, he is not expected to become a man; there is no formal societal mechanism to educate him in his new way of life. It would be a fallacy to think that in the United States he is willingly incorporated into the older men's group. On the contrary, he represents a definite threat to the adult male both economically and sexually.

The adult must work to support himself and his family, and is expected to gain social status. Does he welcome the competition of the young aspirant? As Kingsley Davis, Talcott Parsons, and others have shown, the intrusion of the adolescent into the adult world of work, play, and civic responsibility is apt to produce tensions, frequently quite serious, and consequent resentment, open and concealed, towards the rising young male.[27] And since Kinsey showed the adolescent to be a potential Priapus, many a mature man casts a "jaundiced eye" on this well endowed, though still youthful, sexual opponent.

What provision is made to teach the adolescent to steer a course through our society? Definitions of roles for him are confusing and contradictory. Parents tell the adolescent that he is a man, but he is still closely identified with his mother and is not ready to assume adult male status. He is treated like a dependent, supported by his parents, and often forced to defer male activities in order to prepare for the distant future. His sexual role is likewise confused and contradictory. He is driven to prove virility by pursuing girls. But at the same time he knows that "good girls" are not supposed to allow themselves to be caught. He, therefore, is apt to experience acute guilt-feelings if he goes beyond the approved limit of amorous play and yet, if he doesn't, it appears to be a reflection on his virility.

The lower class boy on the other hand absorbs dominant middle class values which set goals for him, but sees on every hand that he is unable to pursue these ends. To many a lower class boy, the socially approved objectives for desired manhood are so far-fetched, so unattainable, that they constitute a sort of chimera, a never-never land about which he can dream but actually not hope to achieve. The patterns of living of his father and other adult male figures in his environment appear to offer substantial testimony as to the futility of achieving the goals which the popular cult of American success so stridently affirms in the classroom, the movies, TV, and other popular channels of mass enlightenment. What models are offered in the lives of parents and others in his environment, who are closely bound to a limited and constricted routine of seemingly unrewarding toil, appear uninspired and, for many youths, hardly worth the effort. Recognizing the limitations upon his strivings, the values of the working class youth may be an actual negation of the very things which the calculated prudence of the middle class hopes to foster among its own young. The source of such negative values, frequently an outright contradiction of values venerated by middle class culture, comes from those most intimately associated with him. Where else, realistically speaking, can the slum youth learn the appropriate behavior to men's status in a great many cases? Really, from only one source—his own peer culture.

In primitive society the puberty rites are rites of passage from childhood to the next stage—manhood. Adolescence among such groups, if it can be said to exist at all, may actually encompass a very short span of life. In our society adolescence has been lengthened until it now often covers a period of ten years or more. Extreme examples of delay in conferring adult status may be found in East European villages where, until the birth of the first child, the Jewish father, for example, is not considered a real man. The Irish system of delaying marriage until the father of the prospective bridegroom makes economic provisions for him is still another example of the prolongation of adolescence. Thus, because of this prolongation, we are faced with a situation in our modern western culture which is very different from the brief period of adolescence found in preliterate cultures. Gang lore and practice, with its own involved techniques and values, may become the curriculum in which the member learns proper behavior in preparation for the next age group. Here, however, the next step for the teen-ager is not maturity, but this peculiar "middle world" of adolescence. In this respect, the teen-age gang life is a remarkably effective school. Pupils learn lessons quickly, easily, and permanently. It matters little that the basic curriculum does not meet with the approval of the dominant middle class in American life. However, it does offer many elective and compulsory "workshop" courses in popular sociology, including such courses as Class and Status in Tenement Areas; Cooperation and Competition Among Ethnic Groups; The Impact of Middle Class Culture on the Working Class; Criminology and Juvenile Delinquency; Marriage and the Family; and, certainly not least, Urban Adolescent Sexual Behavior.

It is very disconcerting for an informed police officer to hear from the lips of these sophisticated juvenile "scholars" realistic sociological appraisals of society that would make many a college sophomore (and possibly even their mentors) appear very naive by comparison. Admission to this adolescent subculture has become the principal and, in fact, the only means for many a modern urban youth—especially in lower class neighborhoods—to accomplish the transitional growth expected of the normal teen-ager.

IX. *The Sex and Fertility Theme in Puberty Rites.*

As lower class adolescents reach their late teens, they find that the gang gives them increased opportunities for heterosexual contact with girls. Cellar clubs, the "line-up," auxiliary gangs of girls, and the individual girl who "belongs" to the whole gang, are some features of the sexual life in the older adolescent gang. Middle class boys find new courage in handling girls when they are in a group situation as, for example, when they are crowded in an automobile. Kinsey, on the basis of his impressive statistical evidence, asserts that "the maximum sexual frequencies (total frequencies) occur in the late teens," adding a little later that "the peak of actual performance is in the middle or later teens."[28] In respect to adolescent group sexual activity, he draws the following conclusion:

> There is a social value in establishing one's ability and many a boy exhibits his masturbatory techniques to lone companions or to whole groups of boys. In the latter case there may be simultaneous exhibitions as a group activity. The boy's emotional reaction in such a performance is undoubtedly enhanced by the presence of the other boy. There are teen-age boys who continue this exhibitionistic activity throughout their high school years.[29]

Sociologists have indicated for a considerable period the effects of the puritanical tradition as a significant phase of our general cultural orientation to sexual behavior. Although primarily a middle class cultural complex, its general effects have been diffuse and, in some way, have affected the folk patterns of all segments of the culture. One of the results of this historic tradition has been an ambiguous public attitude concerning sexual standards and the confrontation of the issue of a contradictory sexual morality squarely in its implications for teaching the young. The problem of teaching children and adolescents about sex, and whether indeed it should be taught at all, still remains a controversial subject among educational theorists. In the majority of cases as we so well know, and in spite of the rise of a so-called modern and liberal outlook, the adolescent learns the "art of sex" from his street corner companions.

X. Death and Rebirth Myth

In this category, correlations between primitive and modern rites appear more difficult to find. Yet, there is substantial evidence to support the analogy, depending on the interpretation of a symbolism which may appear ambiguous and vague. Correspondence may be found in such separate processes as the wailing of mothers at the loss of their sons, the emergence of a new language and new names, the different types of clothing worn, and even the bodily scarification that anthropologists have connected with the central theme of death of the boy and his rebirth as a new person. In a culture where the temper is scientific and naturalistic, such practices appear singularly inappropriate. Our secular, materialistic, and pragmatic society could hardly be expected to adhere precisely to such a symbolic, mystical, and quasi-religious ideology, especially in a culture where the principle of separation of church and state has been so deeply imbedded.

If, however, we examine closely the human meaning and striving in such experiences concealed by the symbolism, certain analogies begin to emerge with stark clarity. Radin, for example, interprets death and rebirth in this manner: "Sociologically, death is here the equivalent of absence of status, and rebirth, the equivalent of possession of status."[30] Seen in this light, the interpretation becomes definitely applicable to a significant phase of the gang function. We have simply to observe the younger boys in any lower class urban area yearn for the time when they can join the gang, when they may receive the status which such membership provides, and when they can really begin "to start to live." If any credence may be given to the views of Bettelheim and Mead already analyzed in this study under the classification of "Sexual Ambivalence" (Section V above), then other points of equivalence become amply evident and provide a substantial basis for the view that the modern gang boy finds a "new life".

Frazer's thesis[31]—that death and resurrection ceremonies are concerned with placing the novice's soul in the safe-keeping of the totem—must be mentioned here. The concept of rebirth in this context consists of "the infusion into him of fresh life drawn from the totem." We may translate this concept into modern terms by indicating that by membership in the adolescent gang, the youth "gives up" his life as a child and assumes a new way of life. It is highly suggestive to find that gang names themselves are often strangely reminiscent of primitive totemic ancestors. Such resemblances, as superficial as they may appear, may be seen in such common designations as the Ravens, Bears, Jaguars, Eagles, Falcons, and a host of others too numerous to mention. Although Tylor, and Spencer and Gillen, have criticized Frazer's view as being unsupported by the weight of evidence found in Australian rites,[32] there can be little doubt of the gang youth's total surrender to the protective custody of the gang's objectives conceived in its own totemic terms.

Postscript

In the sections above, an attempt was made to break down puberty rites into their most important categories and then compare them with modern teen-age gang practices. Reference has been made not only to gangs but also to adolescents in general, as constituting in varying form (reflecting regional, class, and cultural differences) a distinctive subculture within the larger society. However, it is not contended that the gang necessarily transforms the adolescent boy into a personality type widely different from his adolescent counterpart in other parts of the social order. Gang members as a class have the same basic needs and impulses as those adolescents who remain outside the gang. But gangs, because of their highly charged interactive situation, often crystallize in visible, dramatic, and overt form the traits that are repressed or dormant in the non-gang teen-ager. Particular gangs will not necessarily exhibit all of the characteristics described; by the same token, neither will one primitive society invariably combine every element of the puberty rite complex found in all parts of the world.

---

1. William F. Whyte, **Street Corner Society** (Chicago: The University of Chicago Press, 1955).
2. As a point of added interest, this was to prove their downfall several years later. While on prowl car duty responding to a "Signal Thirty Two," a fight in a neighborhood tavern, one of the writers observed an adolescent running from the scene. The youth was picked up and brought back to the place where the brawl had occurred. The complainant identified the boy as one of a group who had viciously demolished the complainant's bar and grill. During the course of interrogation, the culprit inadvertently moved his arm exposing the tattoo mark "Corner Boys" on his wrist. From previous experience with this group, the tattoo mark resulted in the round-up of the entire gang. This group had in the course of two years graduated into a predatory gang that terrorized the neighborhood.
3. Bettelheim, op. cit., p. 163.
4. **Ibid.**
5. Chapple and Coon, op. cit., p. 494.

6. Thrasher, op. cit., p. 221.
7. Bronislaw Malinowski, **The Sexual Life of Savages** (New York: Eugenics Publishing Co., 1929).
8. Paul Crawford, **Working with Teen-Age Gangs**, (New York: The Welfare Council of New York, 1950), p. 11.
9. See, for example, Lowie, op. cit., pp. 431-33, which concerns itself with the Canella Indians.
10. See Chapple and Coon, op. cit., pp. 484-506.
11. Ibid.
12. Frankwood Williams, **Adolescence: Studies in Mental Hygiene** (New York, 1930), pp. 102 ff.
13. Cohen, op. cit.
14. Talcott Parsons, "Age and Sex in the Social Structure of the United States," American Sociological Review, Vol. VII (1942), pp. 604-16.
15. Philip Wylie, **Generation of Vipers** (New York: Farrar and Rinehart, 1942).
16. Parsons, op. cit.
17. Margaret Mead, **Male and Female**, op. cit.
18. Alfred C. Kinsey, Wardell B. Pomeroy, and Clyde E. Martin, **Sexual Behavior in the Human Male** (Philadelphia: W. B. Saunders Co., 1948), p. 629.
19. Significantly, for many adolescents who now attempt to assert openly their maleness, a new vogue is currently popular in the growing of beards. Some of this may be a partial compensation for the suspected presence of feminine traits.
20. Bettelheim, op. cit., p. 107.
21. Ibid., pp. 28-37.
22. Ibid.
23. Margaret Mead, **Male and Female**, op. cit., pp. 103-104.
24. Paul Radin, **The World of Primitive Man** (New York: Henry Schuman, 1953), p. 165.
25. Webster, op. cit., pp. 60-61.
26. See Whyte, **Street Corner Society**, op. cit., for a realistic and astute account of the methods employed by politicians to manipulate gangs to further the politician's own purposes.
27. See, for example, Kingsley Davis, "Adolescence and the Social Structure," The Annals of the American Academy of Political and Social Science, 236 (1944), pp. 9-16; also, Talcott Parsons, "Age and Sex in the Social Structure of the United States," American Sociological Review, 7 (1942), pp. 604-16.
28. Kinsey, op. cit., p. 219.
29. Ibid.
30. Radin, op. cit., p. 265.
31. Frazer, op. cit., p. 692.
32. Webster, op. cit., p. 46.

CHAPTER VI

THE UNIVERSAL PATTERN OF
ADOLESCENT STRIVING

At first glance there seem to be many logical reasons why puberty rites cannot be compared with gang activities. This chapter will attempt to set forth the most cogent criticisms of the hypothesis advanced in this book. For each objection, a reasonable and cogent explanation will be attempted in order to sustain the consistency of the views expressed thus far.

I. The first criticism that would reasonably appear to cast some doubt upon our analysis is that consideration must be given to the fact that puberty rites in primitive society seem to be imposed by society on unwilling novices, whereas gang practices are voluntary and spontaneously developed All too often the condition seems to be one in which the gang imposes its practices on an unwilling society. What is overlooked in such criticism is the psychological state of mind of the novice himself, whether primitive novitiate or the modern gang aspirant. Whether forcefully imposed or voluntarily assumed, the young boy eagerly awaits the ordeal and is willing to accept it. This appears to be the major point. In fact, as we have learned, when society or its delegated agencies refuses to impose satisfactory standards of admission and ordeals for acceptance, the young aspirant himself frequently demands that he be put to the test.

The view of society forcefully imposing its conditions upon the young novice is dramatically portrayed in one of the articles of *Life Magazine's* recent series on the "Epic of Man." A primitive boy is seen to be screaming in agony as he is forced to endure circumcision.[1] However, when we consider that for the boy to be accepted as a respected member of his society he must be incorporated into one of the men's societies, the boy's attitude takes on a different aspect.

We may assume that in the ordinary course of events it is perfectly normal for a boy to want to reach social maturity and assume respected adult status in his particular society. If attainment of this goal depends on undergoing ceremonies, no matter how mysterious and painful, most boys will voluntarily choose to endure whatever ordeal is involved. How many college freshmen refuse to join fraternities when tapped, even though it may mean a painful and dangerous hazing? In fact, they glory in the prospect of the hazing as an indication of their proven manhood. Bettelheim[2] shows that in the case of the Masai, the Nandi, and the Tikopia, the boys express happiness at the prospect of initiation. They dance and decorate themselves because "they will soon enter the privileged class of initiates." He reports other cases where the traditional rite of circumcision was opposed by chiefs of certain tribes. Yet the custom became even more prevalent because of the popular desire for it and not from pressure from above. That the young boys willingly look forward to their initiation is partially supported, according to Bettelheim, in terms of accepted modern theories of learning. It is a well-known fact that learning imposed against the will often results in behavior that is just the contrary of what was taught. Since observations have shown that youths inducted by puberty rites turn out, with rare exceptions, to be conforming members of society, he feels justified in concluding that puberty ceremonies correspond to the desires of the initiates.[3]

II. Can one, however, really compare adolescence in primitive and modern society? Can our hypothesis of adolescent group behavioral similarities be maintained in the face of the objection that puberty rites in some societies occur at *any* age, depending on the availability of the requisite number of initiates? The Mundugumor may be presented as a case in point. If puberty rites are traditionally restricted to young boys about thirteen or fourteen years old, have they the same relevance socially as gang practices in which the participants may be sixteen years of age, seventeen, or even older?

To interpret this problem adequately, it is necessary to analyze the social significance of adolescence. In our culture, the period of adolescence may last for ten years, or even longer. Yet in some primitive cultures the period of adolescence passes so quickly that it seems hardly to exist at all. In her analysis of puberty institutions, Ruth Benedict has stated:

> In order to understand puberty institutions, we do not most need analyses of the necessary nature of *rites de passage;* we need rather to know what is identified in different cultures with the beginning of adulthood and their methods of admitting to the new status. Not biological puberty, but what adulthood means in that culture conditions the puberty ceremony.[4]

The length of time, apparently, is not the significant element since the crucial question is the particular social definition of the situation determining adulthood. The crucial question is at what point is it most important, psychologically and socially, to *become* an adult. There are examples to be found among primitive societies where adolescence is prolonged almost to the same extent as it is in America. The adolescent in Mundugumor culture may wait five years until a sufficiently large class of boys can be gathered for an initiation ceremony. The Poro Bush school lasts for four years.

According to most authorities, transitional rites usually cluster around the biological age of puberty—at the ages of thirteen, fourteen, or fifteen—in spite of Ruth Benedict's contention that the rites can occur at any time. Gang activities on the other hand seem to occur anywhere from the age of twelve to the late twenties. In this analysis, we have concentrated on adolescent gangs in the seventeen to twenty-one year old age group. In our urban society where school attendance is commonly compulsory until seventeen, and employment certificates frequently necessary until eighteen, there is very little chance for the adolescent to strike out on his own until he reaches the seventeen to eighteen year old period.

Sociologists have observed how adult status has been deferred for increasingly lengthier periods in the United States. Therefore, the late teen years in America are roughly equivalent to the thirteen to fifteen year old level in primitive society. This is particularly true in respect to the following socio-psychological characteristics preceding adulthood: (1) The self-conception of the adolescent boy. (A thirteen year old boy in primitive society begins to look forward to his imminent initiation into the men's group, the opportunities for approved heterosexual activity, and his assumption of certain coveted adult responsibilities, such as joining war parties, hunting expeditions, etc., etc. Our modern thirteen year old boy is still in elementary school and knows that it will be years before he can hope to accomplish a comparable role. At seventeen, however, the sense of urgency is already upon him and he more closely corresponds to the primitive initiate in respect to his adult expectancies.); (2) Society's conception of his role, which complements the boy's social awareness described above; (3) The barriers and social realities to which the boy is exposed. (If, in exceptional cases, the fourteen or fifteen year old boy in our culture attempted to perform the role of a man, he would receive the attention and notoriety that greeted the legendary Sonny Wisecarver,[5] even though Kinsey has now seemingly prepared the way for him.)

No matter how abrupt the change from childhood to manhood in primitive society may appear, there is inevitably at least a short period of preparation for the puberty ceremonies, and invariably a time for adjustment before realistic incorporation into the men's group occurs thereafter. This period, at least, is the functional equivalent of adolescence in our society and may serve as a universal basis for comparison. To repeat, it is *social puberty, not biological puberty,* that the rites celebrate.[6]

Regardless of the tensions and problems of adolescence, which admittedly may be peculiar to our own society and not a ubiquitous characteristic of adolescence in the larger sense, there are institutions and psychological states connected with this age-status which may nevertheless be considered universal. From the social viewpoint, institutional rites of passage are so widespread that they come near being universal. In other words, there are accepted roles and behavior patterns laid down for the adolescent period. When such institutions break down or fail to develop adequately, however, and the roles ascribed to adolescents are confused or contradictory, problems will develop similar to those in our society.

In any scientific and realistic approach to the problems of adolescence, therefore, the universal striving towards adulthood finds its own peculiar expression in accordance with variations in societal, class or subcultural, and individual standards. The basic pattern—what the late Kurt Lewin might have referred to as a "genotype"—remains fairly constant; what is different are the expressions of a common motivation in terms of varying permissive and inciting conditions determined by societal, class, and individual contexts. In each case, whether we are examining societal, class or individual variations, the social and psychological expressions of adolescence may be viewed as existing along a common spectrum while varying for a particular society, class, or age group.

Adolescence in any society, thus, from a broad societal view, may be seen as extending along a continuum ranging through the following gradations:

(1) Highly developed puberty rites, as among the Poro, to the absence of well defined formal puberty rites, as among ourselves.
(2) From consistent role development, as in the Samoan society, to confused, contradictory, competitive roles as among the Manus, the Mundugumor, and ourselves.
(3) From adolescence in a relatively stable and homogeneous society to adolescence in a complex and heterogeneous one as in America.

Likewise, observed from the vantage point of class, subcultural and group differences within the same society, the reasons for adolescent variations may be resolved in terms of the following queries:

(1) Are there class and hierarchical gradations in primitive society which modify the expressions of behavior of adolescent groups in each society? If so, do such gradations make for conflict between such groups?
(2) What of the conflict of generations? Is the rising adolescent group received with friendship by the older generation or with hostility as among the Mundugumor, where the adolescent becomes the father's rival for the available women?
(3) Are the expressed strivings of the adolescent group in accord with societal values or are they in rebellion against acknowledged standards, as in the case of certain adolescent groups found among the Comanche?

Finally, adolescence may be viewed from the standpoint of differences within the individual himself and raises such questions as the following:

(1) What are the psychological states of mind that characterize the individual adolescent? (There probably are clusters of types at various points in a continuum denoting differences of attitude, ranging from eagerness to become an adult to a confused ambivalent midway state and terminating in a position where certain young people express an extreme desire to remain on the childhood level.)
(2) What is the adolescent's relation to his family? To the male and female parents? To what type of family structure does he belong? How do such membership and oedipal relationships affect his psychological preparation for adolescence?
(3) What is his reaction to the physical changes which he undergoes as an integral phase of adolescence and to the ways in which these changes have been interpreted to him?

(4) What is his relation to his peers: superordinate, subordinate, hostile, friendly, accepted as a member of the peer group, or an outcast?

Examined from these categorical positions, adolescence in any society may be adequately described and compared with profit. Indeed, this is very likely the only way in which adolescence as a universal phenomenon may be adequately understood. Nevertheless, irrespective of the theoretical standpoint employed, puberty rites in any event would have to be considered as a response to a universal cultural imperative. Implicit in this imperative is Malinowski's insistence that "the human material by which every institution is maintained must be renewed, formed, drilled and promoted with full knowledge of tribal tradition." [7]

III. Is too much being read here into the meaning of puberty rites? May these similarities be mere coincidence? Theoretically, puberty rites may be empty survival forms and have very little psychological meaning for the initiate. If this is so, our entire point of view may be seriously questioned. It has been said that "(the) popular use of ceremonialism and esoterism are merely survivalistic forms and functionless trappings." In the case of modern secret societies and ritualism in our impersonal, technical culture, the meaning of such ceremonies may have been largely emasculated. Nathan Miller, for example, states: "In the case of college and purely ceremonial societies the rudiments of the psychology which govern the true society become irrelevant and gratuitous."[8] We may agree that an arid and empty ritualism too often surrounds modern ceremonies. For example, the Bar Mitzvah rite of the Jewish youth today, aside from peculiar religious aspects, may mean little to the boy as a puberty rite even though he piously intones the familiar words, "Today I am a man."

It should be noted, however, that Miller, in the passage quoted above, distinguishes such "mock esoterism" from the psychology which governs the true secret society—that is, the society or subcultural group which is intimately concerned and deeply involved in the transition accompanying adolescence. A formal ceremony, for example, may represent a kind of archaeological museum piece of the past, with little of the emotional fervor and throbbing excitement which originally accompanied its appearance. In this sense, the anthropologist Tylor's view of ceremonials as purely a vestigial survival might apply, for example, to a large variety of modern ceremonies, including confirmation and Bar Mitzvah exercises. However, rituals, ceremonials, social ordeal, and institutional practices must likewise be regarded in relation to the functions they serve—not the least of which is the function to the active participant himself. Malinowski, in recognizing that original meanings of such social forms may change, asserts that the ancient practice may serve a vital new function in the life of the group and the individual. Consequently, the "present function, vitality, and adaptability" of such procedures must be stressed and "not the shape and trappings of the past." [9] This realistic view seems completely in accord with the social function of gang practices.

Almost all anthropological authorities are agreed that puberty rites, irrespective of their ceremonial importance in the life of the group, are very important dramatic events in the life of the novice. It is not likely that one could consider unimportant an experience that may mean any one of a variety of dramatic and dangerous consequences for him: his death (symbolically or actually), a physical and emotionally harrowing ordeal, unusual hardship, new status, vital religious experience which can alter his whole life, increased sexual activity, and similarly compelling experiences.

For these reasons, the impact of the ceremony on the initiate may not in any way be minimized. Certainly, it is a paramount crisis in the adolescent boy's life, often a crucial test of his ability to survive as an individual and as a recognized member of his group.

> Sometimes they (i.e., the ceremonies) are so severe as to ruin the health, and even to cause the death of the young novice, an outcome which is always defended by the old men on well-known Darwinian principles. Inability to support the torments is of course unusual and would subject the unhappy youth to the direst penalties.[10]

This evaluation of the rites as coming at a critical period of transition, being a crucial test of manhood and even of fitness to survive, is justified when one examines the common experience of a great many societies. In addition, the mysterious preparations, the awe-inspiring paraphernalia which frequently surrounds the ceremony, the religious atmosphere, certainly places the novice in a psychological state of ambivalent dread and expectancy. He knows he is expected to enter the tests bravely. He realizes that it is the gateway to a respected adult life, while at the same time he may fear for his life and for his ability to act strongly and bravely in the presence of respected elders and his peers. Once having succeeded in passing through the ceremony with honor, the psychological aftermath of the experience contributes towards the strengthening of his feeling of manhood, and towards creating bonds of solidarity with those other initiates who have shared this vital experience with him.

Naturally the importance of ritual will vary from society to society, from group to group, and in the case of the informal usages of modern youth, from gang to gang. With some it will merely be a decorative addition to a life which is becoming very exciting; with others it will be the very warp and woof of their social existence and status. For example, the Pachuco tattoo of the Los Angeles gang boy can mean avoiding a horrible beating from some other gang because of the fear that the Pachuco reputation inspires. The "cramping" ceremony (the ordeal described earlier) is a miserable experience that the boy endures only to prove his fitness to join the gang and acquire status. The "blood brother" declarations of loyalty have caused many deaths in gang vendettas to avenge a beating. The rituals, it would appear, cannot be glossed over as empty ceremonialism nor as coincidental.[11] Similarities of structure and function are too great to allow that interpretation.

IV. A continuing assumption in our analysis has been that transitional practices, no matter whether formally prescribed or spontaneously informal, perform a function in alleviating the "sturm und drang" of the adolescent period. Do such practices arise in any society or subcultural group, therefore, where the strains of adolescence are not acute? In the light of the well-nigh classic disclosures by Margaret Mead of the relative ease with which adolescent transition may be accomplished in Samoan society,[12] certain objections may be raised concerning the validity of our position that ritualistic practices of adolescents are virtually universal. Concerning the relative absence of strain in the attainment of adolescence in certain cultures, one of the authors, Professor Herbert Bloch, arrives at a similar conclusion in his analysis of age-level patterning in various societies.[13] If this is so, can we still maintain that puberty rites help the initiate to overcome anxiety over problems related to adolescence if possibly there are no serious problems at all?

However, the problem is not necessarily whether the formal structure of society interposes serious obstacles in the way of the youth's striving towards adulthood. The problem is rather whether the adolescent is able to negotiate successfully the process of social growth irrespective of how smooth the road which society prepares for him may be. In any event, the movement from childhood to adulthood invariably appears to be fraught with some peril. It appears highly unlikely that a certain degree of strain and anxiety is not present. It appears evident that in certain societies adolescence does not necessarily have to be an age of serious tension; but even so it would be a logical fallacy to draw from this premise the conclusion that psychological ease of transition is a universal condition of adolescence in primitive society.

In order to evaluate this viewpoint, let us examine more closely that very Samoan culture which has frequently been cited as an illustration of a relatively idyllic and tension-free adolescence. Upon examination, it appears that even in Samoa there are many evidences of adolescent activity which resemble closely the formal and informal practice that we have been discussing in this book.

Certainly there is a well-defined age grading and ganging process. "The fifteen and sixteen year old boys gang together with the same freedom as do the twelve years olds."[14] Circumcision comes for the boy at the time of puberty just as it does in other societies with well-defined ceremonies.[15] Young males have no status until just after the time of puberty when they are inducted into the *Aumaga,* a flourishing adolescent "bachelor society" that is an imitation and replica of the central adult male society, the *Fono.*[16] Casual homosexual practices are indulged in as part of the *Soa* relation, wherein two boys become intimate friends after being circumcised at the same time.[17] Here, once more, we find some evidence of the typical sexual ambivalence displayed by adolescents during puberty rituals.

Therefore, it is apparent that even in Samoa where adolescence in the recent past appeared to be marked by an absence of stress or strain, the institutional practices centering around the *Aumaga* have been necessary, apparently, to confer status and a sense of maturity upon the adolescent male. The society still practises the ceremony of circumcision at the time of puberty. Adolescents here also show informal practices which correspond to both the traits of formal puberty rites and also to informal practices of modern adolescent gangs.

It may well be that what we see in Samoa today is a "watered down" version of puberty rites due to the Europeanization of Samoa and the results of American naval rule. Margaret Mead, herself, has shown that before falling under the influence of the dominant western culture, Samoa was far from the easy-going, casual, relaxed and indolent culture it appeared at the time of her first writing.[18] During that earlier period, the head of the household maintained life and death powers over every individual under his roof.[19]

> Present day Samoan civilization is simply the result of the fortuitous and on the whole fortunate impetus of a complex intrusive culture upon a simpler and most hospitable indigenous one.[20]

Concerning the process of adolescence, Margaret Mead makes the point that "puberty was formerly much more stressed than it is today . . . . The adolescent boy faced tattooing, a painful wearisome proceeding, additionally stressed by group ceremony and taboo." [21]

To these observations, Webster adds the following confirmation:

> At Samoa a boy until tattooed was in his minority. He could not think of marriage and he was constantly exposed to taunts and ridicule, as being poor, and of low birth, and as having no right to speak in the society of men.

To recapitulate, thus, it appears that even in Samoa, the society frequently regarded as presenting glowing evidence of the absence of adolescent strain, institutional derivatives of well-developed puberty ceremonials are found. The absence of such adolescent strain has been considered as closely correlated with the ease of intergenerational transition and the state of integration and homogeneity of the culture. Although their historic importance may have diminished, the ceremonials still serve to help the boy surmount whatever the major problems of adolescence may betoken in his particular society. This basic fact seems to hold no matter how trivial these problems may appear to be as compared to those of American adolescence.

The problem of how societies cope with adolescence, either formally or informally, has occupied the thinking of many of our outstanding students. In devoting much of her interest to this same fundamental question, Ruth Benedict has asked: "Do not all cultures have to cope with the natural turbulence of this period even though it may not be given institutional expression?" [22] Taking Margaret Mead's description of Samoan life, but focusing on the adolescent life of girls (*not boys*) in that society, she concludes that:

> (1) adolescence, therefore, may not only be culturally passed over without ceremonial; (2) it may also be without importance in the emotional life of the child and in the attitude of the village toward her.[23]

The fact that a culture may learn to give little stress to adolescence in terms of an elaborate institutional pattern, because of historic fortune or accident, may readily be recognized. The assumption that the transitional period of youth may have little emotional significance to the child and in respect to the attitudes of those about her, however, is seriously open to question. Further, it should be noted that Ruth Benedict's observation refers essentially to the female adolescent period—a period which rarely achieves the importance attached to male adolescence in primitive cultures. Further, it is based on a study which merely affirms that there once was a well-developed Samoan puberty rite which has since broken down, together with the spirit and morale of the people in the culture, as a result of the disintegrating influence of an alien and compelling culture from the outside.

It seems reasonable to assume, therefore, that even where adolescence presents no particular pressing threat or problem (and this, we would hold, is relatively rare), puberty rites or related institutions (as in the case of the Samoan *Aumaga*, for instance) still serve a functional purpose in facilitating the adjustment of the boy to his new status. Whether of short or long duration, adolescence always involves a change in status from childhood to something new. New roles and duties are assumed whether or not they are consistent with the training received in childhood. Any important change in status may be considered something of a crisis.[24] Between childhood and the next stage of life which leads to maturity and responsibility, psychological conflicts often develop because of the unavoidable tension between nostalgia for the old and the mystery of the unknown future status. Puberty rites and institutions can serve, and *do* serve in many cases, to help tide the adolescent over the transitional phase towards adulthood, and also to help him meet the problems of his newly acquired status. However, where formal facilitating institutions are not present, adolescents tend to develop informal substitute systems of their own.

V. As we observe the informal rituals and procedures of gangs, we are led to wonder how much of this behavior is imitative and how much has been developed through the spontaneous interaction of group dynamics. In modern societies, for example, how much tradition from former and older groups, in the way of ordeals, rituals, and ceremonial practice, has been handed down to serve as a model for imitation by the young? In view of the fact that whenever ceremonies are found, among boys' groups as well as among adult secret societies, the content is apt to vary, a real possibility remains that there are inherent factors within the adolescent group process itself which produce the similarities observed.

The tendency of adolescent age-mates to band together into closely knit in-groups is universal. As an aspect of group solidarity, certain distinctive decorations might well be utilized. Tattooing, for example, might be one such device, reflecting at the same time a type of imitative magic. This, however, is largely conjecture and falls beyond the purview of this analysis.

Puberty rites, wherever they are seen however, are shaped particularly by their purpose and structure, and in association with the adolescent group within which they have been developed. Other groups may have some few rituals which appear similar—as in fact they do—but the striking similarities among adolescent youth in all cultures produce such an overwhelming pattern as to establish what appears to be a very impressive case. This does not mean that exact replicas of ceremonial usages are followed by different adolescent groups—particularly those in different societies and cultural contexts. The ceremonial is a social mould fashioned by the needs of a given society. While the moulds may be distinct and dissimilar, the psychological content and urge to expression may be much the same. In a descriptive analysis of a variety of different groups, psychologists of the Kurt Lewin school of "Group Dynamics" make no mention of any group that employed a set of similar ceremonies.[25] Miller's discussion of secret societies,[26] cited previously in connection with ritualistic survivals, gives little basis for a comparison between boys' gangs and organized groups such as the Masons, the Elks, and the Rotarians, even though some of their ritualistic ceremonies are faintly reminiscent of puberty rites.

In the history of gangs in the urban centers of America, there is little evidence to show that earlier gangs have served as a model for today's youth, although certain types of gang practice may have been transmitted. New York City, for example, has always been a fertile field for the growth of gangs. Its history is replete with examples of older gangs who left their mark in the annals of the city as far back as the days of the Civil War Riots and up to the more recent times of Little Augie, Kid Dropper, and many others.[27] The legendary exploits of the *Bowery Boys, Dead Rabbits, Plug-Uglies, Roach Guards,* and of such picturesque leaders as *Mose, Bill the Butcher,* and *John Morrissey* may well live on in the legends of the underworld. However, they can hardly be said to have served as a model for today's adolescent gangs. Asbury's account[28] of these older gangs rarely indicates that they employed ceremonies that may be conceived as comparable in any way to puberty rites.

VI. There is, however, one significant element, characteristic of primitive puberty rituals, which appears—superficially at least—to be lacking in the comprehensive theory being advanced here. Puberty rites in primitive societies invariably are in some way connected with profound and ramifying religious and magical meanings for the individual and his society. In the case of modern gang practices, it would be stretching our facts too far to claim such a religious and supernatural significance.

When we observe the connection with mythical gods, totems, visions, churingas, bull-roarers, and the rest, it is obvious that religious values play a vital part in such ceremonies for the primitive youth. It is naive in the extreme to dismiss such supernatural expressions completely as a passive reflection of economic factors, as Paul Radin appears to have done.[29]

In primitive societies, the sacred and profane are not very far apart, if, in fact, they are separated at all. The belief in animism, animatism, ancestor worship, and totemism is an integral part of primitive daily life. Priest and shaman officiate at all important ceremonies. Since puberty rites constitute a crucial ceremony in the life of the individual,[30] it is necessary for the religious element to be present and conspicuous. This does not necessarily mean, however, that primitive societies have not been able to distinguish between natural and supernatural phenomena. It simply means that important events in the life of the individual receive their principal meaning in terms of supernatural sanctions.

Modern gang practices, however, are not institutionalized. Certainly, they receive no sanction from organized religion or the blessings of the church. More usually, they are conceived and executed over the protests of religious organizations and in defiance of society. The traditions of our culture have led to the acceptance of the complete separation of the religious and the secular ways of life. This is most clearly expressed, perhaps, in our political institutions which emphasize the sharp dichotomy between church and state. In the field of public education, formal religion has made very few effective inroads. In business and economic life, our dominant values function in an atmosphere apart from the main religious tenets of our culture, even though the rise of capitalism has been historically associated with the Protestant ethic. Studies by George Mursell, Professor Hightower, and W. C. Kvaraceus show that formal religion has not figured as an important element in the lives of delinquent youth, as far as preventing them from embarking on a life of crime.[31]

Since religious patterns are separated from so many aspects of institutional life, it is hardly surprising to find an absence of conventional religious meaning in activities which society and the church so strongly disapprove. In fact, because of conditions in the surrounding society and the frequent inversion of values by adolescent gangs, formal religious values, if they exist at all for the gang boy, serve no useful purpose in his gang activities. If, on the other hand, we recognize that there are values and experiences which transcend the self and which appear to give a higher sanction to the activities of the individual than afforded by his everyday activities, then gang life is suffused with its own "religious" meaning. Within the gang certain activities are indulged in with such fervor and almost religious intensity that they appear to serve as surrogates for the institutional religious element in puberty rites.

If a little latitude is permitted, it may be possible to suggest certain contemporary analogues of such primitive devices as the churinga and the bullroarer. The automobile, and its meaning to modern youth, immediately comes to mind. To understand today's adolescent, important consideration must be given to the role of the auto. Is the bullroarer, as commonly believed, the primitive masculine symbol *par excellence*? If so, no more so perhaps than the automobile is today to the modern youth. Is it a male sexual symbol? One need not be a thoroughgoing Freudian to analyze the feelings of the adolescent sitting at the wheel of a high-powered car. Feelings of dominance and mastery suffuse his spirit when he controls all the horsepower under the hood in that long engine up front. The hum of the twirling bullroarer is matched by the roar of the motor. Indeed, special mufflers are now installed to achieve that special noise of power which warns all and sundry that "Mr. Hot Rod is going to town."

Frazer indicates that the churinga, often used as a bullroarer, was probably considered the repository of the candidate's soul.[32] Without intending to stretch the analogy too far, can it be denied that the youthful owner of an automobile does not likewise put his "heart and soul" into his car? He adjusts it, tunes it, cleans it, polishes it, communes with it, cherishes it. The religious symbolism, as well as the sexual, invests the intense relation between the adolescent and the auto with a mystical significance that almost verges on the supernatural.

---

1. Lincoln Barnett, "The Epic of Man, Part II: The Dawn of Religion," **Life**, Vol. XXXIX (December 12, 1955), pp. 88-89.
2. Bettelheim, **op. cit.**, p. 85.
3. **Ibid.**, pp. 94-96.
4. Ruth Benedict, **Patterns of Culture** (New York: New American Library, 1934), p. 23.
5. In the celebrated case of fifteen year old Sonny Wisecarver of a few years ago, he so attracted a married woman of twenty-five by his sexual prowess that she deserted her family to stay with him. When brought to trial for impairing the morals of a minor, she gave such glowing reports of Sonny's amatory technique that he became famous throughout the United States.
6. Benedict, **op. cit.**, p. 22.
7. Bronislaw Malinowski, **The Dynamics of Culture Change** (New Haven: Yale University Press, 1945), p. 42.
8. Nathan Miller, "Secret Societies," **Encyclopedia of the Social Sciences** (New York: The Macmillan Co., 1942), Vol. XIII, p. 622.

9. David Bidney, **Theoretical Anthropology** (New York: Columbia University Press, 1953), p. 233.
10. Webster, op. cit., p. 34. For other supporting evidence see the rites of the North Carolina Tuscarora Indians, the Poro Bush Society, the Macquarrie, and Euahlayi, among many others.
11. Ernst Cassirer, **The Myth of the State** (Garden City: Doubleday and Co., 1955), p. 33. Cassirer says that rites disclose fundamental needs and are not mere meaningless representations.
12. Margaret Mead, "Coming of Age in Samoa," in **From the South Seas** (New York: William Morrow and Co., 1939).
13. Herbert A. Bloch, **Disorganization - Personal and Social** (New York: Alfred Alfred A. Knopf, 1952), p. 134.
14. Mead, Coming of Age in Samoa, op. cit., pp. 69-70, 73.
15. Ibid., p. 107.
16. Ibid., p. 74.
17. Ibid., p. 70.
18. Ibid., pp. 272-74.
19. Ibid., p. 273
20. Ibid., p. 273.
21. Ibid., p. 273.
22. Benedict, op. cit., p. 26.
23. Ibid., p. 27.
24. Chappie and Coon, op. cit., p. 484.
25. Dorwin Cartwright and Alvin Zander, eds., **Group Dynamics** (Evanston: Row, Peterson and Co., 1953).
26. Miller, op. cit.
27. Herbert Asbury, **The Gangs of New York** (New York: Alfred A. Knopf, 1928).
28. Ibid.
29. Paul Radin, **The World of Primitive Man**, op. cit., pp. 156-165.
30. See Chapple and Coon, op. cit., p. 484; Lowie, op. cit., p. 317; Radin, op. cit. p. 152.
31. Negley K. Teeters and John O. Reinemann, **The Challenge of Delinquency** (New York: Prentice Hall, Inc., 1950), pp. 159-60.
32. Frazer, op. cit., p. 692.

CHAPTER VII

THE GANGING PROCESS AS SYMBOLIC EVIDENCE OF THE URGE TO MANHOOD

If these comparative analyses are valid, certain limited inferences may be drawn. For example, where puberty ceremonies lose their functional significance and become mere "survivals," then adolescents will search for other paths leading to adult status. In addition, there will always be a certain number of deviants who cannot find emotional satisfaction within the prescribed institutional pattern. These, too, must seek different roads to attain satisfaction of the drive "to become a man." Societal conditions may impose barriers and difficulties which block this goal. Youth often retreats from this struggle into a type of life wherein symbolic appearances and evidences of maturity assume more importance than reality. It is preeminently within the gang framework that this "substitute" ideology holds sway. Harlem gang boys address each other as "Hey, man!" "Daddy-O" is now a popular form of salutation among teen-agers. These minor illustrations are merely suggestive. In primitive society, under similar conditions, the gang phenomenon should appear with the same implications that have been described. Actually, it does not require any distortion or reading "between the lines" to find corroboration for this expectancy. A review of some of the literature cited gives ample evidence in support of this statement.

Case 1: The Mundugumor[1]

The Mundugumor puberty ritual has degenerated into an opportunistic device used by the powerful elders to acquire a group of sycophants. Their kinship system of *ropes* sets father against son as rivals for property and women, making it extremely difficult for the younger generation to gain respected adult status. According to our view, gangs should develop in this situation. We find, in fact, that they *do* exist; young male adolescents "band together in outlaw activity, going off to live in the bush, steal from the gardens and cook their own game." [2]

Case 2: The Manus[3]

In the study of the Manus people, it has been demonstrated that rites are inadequate in preparing adolescents in that society for the abrupt transition from a happy childhood to the anxiety-ridden life they lead as adults. This should be fertile territory for the growth of gangs. Here again we find evidence of the formation of groups of dissident and roistering adolescent males.

> War, war dances, heartless revels with one unwilling mistress after another, occupied the energy of the young men before marriage in the old days. The years between puberty and twenty to twenty-four were occupied in learning no peaceful art, in forming no firmer bonds with the society. They did no work except casually, as when a thatching bee followed by a feast or house raising involved the whole village. They were a group of arrogant roistering blades, the terror of their own village girls, the scourge of neighboring villages.[4]

Case 3: The Kaffir[5]

Gangs may be a positive defense mechanism of youth cut off from meaningful participation in the adult world.

> This has happened with Kaffir children in South Africa where the world of grown-ups treat children as little nuisances, lie to them, pack them off to watch the grain fields, forbid them even to eat the small birds of their own catch. This play-group of children put on its mettle by adult measures, organizes into a children's republic with spies and guards, a secret language, certain conventions of its own, which reminds one of the city boys' gang of today.[6]

Case 4: The Comanche and the Plains Indians

Even where puberty rites have a vital function in building a warrior class as they frequently do in North American Indian societies, the investigator can find adolescents who do not conform to the established pattern. The peculiar, inverted form of behavior found among the Plains Indians, in which the individual appeared to reverse the usual order of things, frequently brought membership in the esteemed men's war societies known as the Crazy Horse Societies. Although the Comanche had no such societies, there were deviant individuals who, by their depredations and reckless courage, earned the sobriquet of "the contrary ones." [7] Both Herbert Bloch and Abram Kardiner[8] point out that while such gangs or individuals represent a definite threat to the peace and harmony of the community, they are tolerated because this same reckless behavior is demanded of the "Contrary Ones" in war. In this way, non-conforming "delinquent" activity, whether gang or individual, is channeled into constructive paths. It is instructive to note that a "primitive" tribe has succeeded in applying a principle to which our enlightened civilization pays great lip-service but has failed dismally to convert into actuality.

We still are searching vainly to turn the gang from antisocial to socially approved action patterns. Much of our inability to divert delinquent gang activity into constructive channels may be due to the fact that the values, attitudes, and emotional orientations of the gang are warlike and militaristic in character. Thus, in a simple society in which aggression may pave the way to esteemed exploits in war, youthful intransigence may find a salutary and socially approved outlet. In contemporary American society, the loyalty, self-sacrifice, hostility, and courage of the gang boy may have little opportunity for expression in a social order which demands lawful cooperation and mature self-discipline towards peaceful ends. On the other hand, there is reason to believe, on the basis of study of parolees from penal institutions in the armed services, that the former delinquent youth may become a highly valued member of a combat unit in modern warfare. However, depending upon the circumstances and the youth involved, the lawless propensities of delinquent youth does not always work out so satisfactorily in modern military units. The same uncompromising hostility to superimposed authority frequently becomes intensified under the more rigid controls of army life.

There are, however, a number of insights to be derived from the psychological experience of gangs which modern society has not adequately employed as yet. To paraphrase William James, we have not as yet learned to utilize "moral" and "emotional equivalents" of the positive virtues of courage and loyalty which the gang fosters. One of the authors (Bloch), in his early work with delinquent youths in a New York City social settlement, found that the positive aspects of youthful gang life could find wholesome expression through positive means of constructive aggression. Such a means was found in the organization of secret fraternal orders in which the loyalty of the gang boy was expressed in rudimentary forms of community service. The use of such secret fraternities—interesting, since they follow so closely the motivational strivings of primitive youth in puberty ceremonials—is only one of a variety of organized means which might conceivably be employed to give positive direction to the attitudes of delinquent youth. Part of the problem, however, in the effort to discover positive and "moral equivalents" of hostility and anti-social behavior, is to recognize how the adolescent peer-age group reinforces the basic ego needs of the economically deprived and socially rejected teen-age gang youth.

To recapitulate, there is strong motivation among normal adolescents to gain adult status. Puberty rites help to smooth this transition. Puberty rites often fail to accomplish this purpose, however, for any number of reasons, of which the personality of the individual adolescent may play a significant part. Youth, blocked in such normative efforts, finds in the gang (among other things), informal and gang-approved mechanisms of "symbolic" adult status, as well as informal ritual devices which appear to resemble very closely the institutionalized puberty ceremony. In the second part of our analysis, this motif of symbolism in the gang will be elaborated upon and analyzed.

1. Margaret Mead, Sex and Temperament, op. cit.
2. Ibid., p. 214.
3. Margaret Mead, "Growing Up in New Guinea," From the South Seas (New York: William Morrow and Co., 1939), 195-96.
4. Ibid.
5. Ibid., p. 128.
6. Ibid.
7. Bloch, op. cit., p. 141.
8. Abram Kardiner, Psychological Frontiers of Society (New York: Columbia University Press, 1945), p. 62.

CHAPTER VIII

SUMMARY: SOCIETY AND ADOLESCENCE

In this section, a considerable amount of comparative anthropological material on adolescence has been carefully examined. It was noted that there was a conspicuous lack of comprehensive field material on adolescence dealing with this significant phase of primitive life, although broad descriptive materials dealing with certain phases of adolescent life are commonly found. In the comprehensive survey of such materials, the subject of adolescence is usually discussed in connection with puberty rites. The correspondence between puberty ceremonies and modern adolescent gang practises appeared so striking as to lend substance to a theory of adolescent gang behavior.

Basic to this study is the assumption that side by side with the frequently found stereotype of the adolescent who is overwhelmed by internal and external problems and retreats into solitude to meditate *a la* young Werther, there exists and has always existed the opposing type. This more commonly found adolescent in the Western World does not flee from society to a state of isolation and "weltschmerz" but finds security and solidarity in the company of his peer-age group and, through them, finds a structured outlet for his hostility to the adult social world.

Whatever personal problems each may have, adolescents are *all* faced with the prospect of assuming a new way of life, one that entails added burdens and responsibilities, a different interactive relationship with his past and future reference groups, a new conception of the roles he must play, and an entirely different status. Psychological tension is generated by his ambivalence in attitude towards the old and the new statuses. Societies differ in the range of permissive and approved institutional structures which can provide support for the adolescent during this period of transition.

Primitive societies have developed well-defined puberty ceremonies aptly called "rites of passage." These ceremonies serve the dual purpose of integrating the initiate into the social order and softening the conflict between generations, a procedure facilitated by the older men who look with mixed feelings upon these new additions to their ranks. The social needs of the community and the psychological needs of the individual may thus be satisfied by these institutional safety-valves.

The lack of provisions for adolescents in our society has engendered much of the confusion and conflict which permeates modern youth. The reason for this condition reflects many factors in our rapidly changing culture: change from a rural to an urban way of life; the vast population flux and mobility of our age; the breathtaking technological changes within a few brief generations; the monumental transformation in age composition of our population from a relatively youthful to a relatively old-age people; the shattering of the time dimension through modern communication and transportation; change from an inner to an other-directed emphasis in personal relations; the peculiar impersonal character of modern urban life; the frequently misunderstood but absolute revolutionary change in the structure and responsibilities of the family; the dynamic changes in the roles of women, particularly married women; the changing social character of adolescence itself, including its prolongation; and the many other forces which have shaped our confused and modern world. Aside from the historic trends which have shaped this ambiguous attitude towards adolescents, the resultant condition forces our teen-agers to develop their own folkways to deal with this universal experience of growing up. Our analysis thus far has attempted to illustrate the remarkable similarity between these spontaneous expressions of modern youth today and the formal, institutionalized puberty rite complex of primitive cultures.

To place a proper perspective on this study and to moderate the tendency to manufacture connecting links where in reality none may exist, we should be mindful of a very timely warning from Bettelheim.[1]

> No single set of theories can cover more than the essence of these rites, because they are infinitely complex, they seem to originate in and to serve a wide variety of psychological and social needs, and they differ very much in form and content. Many ritual details are explainable only on the basis of conditions prevailing in the society in which they occur.

Although the precaution pointed out by Bettelheim is worthwhile noting, it appears evident that the strains towards adulthood in all cultures provide only a limited number of alternatives—a limitation of possibilities—in which the adolescent may express himself, irrespective of how widely such expressive forms may differ in content. Thus, what we may be observing is a universal psychodynamic pattern during the adolescent stage which is present in all cultures but which may assume a wide variety of expressive forms.

Whether the close resemblance we have observed has resulted from transmission of a cultural heritage that has never really disappeared, whether it is a result of historic diffusion, or whether it represents a common functional need of adolescents in all social structures as suggested by the work of the anthropologist Malinowski, it may be still too early to say. Our own view inclines rather strongly to the latter functionalist interpretation, with the added emphasis that the functional needs of adolescence socially interpreted are universal in their importunate demands for admission to the adult world. In this sense, our analysis does show vividly and rather conclusively that, emotionally and psychologically, the adolescent of today is still in many respects a close relative to the primitive youth.

---

1. Bettelheim, op. cit., p. 104.

PART III

YOUTH AND THE SPIRIT OF OUR TIMES

CHAPTER IX

CONTEMPORARY ADOLESCENCE AND DELINQUENCY: SOME GENERAL OBSERVATIONS

The conclusion seems inescapable that the primary goal of the adolescent has been, and still is, the attainment of manhood—"to be or not to be a man." Where social institutions fail to satisfy this need, youth will develop behavior patterns which appear to be psychologically satisfying substitutes for adult status. Symbolic activities, then, are a prominent part of adolescence and vary inversely in proportion to the ease with which the transition to adult status may be accomplished. The gang provides a "custom-built" answer to the adolescent's strivings for adult fulfillment.

Tannenbaum well illustrates the significant dimensions which the gang may assume to American youth:

> Once the gang has been developed, it becomes a serious competitor with other institutions as a controlling factor in the boy's life. The importance of the gang lies in its being the only social world of the boy's own age. And, in a sense, of his own creation. All other agencies belong to elders; the gang belongs to the boy.[1]

It is a fascinating paradox of American culture that mature people want to remain perpetually young, while youngsters yearn to leave youth behind and become adult as rapidly as possible. This tendency is, upon occasion, almost obsessive. Thus, the need of the adolescent boy to become a man may be added to an already imposing catalogue of needs. The classification of presumed needs and wishes has been a favored device of sociologists and psychologists for some time, as may be seen in the writings of Ratzenhofer, Small, Thomas,

Malinowski, Maslow, and many others. In one sense, the need to be a man may be viewed as more fundamental than even the wish for security or the wish for new experience, which are basic to W. I. Thomas' highly regarded system. The person, rebelling against the wish for security, may become a hero because of his reckless bravery. Suppressing the wish for new experience may well lead to a settled conforming type of life that is nevertheless acceptable to our standards. But frustrating the need to be a man, with all that this entails, allows only the alternative of remaining a child or retreating from masculinity, both of which courses are condemned for males in our society.

Observation of male adolescent behavior suggests strongly that this wish cuts across class lines and can be considered the cultural imperative of gang behavior. Widespread observation of this compulsion invites modification of several commonly held theories relating to class differentials in adolescent behavior.

In Alfred Adler's analysis of demoralized adolescents in Vienna shortly after World War I, he recognizes this same motivating force. After discussing the desires and goals of youth, Adler concludes as follows: "The meaning of this desire for power is: 'I want to be a man.'" [2]

Valid sociological analysis studies the social phenomenon as a function of a dynamic interactive social process. This frame of reference must consider at least four components:

(1) the cultural system in which the action takes place, including the impersonal superorganic forces that structure the interactive field;

(2) the social system and the definition by society;

(3) the personality system and the definition of the situation by the actors;

(4) the real situation, to the extent that this may be determined objectively.

The following discussion will be a composite of these four levels of analysis, since they are inextricably interwoven.

We may begin by considering the broad cultural drifts that influence the contemporary adolescent generation regardless of class. Our purpose in this discussion is to develop a unified theory to explain gang activity. Beginning this way, we may be able to avoid the fallacy of generalizing about all adolescents from material based mainly on lower class gangs who are the inhabitants of urban slums.

Concentrating on broad cultural processes at the outset possesses the virtue of establishing some order and regularity among the multiplicity of adolescent groups, made up of different personalities, of different classes, from different localities, with different goals, subject to differing tensions, and other differences. This perspective can only be obtained by taking into account the ethos of our times and the social currents whose broad effects may be felt by all.

Are there certain dominant and recognizable trends of our age which distinguish it from past epochs? Many popular critics suggest that widespread culture characteristics of our age are manifested in anxiety, pressures towards conformity, and feelings of alienation.

A number of sensitive observers, poets, and intellectuals of our age have maintained that these sinister moods are becoming epidemic. This has been called the "Age of Anxiety" by the poet, Auden. Conformity is really the reverse face of the "other directedness" of David Riesman. Alan Valentine labels our age, "The Age of Conformity".[3] Alienation is the crucial problem of contemporary man according to Erich Fromm.[4] In his analysis of contemporary social problems, Lawrence G. Brown has stated:

> Just now, social psychological epidemics of an abnormal nature seem to be the main form of social disorganization, involving the entire world. These epidemics bring into prominence the pathological behavior reserve.... They feature the mass man in a sick society.[5]

Different segments of society react to these forces with varying intensity and at different time intervals. During the past fifteen years, adolescents appear to have become particularly affected. As each new age group reaches adolescence, it appears to become increasingly more susceptible. In childhood, such groups were unable fully to experience these powerful influences, perhaps, because of lack of understanding, protective shelter, or age level goals which focused on other aspects of life.

Many who feel they are well qualified to discuss the matter may point out that from time immemorial there have always been gangs and delinquencies. They ask, "Why all the fuss now?" Reflecting this point of view, Dr. Lauretta Bender, senior psychiatrist at Bellevue Hospital, has recently reported, "The delinquency crisis is the creature of alarmists." [6]

We may well wonder whether such apologists have gone out in the streets to watch gangs gather for a fight. Have they observed apparently peaceful groups on the corner stop everything to watch apprehensively a speeding car go by because they anticipate the sneak attack of a rival gang? Have they ever searched a teen-age group and found in the hallway, where the boys had been standing, guns, knives, meat cleavers, and oars with long nails protruding? Have they ever talked to residents of neighborhoods in a grip of terror because of gang depredations?

Few sociological statements can be as cold and lifeless as a column of statistics. However, the writers have attempted to introduce personal experience in order to infuse life and reality to the statistical analysis which follows. This will also serve to buttress the conviction that adolescent gang delinquency has increased to a deeply disturbing extent. The quality and nature of the crime is growing more outrageous. It shows a wanton, brutal, irrational contempt for humanity.

The following table breaks down crimes and criminals according to five year groupings, of which the sixteen to twenty year bracket is of special interest to us since it coincides with the age of the groups in which we are primarily interested.

TABLE 2

ADOLESCENT CRIME IN NEW YORK CITY DURING 1955-7

Type of Crime	Total Arrested of all ages	Total of 16-20 Group Arrested	Position of 16-20 Group
Destruction of Property	950	288	1
Robbery	2,195	721	1
Grand Larceny from Highway, Vehicle, etc.	2,384	1,371	1
Burglary	2,772	1,175	1
Petit Larceny from Highway, Vehicle, etc.	762	344	1
General Criminality Felonies	838	238	1
Homicide Unclassified	107	26	1
Homicide by Shooting	63	17	1
Assault on Officer Felony	768	177	1
Kidnapping	53	13	2
Rape, Age of Female Not Reported	76	18	2
Rape, Female under 18	560	144	2
Abduction	32	19	1
Sodomy	176	26	3
Impairing Morals of Children, Misdemeanor	263	45	1
Arson	74	15	2
Malicious Mischief Felony	41	15	1
Malicious Mischief Misdemeanor	835	258	1
Extortion, Felony	74	12	2
Larceny of Auto	1,894	1,262	1
Dangerous Weapons	693	204	1
Burglars, Tools	117	28	2

This is the recent crime picture in New York City. Reports of other major metropolitan areas in the United States, as well as the more recent *Uniform Crime Reports* of the Federal Bureau of Investigation, indicate the same general type of distribution. It shows that the adolescent group is the first or second highest in practically every crime category. The juvenile group under 16 years of age many exceed the 16-20 group in the two crimes of burglary and auto theft, but this only lends strength to the conclusion that adolescent crime has become a significant threat to the peace and safety of the community. The Police Department Report soberly announces that,

> Among youth, as in the community at large, crime has grown in recent years. It is evident that there is a steadily rising trend of criminal and anti-social behavior among our young people . . . . But today's delinquency figures do not merely represent improved reporting—educators, clergymen, social workers and police agree that the problem grows increasingly serious.[8]

Authoritative opinion supports the contention that adolescent crime of late years reveals a sinister quality that demands a reconsideration of traditional theories. If, on the other hand, it can be shown that the quantity and quality of youthful crime in our day is approximately the same as it was many years ago, then our hypothesis which attempts to explain the whole configuration, loses much of its vitality and timeliness. The difficulties are multiplied by the notorious unreliability of comparative statistics relating to youthful crime, in which much of it is treated as juvenile delinquency, and in which different jurisdictions set up different criteria. In addition, age categories and crime classifications have been changed, as well as the manner of reporting the information. All this occurred within the period covered by this analysis.

Considerable recent evidence suggests rather strongly that the rising trend of modern delinquency is characterized by pathological states of mind. The frequency of psychopathies and emotional disturbances among young offenders may be reaching significant proportions.[9] Underscoring the same point of view, Dr. Robert Lindner, formerly of the psychiatric staff of Lewisburg, Pennsylvania, describes today's youth in terms of mass psychopathic personality.[10]

In their disclosures, Richard Clendener and Herbert W. Beaser, executive director and chief counsel, respectively, of the special Senate sub-committee investigating delinquency, state unequivocally that: "Today's delinquency problems are incomparably worse than those of the past." They feel that chalking these problems up to the concern that every older generation feels about its young counterparts is pure wishful thinking.[11]

The New York City Youth Board feels that not only is juvenile delinquency at an all time high, but it is breaking through class lines:

> No longer is it limited to underprivileged urban areas. Incidence is rising sharply in the smaller towns and suburbs. Also there has been an ominous shift in its character—from petty and mischievous offenses to crimes of major violence.[12]

Bradford Chambers, who has extensively studied New York gangs, concludes:

> But recent gangland eruptions in certain sectors of New York (and the same pattern is evident elsewhere) make the youthful blockfights of yesteryear seem as tame as a game of hopscotch.
> For sticks and stones and bottles they have substituted ice picks, knives, and ingenious home-made revolvers and rifles. Last year in New York City more than 12 youths were killed as a result of these gang wars.
> Although the ferociousness of gang conflict reflects the rising tide of juvenile delinquency, its real significance goes deeper. Today, gang wars are based to a large extent on racial and religious hatreds and frustrations.[13]

The following newspaper accounts indicate the scope and gravity of the modern adolescent problem: In Johannesburg

(South Africa) young gangsters have established a "night terror" which "produces cracked skulls, chest wounds, and murders." These gangsters rule the township at the point of knife or pistol.[14] Even Sweden, which until now had no conspicuous juvenile delinquency, has now "become the promised land of the automobile thief, the unenvied holder of the world's record for cars stolen in relation to the number of cars owned. These findings suggest that the practice of handing out suspended sentences has led to adolescent immunity to consequences and a callous disregard of property rights." [15] It is obvious that the authorities in Sweden feel that adolescents are responsible for this condition.

"52.7% Rise Reported in Youth Crime"; "Increase Called Unprecedented"; "The delinquency rate of New York City youths between the ages of 16 and 21 jumped an unprecedented 52.7% during 1954," Ralph W. Whelan, Executive Director of the New York City Youth Board, reported.[16]

"Venereal disease is on the increase throughout the United States. Maladies among the young a chief concern." "Teenagers and young adults," the article concludes, "make up more than one half of the infectious case load."[17]

And finally, important corroboration can be found for the major thesis of this study, in the concluding sentence of the New York City Police Department Report which deals with arrests for violations of gambling, liquor, and public morals ordinances during 1955. The sixteen to twenty year old group increased over 9% in this classification of crime rather than in the traditional property offenses.[18]

In 1956, Police Commissioner Kennedy of New York City reported a continuation of this disturbing trend, a major increase in crime for the sixteen to twenty year group. The overall jump from 1955 was 12.7%. However, "arrests for major crimes in this group climbed 15.9%. As among juveniles below sixteen there was a large leap in arrests for felonious assault with 1,141 arrests in 1956 as compared with 836 in 1955, a rise of 36.5%."

An ominous warning is sounded by the juvenile group just below the sixteen to twenty age category. This group revealed the greatest percentage increase of arrests in 1956.

Specific offenses for which there were large additions in arrests for juveniles were as follows:

> Arrests for possession of dangerous weapons, both felony and misdemeanor, rose 92.1%; unlawful assembly, 54.6%; felonious assault, 39.3%; grand larceny auto, 36%; burglary, 15.3%.[19]

In New York City, then, adolescent crime is more threatening than ever. Case-hardened police critics of this view object that because of the increased mechanization of our culture, it is only a normal progression from the sticks and stones of twenty-five years ago to the guns and knives of today. Their argument runs along the theme that lethal weapons are now more accessible and familiar; therefore, to employ them is a result of technical progress rather than a symptom of ethical demoralization. Possibly, guns, knives, and meat cleavers are the equivalent of yesterday's sticks and stones. But the moral problem still remains. Why are gangs ready to kill or be killed, to maim or be maimed? Youthful gunfights used to be a rarity. Now they are commonplace. It was the practice years ago to break up the fight if one of the participants was seriously injured.[20] Only death settles the issue in some "rumbles" of today. A further answer to such criticism involves the use of the atomic bomb which is, in the abstract, just a more efficient "blockbuster". Nevertheless, the whole world, even including those who have exploded the bomb, recognize the vital ethical principle which is implicit in this opportunity for wholesale destruction. The arsenal of the modern delinquent adolescent gang, with its guns, cleavers, razors, nail studded belts and boots, fits this ominous configuration of the gang's desensitized and dehumanized life style.

---

1. Frank Tannenbaum, **Crime and the Community** (Boston: Ginn and Co., 1938), p. 10.
2. Alfred Adler, **The Practice and Theory of Individual Psychology** (New York: Harcourt Brace & Co., 1932), p. 85.
3. Alan Valentine, **The Age of Conformity** (Chicago: Henry Regnery Co., 1954).
4. Erich Fromm, **The Sane Society** (New York: Rinehart and Co., Inc., 1955).
5. Lawrence G. Brown, **Social Pathology** (New York: F. S. Crofts and Co., 1945), p. 549.
6. New York Times, July 20, 1955.
7. New York City Police Department, **Annual Report,** 1955.

8. Ibid.
9. Herbert A. Bloch and Frank T. Flynn, **Delinquency: The Juvenile Offender in America Today** (New York: Random House, 1956), pp. 50-51. See also **New York Post**, February 15, 1955.
10. Dr. Robert Lindner, "Adolescents in Mutiny," **The Pocket Book Magazine** (New York: Pocket Books, Inc., 1955) p. 47.
11. Richard Clendener and Herbert W. Beaser, **Saturday Evening Post**, January 1955.
12. **New York City Youth Board News**, Volume VII (January 1955), p. 3.
13. Bradford Chambers, "Juvenile Gangs of New York," American Mercury, LXII (April 1946).
14. New York Times, December 12, 1955.
15. New York Times, January 15, 1956.
16. New York Times, February 14, 1955.
17. New York Times, February 23, 1955.
18. **Spring 3100**, Volume XXVII, No. 3 (March 1956), pp. 4, 5, 12.
19. New York City Police Department Press Release No. 21: Monday, February 25, 1957.
20. For a good example, see Whyte, op. cit., p. 6.

CHAPTER X

CULTURAL DRIFTS: ANXIETY AND CONFORMITY

Anxiety and Conformity

Rollo May, the well known psychiatrist, stresses the fact that our civilization is gripped by a pervasive anxiety. In common with many other social philosophers, he finds the roots of cultural neurosis in the following areas:[1]

(a) Our culture's dominant goal is individual competitive success which is the "most pervasive occasion for anxiety."

(b) The son's relation to the mother.[2]

(c) Monopolistic phase of contemporary economic processes.

(d) Threat to society's basic values due to war, technological change, and the revolution in traditional world outlook.

We have already seen that adolescents in particular are confronted with more immediate anxiety-producing social considerations. These include the characteristic role contradiction and confusion, the lack of institutional support, the prolongation of the adolescent period, and social latencies. Anxiety is a "generalized apprehension which engulfs the whole personality." Something unknown and horrible appears to threaten the person's very existence. The attack can come from any quarter at any time. It must be distinguished from fear which is a reaction to danger from some specific instrumentality.[3]

In the appraisal of a personality it is a fair assumption that anxiety has certain deleterious effects:

(a) "Anxiety and hostility are interrelated, one effect usually generates the other."[4]

(b) "Failure in the struggle for competitive success leads to anxiety, and involves not only social contempt but, more important, self contempt and feelings of worthlessness." [5]

(c) Mechanisms of escape from anxiety are:
    1) "Automaton conformity;"[6]
    2) "Sado-masochism and destructiveness."[7]

May concludes that automaton conformity is the mechanism most frequently employed in our culture.[8] An individual adopts entirely the kind of personality offered to him by cultural patterns;[9] and he, therefore, becomes exactly as all others are and they expect him to be. "Though this conformity is acquired by the individual as a means of avoiding isolation and anxiety, it actually works the other way; the individual conforms at the price of renouncing his autonomous strength, and hence he becomes more helpless, powerless, and insecure." [10] Adolescents are abandoning solitude and their traditional privacy, Lindner informs us. "They run in packs, lose individuality." [11]

This conformist personality is described in different terms by David Riesman. He labels it "the other directed" type and finds it prevalent in large metropolitan areas in the United States especially among the middle and upper middle class. Such individuals "conform to ever changing expectations of ever changing contemporaries." [12]

The etiology of this trend to conformity is very similar to May's derivation of anxiety, containing several of the same factors, such as the sweeping change of contemporary industrial society, preoccupation with consumption rather than production, loss of parental authority, and similar conditions of our modern industrial society.

Riesman gives some interesting examples of what "other direction" means in interpersonal behavior. The resultant anxiety and indecision of the adolescent are well illustrated in an interview with teen-agers to determine their musical preference.

> At the same time the teen-agers showed great anxiety about having the right preferences. When I had the occasion to interview a group, its individual members

looked around to see what the others thought before committing themselves . . . . Readers who have not themselves observed the extent of this fear of nonconformity may be inclined to dismiss it by remarking that young people have always been conformists in their groups.[13]

Alienation

Pointing an accusing finger at society for the feelings of alienation it has engendered, May explains:

> Thus contemporary economic processes have contributed not only to an alienation of man from man but likewise to 'self-alienation' . . . . an alienation of the individual from himself. Feelings of isolation and anxiety consequently occur not only because the individual is set in competition with his fellows, but also because he is thrown into conflict about his inner valuation of himself.[14]

Fromm offers a different explanation for feelings of alienation.[15] Workers have lost a sense of creativity. The worker is just a cog in a huge machine, one of a mass. His assembly line contribution has little relation to the finished product. His work becomes an abstraction. The rationalization of industry thus leads to irrationality in human relations. Our marketing orientation leads to quantification and descriptions in terms of money. These abstractions are carried over into interpersonal relations and men become commodities worth just so much. Sociologists have long realized that urban life with its congestion, mobility, diverse ethnic groups, and attitudinal multivalence, prevents real intimate face to face relations. People are placed into categories or stereotypes abstractly on the basis of superficial qualities and roles.

In 1920, Alfred Adler applied a similar frame of reference specifically to the youthful gangs of his culture. Discussing demoralized children, he states:

> They play the role of people whose feeling for society is defective, who have not discovered the point of con-

155

tact with their fellow men, and look upon them as hostile. Traits of suspicion are very common among them; they are always on guard lest someone take advantage of them and I have often heard these children exclaim that it is necessary to be unscrupulous, i.e., that superiority must be attained.[16]

Our push button age, automation, etc., have exaggerated man's dependence on anonymous, invisible authority to get things done for him. Psychologically, his own self-reliance is short-circuited every time he turns a switch and the gigantic machines do all the work that a hundred employees formerly did.

A new conception of self and humanity is gradually emerging as this spiritual blight spreads. Human beings are amorphous objects, parts of a mass, vaguely perceived, remotely related. The personal sense of identity, the ego, the self, grow dimmer and worthless. Adler would call it a "loss of social feeling." [17]

A philosophical investigator might apply this frame of reference to certain prevailing language patterns concerning the use of such expressions as "It is me." Or, responding to the question, "Who is there?," by answering "Me." Most people, educated or not, attempt to speak fairly grammatically. Why do they observe rules of grammar in most cases, but fail to follow in the instances cited, the principle requiring the use of "I" in the nominative case? What is the emotional involvement which makes people feel so uncomfortable about asserting ego according to proper grammatical construction? Why do they avoid the "I" which connotes pride and certainty of identity? Why do they invariably choose the word "me" although they know that it is definitely wrong usage? They rationalize the mistake by such ephemeral thoughts as " 'Me' sounds more pleasing to the ear." "It is an idiom." They justify it by esoteric semantics dealing with popularization of common mistakes. It seems that this insistence upon the use of "me" instead of "I" is connected with this same alienation, *anomie,* and concept of mass man that forms the major part of this discussion. Notice that "me" is the objective case (man as an object) and/or the accusative case (the self accusation of neurotic anxiety and guilt feeling); "me" stands for the self, the object that receives the action, that is manipulated, the mass man of our society.

This gradual loss of the self has been a major concern of humanistic scientists in our century. Perhaps, it results from the modern reified concepts of Relativity, Probability, and Functionalism, tearing down the foundation upon which our *weltanschauung* has been built. One of these basic building blocks was the concept of human nature arising from the previously conceived God-given self, the central core of the personality. Little by little, however, the trend of the times emphasizing interpersonal relations and the social process has whittled away the integrity of the self. Before the turn of the century William James and James Baldwin had split the personality into fragmented selves. Shortly thereafter, Charles H. Cooley advanced the hypothesis of the "looking glass self".[18] and soon was joined in theory by George Mead and his "generalized other".[19] John Dewey supplied the philosophical substratum of the "social process" theorists with pragmatism.[20] The field concept of Kurt Lewin considered the person as little more than a dynamic particle buffeted by field forces. Psychology finally went all the way in demolishing the idea of an independent integrated self when Harry S. Sullivan based his therapeutic methodology upon the thesis that the self was a construct of reflected appraisals. The latest development in sociology[21] is the building of a complete model of systematic theory upon the cornerstone of the interaction of individuals as status-role occupants.

As Fromm points out, whereas the loss of the self had been considered a tragedy (*Peer Gynt,* Ibsen) a few decades ago, then a symptom of psychosis or neurosis, now it is accepted as a normal concomitant of modern life.[22] Cogently analyzing the relation between the development of these ideas and the world situation, the French existentialist philosopher, Gabriel Marcel, writes:

> As often happens, the idea and the word together make their appearance as the mark of a kind of internal

collapse and what the word really seeks to indicate is the place where the collapse has taken place.

It seems to me that the development in philosophy of what is called "personalism" would only have been possible in an increasingly dehumanized world, in which the reality of what one means by 'the person' is every day trampled underfoot.

It would be permissible to suppose that we are here in the presence of some process of compensation! An almost illusory process, to be sure, since it seeks to reconstitute at the level of the ideal—or fundamentally at the level of the imaginary—what at the level of the real, is tending on the contrary to be destroyed. People would not bother to appeal to the idea of "the person" so constantly if human personality were not on the way toward its disappearance.[23]

The adolescent of today, therefore, moves in a social world structured by these inimical forces. We can see connecting links; these currents, the subethereal waves of our culture, are in turn shaped and directed by our social time and space. Perhaps some general field equation combining all the cosmic unknowns as they interact with contemporary life may yet be hammered out by the future Einstein of sociology, psychology, and philosophy.

The inevitable shift in attitudes and values reflects this "cosmic picture." New criteria are established for truth, good, evil. Validation requires answers to a different set of questions formed in the image of this new man: Does it work? Does the majority approve? Does the reference group approve? Will I gain power? Does it prove me a man?

This warping of traditional ethical absolutes is not a denial of society. It is a logical affirmation of the social process which starts from pragmatism, cross-cultural relativism, and ends up with the ideology of mass man in the contemporary world.

The English physicist and philosopher, J. Bronowski, comments:

> The grave danger is that little by little, a whole generation will be drawn to believe that society is in a con-

spiracy against it. The personal sense of having a place in the civilized state grows fainter; and if it collapses, the young become in fact, and the old become in spirit, members of those robber bands of homeless children which have now roamed Europe after two wars.[24]

Even more explicitly, Erik H. Erikson has illustrated some of the problems which face the youth of the world today.[25]

Industrial revolution, worldwide communication, standardization, and mechanization threaten the identities which man has inherited from the primitive, agrarian, feudal, and patrician cultures. What inner equilibrium these cultures had to offer is now endangered on a gigantic scale. As the fear of the loss of identity dominates much of our irrational motivation, it calls upon the whole arsenal of fear which is left in each individual from the mere fact of his childhood. In this emergency masses of people become ready to seek salvation in some reactionary pseudo-identity.

Matters do not improve by the insight (in the foregoing indicated only by a few suggestions) that the anxieties outlined reach into adult life and this not only in the form of neurotic anxiety, which after all, is kept in bounds by most, and can be cured in some; but more terrifyingly in the form of collective panics and afflictions of the collective mind.

The study of identity, then, becomes as strategic in our time as the study of sexuality was in Freud's time.[26]

Continuing our attempt to build a comprehensive system, we now descend one step from the superorganic to the societal level. There we find society's definition of the situation, both overt and covert. It is made up of stereotyped elements to which we all pay lip service and those hidden factors which often contradict popular impressions, but exercise a gripping constraint which restricts freedom of choice and action. Some of the more obvious conditions affecting youth follow:

(1) Absence of institutions to support adolescents;
(2) Contradiction and confusion in roles,
    (a) social latencies;

(3) Hostility of older generation;
(4) Prolongation of adolescence;
(5) Compulsory military service;
(6) Changing family situation;
(7) Class differentials;
(8) Ideational patterns in the environment.

This is the frame of reference which may well serve as a background in this analysis of adolescent groups and gangs.

Our point of departure is in emphasizing the impact of the contemporary *zeitgeist* and the blockade by society against the vulnerable adolescent generation. This provides direction and momentum to social and psychological forces which cannot synchronize with the non-conforming system, the gang. At the same time, the gang member is an agent of a personality system whose compulsion to prove manhood appears to be throttled for him. Necessity compels him to find an outlet in an autistic pattern of action and expressive symbolism. This is the matrix from which propositions can be drawn to build up a model theory that will integrate seemingly unrelated elements of gang life and make meaningful the deviant tendencies of youth.

---

1. Rollo May, **The Meaning of Anxiety** (New York: Ronald Press Co., 1950).
2. For some challenging insights into the mother-son syndrome, see Parsons, op. cit. and Wylie, op. cit.
3. May, op. cit., pp. 9, 191, 193, 222.
4. Ibid., p. 222.
5. Ibid., p. 217.
6. Ibid., pp. 174-175.
7. Ibid., p. 176.
8. May, op. cit., pp. 174-75.
9. Ibid.
10. Ibid.
11. Lindner, op. cit., p. 45.
12. David Riesman, **Faces in the Crowd** (New Haven: Yale University Press, 1952).
13. David Riesman, **The Lonely Crowd** (New Haven: Yale University Press, 1950), p. 76.
14. May, op. cit., p. 174.
15. Fromm, op. cit.
16. Adler, op. cit., p. 348.
17. Ibid.
18 Charles H. Cooley, **Human Nature and the Social Order** (New York: Charles Scribner's and Sons, 1922).
19. George H. Mead, **Mind, Self, and Society** (Chicago: The University of Chicago Press, 1934).
20. John Dewey, **Human Nature and Conduct** (New York: Henry Holt and Co., 1922).
21. Talcott Parsons, **The Social System** (Glencoe: The Free Press, 1951).
22. Fromm, op. cit., p. 143.
23. Gabriel Marcel, **Man Against Society** (Chicago: Henry Regnery Co., 1952).
24. J. Bronowski, **The Face of Violence** (New York: George Braziller, 1955), p. 487.
25. Erik H. Erikson, **Childhood and Society** (New York: Norton, 1950), p. 368.
26. Ibid., p. 242.

CHAPTER XI

THE GANG PHILOSOPHY

The Gang Definition of the Situation

It is almost impossible to render explicitly a coherent gang "definition of the situation" or, in other words, its outlook upon social reality. Too many factors are involved. Rather, it is to be derived from a descriptive analysis of its daily life. However, a very successful attempt to convey the dynamic tension, the reciprocal relation between the gang and society, is that of F. Tannenbaum:[1]

> In the congested neighborhoods where most of the young delinquent gangs arise, the elements of conflict between the old and the young are natural and difficult to avoid. The old want peace, security, quiet, routine, protection of property. The young want just the opposite; chiefly room, noise, running about, unorganized mischief, fighting, shouting, yelling.
> In the conflict between the young delinquent and the community there develop two opposing definitions of the situation.
> In the beginning the definition of the situation by the young delinquent may be in the form of play, adventure, excitement, interest, mischief, fun.
> To the community, however, these activities may, and often do, take on the form of a nuisance, evil, delinquency, with the demand for control, admonition, chastisement, punishment, police court, truant school.
> As the problem develops, the situation gradually becomes redefined.

> Community attitudes harden into a demand for suppression. There is a gradual shift from the definition of the specific acts as evil, to a definition of the individual as evil, so that all his acts come to be looked upon with suspicion. The individual reacts accordingly.[2]

> The young delinquent becomes bad because he is defined as bad and because he is not believed if he is good. There is a persistent demand for consistency in character.[3]

> The community cannot deal with people whom it cannot define. Reputation is this sort of public definition. Once it is established, then unconsciously all agencies combine to maintain this definition even when they apparently and consciously attempt to deny their own implicit judgment.[4]

It is unnecessary to describe in minute detail the frustrations, pressures, goals, and fantasies which lead the adolescent to join the gang. Whether for protection or protest; whether for status or for fear of responsibility; who can say? But one thing is certain. Gangs are developing a style of life that now conflicts with the publicly stated attitudes and values of our culture. A satisfactory explanation has still to be offered. Let us come down to earth now and mix our metaphysics with the reality of the gang. The average adolescent has, by joining the gang, already shown that he is prepared psychologically to surrender his personal autonomy to the gang consensus. This psychological state is potentially very dangerous. Unfortunately, there is little that can be done to alter this fundamental social fact.

Discerning this ideological shift, Riesman makes the following observation:

> At the same time there has been an ideological shift favoring submission to the group, a shift whose decisiveness is concealed by the persistence of the older ideologi-

cal patterns. The peer group becomes the measure of all things, the individual has few defenses the group cannot batter down.[5]

Let us trace a simple ideal-typical case:

(a) Anxiety, which has been conceived as inherent in our culture, induces a state of mind in the adolescent which can be tolerated best within the gang. The gang gives him ego support while he succumbs to conformity and automaton behavior. He thus achieves the "escape from freedom" which reduces his anxiety and guilt feeling.

(b) He soon subscribes to the "cultural imperative" of the gang, "You have to be a man." This is the first commandment of gang life. To be a man, this is the guiding principle that gives an insight into the gang "mysteries." It happens also to be a cornerstone of Alfred Adler's system of psychology which itself is peculiarly applicable to the gang. It is really another version of the "masculine protest" or compensation for the much abused "inferiority complex." The quest for power, to dominate persons and the environment, is the unconscious foundation upon which the gang ideology rests.

We can see here some powerful examples of group mechanisms at work to rebuild a hostile frustrating reality in new symbolic terms which for gang members will establish a "brave new world." Here is another explanation for fierce gang ethnocentrism. From this point of view they are Mannheim's "utopians" fighting against the reactionary "ideological mentality" of society.

Man is defined by the gang in terms of its own symbols and values, and is much different from man as society knows him. This symbolic manly behavior, it logically follows, becomes much more important than being a real man by society's standards.

To be a man, to the gang, means above all:

(1) Fighting to the death, if necessary. (To "chicken out," or to "punk out" are the ultimate taboos of the gang.)

(2) If caught by the police, "Tell them nothing!"

(3) Getting a "rep" (i.e., a reputation for toughness and bravado).

(4) Loyalty to the gang code.
(5) Possessing a car.

Observations of gangs reveal that time and time again, gang boys use the same expressions. "You 'gotta' be a man. You must fight." When asked if this would still hold true if they knew they would be arrested and their futures ruined, invariably the same answer was given, "Yes!" This emphatic response was made by both middle class and working class groups.

Whether this answer was a mere verbal rationalization and contrary to facts as they really existed is hard to ascertain. However, in the writers' investigations, it was observed that although all gang members participated in both group and individual fights, those of the middle class did so much less frequently.

Another interesting and important insight into gang psychology is that these symbolic evidences of manhood are more important than proof of normal adulthood. For example, participating in the gang "shag" (or sexual orgy), is approved for the youth. But getting married and assuming real adult status draws a noncommittal, somewhat cynical response. "Pulling a job" (a robbery or a burglary) is much admired in many lower class gangs. To actually get a job which requires regular work is the stupidity of a sucker. "Only suckers work."[6]

Another symbol of manhood in the gang is the manner of addressing each other. Harlem gangs employ the generic appellation, "Man". In addition to its symbolism this might be construed as a compensatory reaction to the irritating habit of white men who address the Negro condescendingly as "Boy". Similarly "Daddy-O" recently had a fad as a popular name within the gang. Even the adolescent intelligentsia has yielded. Growing a beard is now a "must" in youthful bohemian and be-bop circles.

No matter what part of gang life is surveyed, all the evidence appears to point in this same direction. The boy of fourteen forges his birth certificate. He changes his recorded age to sixteen so that he can enter the sacred portals of the men's house *par excellence,* the pool room. The sixteen year old youngster is far from satisfied with his age status. He uses a stolen draft card to prove that he is eighteen; now he is permitted into that other traditional "hangout" of real men, the bar and grill.

Other activities which partake of the magical aura of manhood attract them with equal compulsion. For example, we could mention the obsessive desire for an automobile, visits to the house of prostitution, serving time in jail, and getting drunk. Smoking and gambling illustrate the same type of pseudo-sophistication. Is it not natural that fighting, the "manly art of self defense," is a preferred sport? Almost every gang has its little coterie of weight lifters who love nothing better than to flex their muscles and strike the approved masculine pose. Charles Atlas has become a rich man on the strength of his insight into this symbolic fantasy world of the young male. "Don't be a skinny weakling! Get a real 'he-man's' physique!" This is the pulsating message that his ads blazon forth from the pages of pulp magazines. From every part of the world he obtains an eager response from the "would-be" men.

In his trenchant analysis of patterns of adolescent subculture, August Hollingshead indicates incisively the close connection between these subcultural folkways and the symbolic assertion of manhood.

> When a boy is able to walk into a tavern, order a shot of whiskey, toss it off, shake a little, belch, and say, 'Gimme another,' he has demonstrated to himself and to his associates that he is, indeed, a man among men.
>
> Smoking is a symbol of manhood to the boys, and of independence to the girls.
>
> As soon as the boy finds a job, he begins to figure out ways and means to buy an automobile, a new one is the ideal, but an old one is the reality.
>
> To have a car is the all important thing.
>
> The lure of the house of prostitution, the pseudo-sophisticated discussion of the merits of the new 'three way girl' at Piccolo Petes. Although there is evidence that picking up a girl not a prostitute and 'making her' is even more a prestige producing affair.

The pool hall is strictly male territory, and the taboo against a female entering it is never broken. If a female has to communicate with a male in the pool hall, she either sends in a man with a message or goes next door to the drug store and telephones. Even tapping on the window or calling through the door is never done.[7]

In his sensitive, autobiographical style, Thomas Wolfe describes the days of his youth in which a typical episode illustrates that the same attitudes colored adolescent life of a generation ago:

These were the boys from Doubleday—the boys named Reese and Dock and Ira—the worst boys in school. These were the boys who taught the foul words to the little boys, told about going to the whore houses, jeered at those who had not gone and said you could not call yourself a man until you had gone and 'got yourself a little.' [8]

From his experience with a teen-age gang, Will Chasan has this to contribute:

Serving time is the surest way to prestige in the gang community—but the feeling is that regular jobs which don't get you anywhere are for drags. "Most gang boys," said Hank, "are driven by a need for what they call 'rep.'" Reputation, standing, is the most important thing in their lives. They're denied it in their homes. The schools, overcrowded and understaffed, can't give it to them. So they look for it in their gangs. That explains why they fight such ferocious wars over the right to softball fields or a stolen girl friend or a casual shove or some imaginary insult.

Frequently the gang boy's model of success is the man "with lots of bread" who rolls through the neighborhood in a "vicious" convertible, stopping here and there to transact his business—women, numbers, and narcotics.[9]

Bertram M. Beck, director of the Children's Bureau Special Juvenile Delinquency Project in Washington, D. C., through whose office is funneled an enormous amount of material on the causation of juvenile delinquency, discloses:

> Increased mobility plus the draft has accelerated childhood behavior, so that young people experiment with the trappings of adulthood at a much earlier age than they did fifteen years ago. Psychologically and physically they are not prepared to cope with the kind of experiences they are subjected to.[10]

It is apparent that every part of the gang's life is colored by this compulsion to be a man. Here can be found the explanation for lower class gangs' singling out the school as a special target on which to vent their spleen. Vicious vandalism, apparently senseless acts of destruction, even defecation in school rooms, truancy, all fit into place. This is not a protest against the middle class in general, so much as it is a reflection of hatred directed against the one institution that shatters their dream, insisting every day: "You are not men but school boys. School boys you must remain until you are seventeen. Only then can you escape from school."

How the Gang Sees Life and People

The alienation, anonymity, formality, stereotyped classification of all those not in the gang, result in a warped perspective on life and people outside the gang. The feeling-tone of the lower class gang boy's world-view has been well captured by Crawford:

> Those adults outside the gang focus are classified roughly into authorities, hoodlums, suckers.
>
> Authorities pushed them around, told them what to do and what not to do, moralized, made demands, threatened, condemned and meted out punishments.
>
> (Policemen, especially, also parents and teachers fall into this category.)
>
> Hoodlums were the smart guys who got along in the world by exploiting, cheating, and outwitting the other fellow.
>
> (Numbers men, pimps, racketeers, and again, policemen are typical examples of hoodlums.)

Authorities and hoodlums were hard, but suckers were softies. They were weaklings who worked for a living, never stepped out of line and always kept their noses clean. They were 'soft touches' and would fall for any 'line.' They could be fooled, exploited, stepped on. (Indulgent parents, 'easy' teachers, naive do-gooders, all fell in the sucker category.) The boys hated and feared authorities, and had a wary respect for hoodlums, but they expressed only contempt for the sucker.

The boys had little, if any, community identification.

As far as they were concerned adults had no use for them and this feeling was mutual! .... Many boys felt that their fellow club members were the only persons in the world for whom they cared or on whom they could count.

Many boys had grandiose ambitions for themselves without a realistic appreciation for the obstacles they faced. Other boys simply drifted without clearly organized life goals.[11]

The center of his world, spatially, temporally, psychologically, is the gang and its "turf," the geographical area it considers its own. At the interface there is contact with neighborhood residents, authority figures, hoodlums, suckers, families, other gangs, girls. Outstanding sport, television, and movie personalities introduce themselves into the gang boy's circle of awareness. As this perceptual field expands, the world refracted through the gang's emotional atmosphere grows vaguer. Those dimly perceived human beings, already anonymous stereotypes, become bodiless stick figures, unknown things of little worth.

The war against police and authority, against other gangs, requires the use of weapons. "Men" no longer use sticks and stones but guns and knives. These are the legendary "equalizers" which make the smallest adolescent the match for the biggest man. In addition, these are the weapons used by military men, the archetype of masculinity. The gang's aspirations, in this direction, once more, are symbolically expressed by adopting uniforms of military jackets, boots, belts, even down to the gloves held under the epaulettes.

Of course, the war and cold war affect its behavior and must be reckoned with in the attempt to explain gang warfare, commando tactics, etc.

In his observations of gangs of Mexican-American youth, Emory S. Bogardus points out:

> Wartime conditions tend to result in increased delinquency and in new tendencies toward gang conflict. Warfare is in the air and in consequence, the gang grows more war-like. As community leadership is drained off into the armed services, gang leaders grow bolder and wield a heavier hand.[12]

The indiscriminate use of lethal weapons, the senseless killings, result from a combination of all these factors. In the total picture, the devaluation of the person, anonymity and stereotyping of humanity outside the gang, the need to prove himself a man, must be assigned a prominent position.

Shooting unknown amorphous vague shapes arouses little guilt feeling. And since his own self is so worthless, what does it matter if someone shoots him, as long as the gang boy proves to his gang's satisfaction that he is not a punk, but a real man?

As already noted above, the gangs of the thirties were of a different calibre. Doc reminisces about his youthful gang days in *Street Corner Society*:

> We didn't have many rallies between gangs. There was a lot of mutual respect. We didn't go out to kill them. We didn't want to hurt anybody. It was just fun. I don't remember that anybody ever got hit on the head with a bottle. Maybe on the leg or in the back, but not on the head. The only time anybody ever got hurt was when Charlie got that tin can in his eye. The rally stopped . . . . after that there weren't any more rallies.[13]

Even if this particular memoir of Doc's is an idealized, nostalgic version of a violent past, the facts bear out a complete disrespect for, and devaluation of the human being in modern gang behavior.

From a sociological, "relationistic" point of view there is

consistency and functional validity in the lower class gang's ideology. Accept their postulates and there is no escape from the existential logic of their outlook. The ruthless expression of this ideology in a concrete pattern of action often rips the veil from the carefully guarded contradictions inherent in middle class mores. Some of the gang's overt values are:

(a) The doctrine that life is war (a realistic extension of sociological doctrines such as Gumplowicz's "competition," Marxian "class struggle," Darwinian "survival of the fittest") On the lower class block, those who don't fight, succumb.

(b) Experience teaches them that they have more chance of success when they join forces against a common enemy. Therefore, join the gang!

(c) Glorification of racketeers.

(d) Contempt for the doctrine that hard work leads to success and happiness. The gang stopped reading Horatio Alger long ago. The squalor of the lower class worker's life compared to the glamor of the racketeer's leaves no choice. The big man, the big shot, is the realistic ideal from which to shape a life.

(e) Conformity—even in school, the group work pattern is deified. Individualists are declared unsociable or worse—asocial (a very popular term), because they do not find conformity to the group an ideal mode of existence. Members of the gang get "A" for conformity, but only within the gang.

(f) They know from bitter experience what philosophers have only imagined in the abstract; that life is hard, that humans are worth little, if anything. They know well the misery, the manipulation of mass man in our urban society.

(g) Life outside the gang with its frustration, society with its agents of repression (policeman, teacher, attendance officer), convinces the lower class youth that he has chosen the right path. He turns to the gang with renewed faith. It offers a refuge, recognition, hope, a mode of life to struggle on to the unknown future with the least amount of failure and frustration.

If we substitute "gang boy" for "criminal" the following excerpt becomes particularly apropos:

The little group stands between the criminal and the world of enemies; it is the protecting wall against the tide that would engulf him. Here is the reason for the criminal's loyalty to the gang he can trust.[14]

Donald R. Taft believes that the gang takes its values from middle class society.

Though the seriously delinquent gang may be an abnormal phenomenon, it is clear that the conventions which ultimately account for the prevalence of the gang and some of its criminogenic characteristics, are imbedded in our culture. The typical gang boy is, in his basic personality traits, a typical American boy. The slum which produced the gang is a by-product of our economic and social system. It is true that gangs are conflict phenomena, and that some of their superficial values are directly opposed to those of the community. Yet the most basic values in our culture are accepted by both the gang and the larger society. We have already emphasized that the value 'gang loyalty' is a widely esteemed social virtue. Materialism and individualism and competition are common to the gang, and the society upon which it preys. Race prejudice is in our culture and helps determine the lines of much gang conflict. Not only are these values held in common, but the very existence of gangs and the slums which manufacture them may be said to result from the acceptance of some of them. The gang does not so much introduce new social values in conflict with society, as determine the form and direction in which common values shall be expressed. In our culture, the unusual force of some of the gang boy's drives, especially perhaps the drive for social recognition, reflects the almost universal fact that Americans must at all costs belong, and must strive for social recognition. Americans have many traits in common with gangsters, and ours is a gang producing culture.[15]

How can one show the gang that it is wrong? It is extremely difficult. Its system is logically sound. Sociological theorists who demonstrate that gang energies must be diverted into constructive channels rarely conceive of the difficulties involved in penetrating the barrier of this well insulated dynamic organization. From the gang definition of the situation, the gang is conforming to an integrated structure of folkways built up from an empirical analysis of reality, forged and tested by bitter experience. Society, on the other hand, says that the adolescent gang is in mutiny, at war with society, or that gang boys are victims of mass psychopathic personality.[16] Karl Mannheim shows how the conservatives (Ideologists) and oppressed classes (Utopians) unconsciously emphasize different elements and conditions in society and blind themselves to the opposing position. They move in two different worlds and there is no common meeting ground. This is a crucial problem because, with all the talk, we don't reach the adolescent since we are, so to speak, in different "universes of discourse." [17]

Admitting that life is a battle and that the gang's philosophy is constrained by this social fact, it is still a fallacy to consider the exclusive guiding principle of the gang as a war against society. Not deviating from the rest of our society in his fundamental goals, the gang boy wants security, recognition, love, family, happiness. He has forged a precarious existence. Gang life is as much a protection, a defense against life's blows, as it is an attack on authority. If, by carrying out his plans to logical ends he does violence to, or breaks accepted social rules of the dominant middle class, this is only incidental and not specifically directed at the middle class, except in isolated instances.

The gang's reaction to dominant middle class values is far from negativistic. In some ways, it is a positive affirmation, the hypostasis, of fundamental middle class virtues such as competition, materialism, "might makes right," loyalty, deification of success, etc., although the gang does not clothe them in hypocritical illusions.

Along with the rest of humanity, the gang boy, subjected to increasing psychological pressures by modern life, is showing an increase in psychopathy. As Fromm emphasizes in his writings, the reaction to alienation, to anxiety, and to isolation is often a resort to sado-masochism and destructiveness.[18] This tendency has been aptly termed the "malevolent transformation" by H. S. Sullivan.[19] There is, however, a very small minority of gangs whose vicious behavior can be explained only in "psychopathic" terms. But it is not reasonable for Lindner to categorize all modern adolescents as victims of mass psychopathic personality. It is an impressive sounding "catch-all" which takes the place of difficult empirical analysis. If popularized, it could be used to stereotype anyone who deviates from accepted norms of conduct.

What is psychopathic personality? It seems to be a classification used to lump together those disturbed personalities who don't fit into the neat pigeon holes psychologists are fond of using.

> The term psychopathic personality is a general classification used to describe all those deviants who cannot, for any of a variety of reasons, be placed in the other accepted categories. It includes many different types of deviants who cannot be diagnosed more precisely because of a lack of specific information. Psychopathic personalities are most heterogeneous and are usually placed in this group since they differ from the normal in their mental life and behavior without being clearly psychotic, neurotic, mentally defective, or psychosomatic patients, per se.[20]

To cut through the obfuscation, psychopathic behavior really involves irrationality which can be broken into two main types:

(1) The inability to control actions which are known to be wrong, and/or

(2) The inability to sense that the action in question is wrong.

How does the typical gang member fit into this picture? Within the orbit of the gang he is certainly not psychopathic. Gang folkways distinguish clearly between right and wrong behavior. Loyalty to the gang is the highest value. Betrayal of the gang is the greatest evil. By conformity to gang norms, the member knows at once what is right or wrong, and this adherence exerts a strict control over his activities. In relation to the outer world, rationality rather than irrationality, controls, with the proviso that their logic is based on an unusual set of postulates. It must be emphasized that these postulates, although not popular, encompass a selected range of typical middle class values, and are not a distortion of reality.

What it comes down to is a matter properly treated by the sociology of knowledge. Mannheim reveals in his essays on that subject, how ideas and attitudes are existentially determined by class, group affiliation, and social experience.[21] Lower class adolescents may be exhibiting symptoms of the contemporary *mal du siecle*. But, in so far as all other groups show analogous traces of the "Neurotic Personality of Our Times," there is no justification for singling out the adolescent, to stigmatize him as psychopathic. He is conforming to this universal trend in our culture.

---

1. Tannenbaum, op. cit., p. 16.
2. Ibid., p. 17.
3. Ibid., p. 18.
4. Ibid.
5. David Riesman, The Lonely Crowd, op. cit., p. 103.
6. Paul Crawford, **Working with Teen-Age Gangs** (New York; Welfare Council of New York City, 1950), p. 19.
7. Hollingshead, op. cit., pp. 314, 397, 399, 409.
8. Thomas Wolfe, **The Web and The Rock** (New York: Sun Dial Press, 1940), p. 54.
9. Will Chasan, "Teen Age Gangs from the Inside," **New York Times Magazine,** (March 21, 1954), p. 17.
10. Herald Tribune, June 9, 1955.
11. Crawford, op. cit., pp. 17, 18, 19.
12. Emory S. Bogardus, "Gangs of Mexican-American Youth," **Sociology and Social Research**, XXVIII (September 1943), p. 66.
13. Whyte, op. cit., p. 6.
14. Tannenbaum, op. cit., p. 179.
15. Donald R. Taft, **Criminology** (New York: Macmillan, 1950), p. 181.
16. Lindner, op. cit.
17. Karl Mannheim, **Ideology and Utopia** (New York: Harcourt Brace and Co., 1938) p. 40.
18. Fromm, op. cit.
19. H. S. Sullivan, **The Interpersonal Theory of Psychiatry** (New York: W. W. Norton and Co., 1953), pp. 203-216.
20. Carney Landis and M. Marjorie Bolles, **Textbook of Abnormal Psychology** (New York: Macmillan Co., 1948), p. 241.
21. Mannheim, op. cit.

CHAPTER XII

THEORIES OF DELINQUENT GANGS: A CRITIQUE

Recently a valuable contribution to the understanding of the culture of the gang was provided by Albert Cohen.[1] The major conceptualization presented is that the locus of most delinquency resides in the lower class subculture. His derivative proposition explains this delinquency as a function of lower class attitudes and values. Non-utilitarian, malicious, negativistic, versatile, these are the descriptive qualities of the subculture which Cohen stresses time and again. By these very criteria he distinguishes lower class gangs from the adolescent groups in other classes. Probably the basic postulate upon which his theoretical system rests is the assumption that this lower class delinquent subculture has chosen its way of life precisely because it is the antithesis of middle class norms. A typical quotation illustrates his point of view.

> It would appear at least plausible that it is defined by its 'negative polarity' to these norms. That is, the delinquent subculture takes its norms from the larger subculture, but turns them upside down. The delinquent conduct is right by the standards of his subculture precisely because it is wrong by the norms of the larger culture.
>
> The hallmark of the delinquent subculture is the explicit and wholesale repudiation of middle class standards and the adoption of their very antithesis.[2]

At this point Cohen cites Thrasher as a supporting authority. Tracing the citation we find at the original source two case histories of gang vandalism from which Thrasher concludes:

> It (vandalism) may be indulged in to satisfy a grudge, 'to get even'. When it takes place as the result of a general soreness against the world, it may be regarded as a kind of juvenile sabotage.[3]

This does not seem to be impressive documentation for the ideas advanced by Cohen unless there is a logical fallacy in equating the whole world with the middle class. In fact, to say that lower class delinquents have developed a value system based squarely upon its contradiction to middle class norms, sounds suspiciously like a middle class projection in order to rationalize processes which are difficult to fit into other sociological categories. It is all too easy from a knowledge of the gangs' predatory activities for an observer to jump to the slogan, "The gang is at war with middle class society."

Observation reveals that this view is too narrow. There is no specific target, or enemy class. War in its proper application to this situation is more diffuse. It is the struggle for survival in a hostile world; it is the battle to assert manhood in spite of society's constraining web; it is the quest for power, to dominate and manipulate others. This war rages psychologically, internally, as well. On the social level it manifests itself in the fierce ethnocentrism of the typical gang. The adolescent wars against parents, the older generation, against rival peer groups. We may categorize it as a rebellion against any authority except that form to which he willingly submits within the gang framework.

It is only directed against the middle class in the sense that the middle class is a part of the enemy opposition. If gangs concentrate attacks on school and settlement house, it is not primarily because they represent a hated middle class. The more reasonable explanation is that these institutions represent a threat to gang values by emphasizing the dependent status of the adolescent. Lower class and upper class receive an equal share of attention from the predatory interests of the gang. The middle class is not alone in being able to display the scars of battle inflicted by the delinquent subculture.

Lower class gang ideology is far from a negative reciprocal to middle class morality. In some ways it can be considered the highest affirmation of the middle class virtues of competitive ambition, and success at any price, stripped of the veneer that softens the harsh reality of the middle class world. To agree with Cohen's hypothesis is to ascribe to the lower class gang boys a sensitivity, an awareness, and knowledge of middle class culture that is hardly within the scope of their limited experience and perspective.

If lower class delinquency is war against the middle class, it should follow then that its incidence would affect the overall quality of the relations between the lower and middle class. There ought to be some correlation between the rising trend of delinquency and the tension between the two classes. Just what do we find in reality? Facts show that there is less class antagonism now than at any time in our history. The accepted distinctions between the two classes are breaking down. Status differentials based on occupation, salary, residence and education, are fast disappearing in these times of high employment, high salaries, new housing developments, and increased educational opportunities under the G.I. Bill. Strikes and boycotts are scarce; ghettos are disappearing; members of the two classes wear the same clothes bought at large department stores. They see the same movies; they are slaves to the same television programs. In spite of these indices of peace and *rapprochement,* juvenile delinquency insists upon growing without regard for class relations. In addition, crime among all classes of adolescents is at an all time high. The qualities ascribed by Cohen to the lower class gang apply equally well to middle class groups. His theory fails to agree with observed facts. A new, more inclusive hypothesis is demanded.

Examining Cohen's charge of lower class gang versatility, its validity likewise appears doubtful. Actually, the average gang existence follows a fairly monotonous routine. Its activities can be predicted in advance. Night after night, gangs can be found at the same street corner hang-out. Weekend nights may bring a slight variation. They may grace a dance or movie. This regular round of activities is broken by auto trips to pick up girls. This is life in the gang. The fighting, burglaries, delinquency, are a very small part of the total range.

Even the delinquent acts that Cohen describes to prove his point of versatility can be subsumed under the heading of "malicious mischief" which unifies their acts rather than accentuates their versatility. The mobility, if it can be said to exist at all, is in their interactive milling sessions where fantasy and symbolism carry them far away from the repetitive monotony of their life. Not versatility, but this regular patterned existence, the same hangout, the endless "bull sessions," the familiar faces day in and day out, these are the very attractions that lure the gang boy. He desperately needs and clings to this security, this anchor, to keep him from drifting aimlessly in the Sargasso Sea of adolescence.

The present authors' investigations of literally hundreds of juvenile crimes, including burglaries and robberies, expose the overwhelming number committed by lower class gangs. Inevitably, money or valuable property was taken. If the scene of the crime was ransacked, it was because the perpetrators turned the place over in their search for the hiding place of the money. It is true that often other articles in addition to the money were taken. But these, too, were apt to be useful to the gang in some way. Frequently, there is a discrepancy between the actual property loss and the alleged claims made by the victims. The theft of the most outlandish property is claimed in the hope of recovering from the insurance company or from the parents of the young burglars if the youths should be caught. Rarely was there evidence to corroborate the non-utilitarian motives which Cohen ascribes to lower class crime. Perhaps with boys younger than twelve this may be true, reflecting their immaturity and lack of social intelligence, rather than class membership.

It is from the crimes of malicious mischief that the non-utilitarian and malicious character of the gang may be deduced. But even here, when thoroughly investigated, it is more often a response to insults which are prone to call forth exaggerated action from the gang. This vandalism, without doubt, has great psychological utility in satisfying personality tensions which demand redress for aggression, real or fancied, against gang values. It is only when viewed with middle class property bias that it is non-utilitarian.

Cohen believes that short-run hedonism distinguishes the lower class gang from its middle class counterpart. No doubt, sociologists are in agreement with him because it is accepted that lower class members think more in terms of the present, whereas the middle class is oriented toward the future. They point to middle class youth postponing many of life's attractions in order to prepare for a better future. Cohen feels on sure ground when he says:

> Another characteristic of the subculture of the delinquent gang is short-run hedonism. There is little interest in long-run goals, in planning activities and budgeting time, or in activities involving knowledge and skills to be acquired only through practice, deliberation and study.
>
> The members of the gang typically congregate with no specific activity in mind, at some street corner, candy store, or other regular rendezvous. They 'hang around', 'rough housing', 'chewing the fat', and waiting for something to turn up.
>
> It is to be noted that this short-run hedonism is not inherently delinquent.
>
> Furthermore, short-run hedonism is not characteristic of delinquent groups alone. On the contrary, it is common throughout the social class from which delinquents characteristically come. However, in the delinquent gang it reaches its finest flower. It is the fabric, as it were, of which delinquency is the most brilliant and spectacular thread.[4]

However, the facts seems to contradict this proposition. In lower class gangs at war with one another, long range plans are prepared and meticulously carried out. Time schedules are budgeted, roles allotted, supplies and weapons laid in, scouts infiltrate enemy territory, alliances are formed, etc. This is not short-run hedonism!

In gangs dedicated to burglaries, robberies, and larcenies, there are careful preparations involving "casing the next job," practicing rehearsals, coordination of efforts according to a master plan. Long hours are spent acquiring mechanical, and electrical skills, checking the patrol habits of the policeman on post. Surely, this is not short-run hedonism!

Lower class gang boys, dreaming of becoming Jack Dempseys, deprive themselves of many enjoyments—food, women, good times—in order to train rigorously for the future. This is not short-run hedonism!

On the other hand, middle class gangs exhibit the same short-run hedonism that Cohen describes as a distinctive quality of lower class gangs. The middle class gang also meets on the corner, 'chews the fat', 'rough houses', and waits for something to turn up. Cohen says that this short-run hedonism "is the fabric, as it were, of which delinquency is the most brilliant and spectacular thread."

It seems that on the contrary, much serious delinquency involves long term planning, not short-run hedonism. From his description of what he means by short-run hedonism, it appears that the activities noted are just those that are not delinquent but a general characteristic of all gangs of all classes. Very likely they are an inherent part of the group dynamics, the typical milling process which is the prevailing social mechanism when young fellows congregate.

In further rebuttal, by the very adherence to the principle of "You 'gotta' be a man," short-run hedonism is the practical manifestation of this abstract long-term goal. The writers have observed middle class boys who were preparing to be lawyers and engineers ready to sacrifice it all, risking arrest in a fight, to prove they were men. This is middle class short-run hedonism with a vengeance. It is a case where the gang code overpowers middle class folkways just as it often conquers the typical Jewish middle class dependence on the family. For example, many middle class gang members confessed that they came to the gang rendezvous every night over the strenuous objections of their parents.

For additional proof that "short-run hedonism, malice, hatred, versatility, non-utility" exist in middle and upper class gangs, one needs only go to Third Avenue in Manhattan where a famous Rathskeller is located. About three A.M. on a weekend night, the Ivy League collegians emerge in groups after celebrating victory in a football or basketball game, to fight, to scream, to break windows, to overturn garbage cans, and often to end up very contrite—after the police have rounded them up.

A further point of disagreement with Cohen relates to truancy. His opinion is that "the member of the delinquent subculture plays truant because 'good' middle class (and working class) children do not play truant." [5]

Again Cohen has taken a limited view of a complicated trait. There is an almost infinite variety of reasons for being truant either occasionally or as a regular pattern. The reasons which might be most applicable are:

(1) Hatred of school because psychologically it keeps him a child, rather than a man;
(2) Failure at school;
(3) Personality difficulties;
(4) Fear of problem situations;
(5) Superior outside attractions;
(6) Summons by the gang to a gang war.

There is little concrete evidence that truancy is related to negative polarity towards good middle class children. It would take a profound interpreter of behavior to justify this conclusion from random observations.

Our position, then, is in disagreement with Cohen's descriptive analysis of lower class gang life. But a further weakness of Cohen's tendency to generalize about the lower class gang is that even if he is correct in the major elements of his description, he is wrong in his conclusion that the selected traits are distinctive of lower class gangs. They are typical of gang behavior on all class levels, and, therefore, are to be explained by theories based on something more than lower class folkways. This is an important point which should be investigated. It seems fairly certain that, in general, the qualities Cohen attributes to the lower class gang are not typical of middle class society as a whole. The question then arises, Why does the middle class adolescent in a gang (a specially selected sector of middle class society) exhibit these lower class folkways which are at variance with his normal middle class attitudes, values? What theory can account for this atypical behavior? The answer may well be found in social currents of our times which, by creating anxiety, dependence, conformity in our adolescents, have made class-patterned behavior subordinate to interactive processes which tend more to satisfy compulsive personality needs in the electric tension of the gang situation. Behavior, then, depends more on mutual interpersonal excitation and group dynamics working on elemental personality levels, and less on class norms, which do not reside in the core personality.

Although we have dwelled on problems which were wider than class differentials, let it be said that class patterns of behavior do structure much gang life. The lower class boy's attitude toward aggression and fighting, his lack of regard for the intrinsic value of property *per se,* certainly play a part in his choice of delinquent acts. However, they are to be seen as part of a *gestalt* and must be dealt with judiciously. It is dangerous to generalize about gang life until facts are far behind and abstractions seem to develop a functional autonomy of their own.

---

1. Cohen, op., cit.
2. Ibid., pp. 25, 28, 29, 129, 130.
3. Thrasher, op. cit., pp. 94-95.
4. Ibid., p. 30.
5. Ibid., p. 130.

CHAPTER XIII

THE AUTOMOBILE

No discussion of adolescent behavior is complete unless its close connection with the automobile is properly understood. Of all inventions, the auto has wrought the most radical revolution upon the contemporary adolescent generation. Some of its quasi-religious significance was suggested in the first part of this book. It also takes its place as a symbol of manhood in accordance with our principal theme. In various ways it symbolizes manhood:

(1) Sexually — symbolically, psychologically, realistically, by increased opportunity for sex experience;

(2) Age—one must be 18 to drive legally;

(3) Possession of material wealth;

(4) In interpersonal relations—since the rest of the group will be dependent and submissive to the owner of the car as he pilots them;

(5) In status—especially if it is a new car, preferably a "vicious" convertible to draw envious glances and admiration.

For the gang of any class or neighborhood, the auto frees it from the humdrum boredom of street corner society. With the auto the boys can escape to their special "Cockaigne." The constricting bonds of authoritarian control are released in the secrecy and anonymity of the car at night. It has become the bedroom in which many of the youth's sexual conquests take place. It is a magical key which opens new vistas of crime. It is not only a means of crime but an end in itself.

This morbid fascination often begins at an early age. When it was reported by police associates that two brothers, members of a Gerritsen Beach gang, started stealing autos when they were so small that one was on the floor pressing the accelerator while the other at the wheel had to stand on the seat to see through the windshield, it seemed incredible. But corroboration came last year when a patrolman in Brooklyn pursued for a mile an auto being driven by an eight year old boy who had to stand up to barely see over the dash board.

Naturally, there is an hierarchic order of importance in automobiles. Flashy convertibles are number one, Cadillacs of any type come next. A graphic illustration of adherence to this automobile social scale even in the face of tragedy occurred recently. The detectives in a Brooklyn precinct arrested two seventeen year old boys, both seniors in high school, for grand larceny of an automobile. Talks with their parents revealed that both were honor students about to graduate that term. In fact, one mother disclosed between sobs that her boy had received a science scholarship to the Massachusetts Institute of Technology. The boys had been caught riding in a stolen Mercury. Detectives, questioning them to see if there were connections between them and a ring of young auto thieves, asked them if they knew another youth who had been arrested the week before for the same offense.

One of the youthful prisoners answered, "Yes, I know him and I knew that he was arrested, but it was worth it; he was caught in a new 'Caddy'." Here is a classic example of short-run hedonism combined with blind adherence to middle class values, shattering the sense of right and wrong, conscience, and long range planning.

It might be advisable for the sociologists, William A. Wattenberg and James Balistrieri, who have labeled "Automobile Theft: A 'Favored Group' Delinquency," [1] to change the emphasis and quotation marks to "Automobile Theft: A Favored 'Group Delinquency.'" This would place them much nearer the truth because autos are stolen by gangs in every class. They steal to keep them, to joy ride, to pick up girls, to get to the scene of a crime, to use as a get-away car, to sell, to transport, to run away from home, etc., etc. For every youth that is caught, ten get away scot-free. What the mystical relation of the adolescent to the automobile signifies is an untapped field for sociologists to explore.

In an attempt to fathom the perplexities inherent in this problem, our starting point is our theoretical frame of reference, the inner conflict and turmoil of the American adolescent in his struggle to assert himself. We have demonstrated how frequently he seizes upon the symbolic expression of his inner need. It is clear that his mood oscillates between polar limits, from fantasies of victory to the bitterness of despair and defeat. His dominant motivations are caught in this web; it would be natural, as a result, to expect the adolescent to be almost compulsively driven to resolve this engulfing situation.

Our material culture has furnished a perfect solution to an otherwise inescapable dilemma. Symbolically, the automobile fulfills the demands of adolescent yearning. It represents victory in the feeling of mastery, both psychological and material, which it imparts. Simultaneously, it allows withdrawal from the battlefield, without any sense of shame or admission of defeat. He can thus displace his anxiety by the strategic retreat to the insulated world of the auto. No longer does he expose himself to the stigma of cowardice, either by the accusations of his comrades or by his internal awareness. In this new situation which is now under his control, the weight of an oppressive society is relieved. By this conjunction of a seemingly universal adolescent need with the ubiquitous vehicle with which satisfaction may be obtained, both on the symbolic and realistic plane, we suggest an explanation for the overpowering affinity of the adolescent to the automobile.

---

1. William A. Wattenberg and James Balistrieri, "Automobile Theft: A 'Favored Group' Delinquency," **American Journal of Sociology,** Volume LVII (May 1952), p. 575.

CHAPTER XIV

ADOLESCENCE AS A SOCIAL MOVEMENT

There is a widespread opinion that the contemporary adolescent generation is in revolt. Perhaps that conclusion may be a little premature. Approaching the situation from a different viewpoint may help to clarify a muddled issue which nevertheless is of great import for our future world. Who will deny that today's younger generations are in a state of social unrest? Blumer, in a perceptive interpretation has analyzed the collective behavior of the mass during the early stage of a social movement in the following terms:[1]

(1) Much of their behavior is random, erratic, aimless, "as if seeking to find or avoid something, but without knowing what it is they are trying to find or avoid."

(2) They are excited and excitable, prone to exaggerated reaction, "alarms, fears, insecurity, eagerness, or aroused pugnacity."

(3) They are characterized by irritability and increased suggestibility. "Their attention is likely to be variable and shifting."

Psychological mechanisms of their collective behavior seem to be marked by the following characteristics:

(1) Milling—the mutual excitation, the rapport, increasing preoccupation with one another.

(2) Collective excitement — emotionally aroused, rendered more unstable and irresponsive to reason.

(3) Social contagion—"the nonrational dissemination of a mood," "lowering of social resistance," "loss of self consciousness."

This description is clearly applicable to the youth of today. The conclusion seems tenable that the vague unrest, the dissatisfaction, the search for new values, the sporadic violence, and destruction mark the beginning of a new social movement. As yet, it is episodic, scattered, amorphous, and inarticulate, the very adjectives Blumer used,[2] but the basic conditions are satisfied. It has not been organized on a large scale, there are no leaders, prophets, agitators beyond those on a local scale, no literature of its own, no formal ideology, no apparatus, no plan of social action, except in specific neighborhoods. Without these prerequisites, youth is hardly in revolt. But the decisive revolutionary elements are latent, ready to burgeon if a charismatic leader appears. There is still time to recognize and correct the social, institutional contradictions which are at the root of the problem.

In 1920, Alfred Adler, the renowned psychoanalyst, threw up his hands in despair over a similar situation in Vienna. He declared, "I am quite at sea as to what can be done in an age of demoralization like ours."[3] Without succumbing to Adler's pessimism, our own prospects may likewise be dim. It may be that the adolescent demoralization is a necessary concomitant of our present social structure, especially when it is in the grasp of ominous psychological epidemics. Stopgap measures have failed as statistics show only too well.

It was assumed that by levelling the slums and erecting decent housing and recreation facilities, the eradication of a large part of gang delinquency might be achieved. Unfortunately, this turned out to be a fallacy. In many low cost housing projects which replaced slum areas, delinquent gangs have been spawned and proliferated where few existed before. Fort Greene and the Red Hook Projects in Brooklyn are two examples.

Vocational schools, which were thought to be the answer to the needs of many lower class adolescents, are now considered by many to be a source for crime, where gangs learn the mechanical techniques to fashion zip guns, "jump" ignitions, avoid burglar alarms, etc., etc.

Settlement houses just do not seem to take hold among lower class gangs. Street worker projects have had a little success. But for every success there are ten failures and this program does not strike at fundamental causes.

Group therapy is the latest approach. It offers some promise. But aiming as it does at individual personality disturbances, it still leaves untouched the social facts. As a realistic technique, Slavson's report of his work does not seem very impressive when applied to delinquent gangs.[4]

The point has been made by certain students, and it appears reasonable, that we may question the sociological wisdom of those whose only aim is to establish a confederacy of gangs in the hope of changing their activities. Assuming that they stopped fighting each other and joined hands, they might pose a serious threat to established authority in large urban centers, because the social conditions which impel them into violent destructive behavior would still exist. In place of small independent gangs, society might have to deal with a powerful organization which could easily become a serious menace.

This analysis gives at least some indication of a plan to ameliorate the situation. It is based on the political analogy of a democratic solution for the disequilibrium caused by a dissenting minority. In politics, our country has techniques designed to pacify social movements before a revolutionary system develops. These techniques can be applied here.

It leads to the suggestion that adolescents be offered political representation and opportunity for civic responsibility, recognizing them as a large group with special problems. This can be applied from the local neighborhood all the way to a national level. If they are old enough to fight for their country, they deserve the chance to have a voice and share in the decisions which affect them so vitally. The mechanisms to desegregate the American adolescent can be worked out.

It is possible that this might meet with less opposition than has desegregation of the Negro population. In several states, eighteen year olds are allowed to vote. It is a step, a breach, in the united front of the older generation. Local ward politicians for decades have been utilizing, sub rosa, the services of adolescent gangs for political purposes. In a way, therefore, it would only be giving recognition to a political practice that already exists in embryo.

Perhaps, in this way, by according a national recognition to the adult status, the dignity, responsibility, and value of the adolescent in the United States, the psychological climate of opinion may be cleared. Youth's self-conception, predominantly a function of "reflected appraisal," might emerge with a new luster from the old chrysalis. A constructive role as a respected partner in our world is one way to direct such latent energy, now bitter and disruptive, into socially productive channels.

Even in theory, the best of solutions to the gang problem will probably leave much to be desired. The sad truth must be faced that in the solution of any problem, risks must be assumed.

> Not everything is soluble. Not everything can be controlled. Some things have to be lived with. Some have to be taken on faith. Such choice as we have is to decide which risk is the lesser one.[5]

---

1. Herbert Blumer, "The Field of Collective Behavior," **Principles of Sociology**, Alfred Lee, editor (New York: Barnes and Noble, 1951), pp. 170-176.
2. Blumer, op. cit., p. 201.
3. Adler, op. cit., p. 349.
4. S. R. Slavson, An Introduction to Group Therarpy (Commonwealth Fund, 1943).
5. Sidney Hyman, "The Issue of Presidential Disability" (New York Times Magazine, February 26, 1956), p. 66.

PART IV

A STUDY OF A LOWER CLASS DELINQUENT GANG

CHAPTER XV

THE SOCIOLOGICAL SETTING

The early chapters traced the connecting links between adolescents of the past and the present. Then the discussion entered into the realm of abstraction and theory. It seems appropriate now to describe a city gang which figured in a dramatic struggle with its arch-enemy, the police. The emphasis will rest on two vital elements of gang life:

(1) Power and leadership in the gang;
(2) Relations between the gang and the police.

The data for this account was derived from:

(1) "Participant-observer" techniques;
(2) Frequent interrogation of the principal characters whose names have been changed to avoid identification.

To aid in the understanding of this struggle for power, a brief description of the sociological milieu is necessary at this point.

In a sense, the ecological pattern and class composition of the neighborhood were determinants which structured the roles of the participants *vis a vis* each other. The gang's headquarters was a stoop on a narrow street lined with tenement houses. But its influence extended over a considerable area. This, in sociological parlance, can be roughly classified as a "natural area" because its boundaries were the river, the elevated railroad along Third Avenue which divided the residential from the industrial section, and finally, the two main cross arteries on the north and south ends.

In addition, there were no great differences in class of housing or population. The average block had its quota of five and six story "old law" tenements looking down upon the smaller rooming houses and these competed with ancient loft buildings for light, air, and access. Residents were from the lower socio-economic levels. The ethnic composition was predominantly Italian, Irish, and Puerto Rican. There was little evidence of prejudice. One could find a Greek "goulash joint," an Irish bar, a Puerto Rican grocery, and an Italian clubhouse standing next to each other without any animosity among the various types who frequented these places.

Dominant environmental landmarks were the East River in which neighborhood youngsters swam, pushing away the floating garbage at each stroke, and Bellevue Hospital which sprawled along First Avenue and imparted a special tone to the whole neighborhood. At the Hospital's north end was located the recreation yard for emotionally disturbed patients. Neighborhood boys gathered outside the fence to whistle appreciatively at the charms of the female inmates who, by their eager response, gave stimulation to the awakening sexuality of the youths.

At the south end stood, until recent years, the Municipal Lodging House which gave shelter to the human derelicts of the city. Here children acquired an insight into the cheapness of human life and the bitter fate in store for those who failed in the struggle for existence. On the west, the Third Avenue El darkened the streets and covered an avenue which was notorious for criminals of every type, drug addicts, prostitutes, hoboes, drunkards. At the same time, this section was truly an area in transition because the antiquated structures were in the process of being demolished to make way for the new hospital designed to be architecturally related to the United Nations buildings a few blocks north. From these sources were derived the ideational patterns which helped to shape the attitudes and values of the boys in the neighborhood.

Small wonder that the radio car sector which embraced this given area was a major problem of the precinct. Every block had its chronic trouble maker. Crime was common. Most serious of all was the growing rate of safe and loft burglaries. This naturally worried the captain of the precinct. It was his primary responsibility to protect the public and keep the crime rate down. In this situation, the captain decided to utilize the singular abilities of Patrolman C.

To comprehend the significance of this decision, the reader must become acquainted with Patrolman C. and his unusual standing in the Police Department. It is a law of social interaction that in a long continued association of human beings, stratification will result. Certain individuals and groups will occupy positions of power and prestige. In our society, without stable hereditary class traditions, those on the lower rungs of the ladder will covet the higher position. In the police status system, the operator or recorder of the radio car is often considered the elite patrolman. It is not unusual for the radio car to perform much of the work of the precinct. Many advantages accrue to the radio car patrolman, such as escape from the tedium and fatigue of pounding a foot post. He rarely feels cold in winter because the car's heater is usually kept in fine running condition. An increased work load gives increased opportunity to gain departmental recognition, which is desirable not only for prestige, but also for additional credit on promotion examinations. Answering so many radio calls he becomes known to superior officers who also must respond to the calls. The superiors, therefore, tend to call upon the radio car whenever police work must be performed quickly and efficiently. Thus, by this circular reaction, the system is perpetuated. Finally, the radio car is an instrument of power not only within the Police Department, but also in relations with the public. Obviously, its speed and mobility help in the pursuit and capture of criminals. Its strong psychological impact may be observed on any parkway when drivers automatically slow down at the sight of the familiar car. Consequently, to hold on to this assignment, the radio car men "must produce." This rather lengthy digression is necessary in order that the motivations and pressures on the patrolmen who are actors in this case history might be better understood.

Patrolman C. was an extremely competent young rookie who gained the radio car assignment by sheer weight of outstanding arrests, clever police work, and strength of purpose. It is no exaggeration to state that his fabulous exploits became a legend throughout the department. His cocky attitude violated departmental mores. Rookies were supposed to be submissive and deferential. Here was one who refused to take a back seat. He was a thorn in the side of the "old guard" who predicted a dire end for Patrolman C. Although a member of the Jewish faith, he was the embodiment of the traditional tough Irish "cop". Even the public sensed this and many began to call him "Reilly," a name in which he gloried.

To return to our case history, the captain called in the radio car team consisting of Patrolman C. and Patrolman X, asked several general questions, and assigned them to Sector 29, the trouble spot of the precinct which has already been described. His instructions were, "Get those burglars and straighten out that sector!" It was an unenviable task. There were no leads, no clues. Detectives had been unable to crack this burglary ring, if indeed it was the work of one "mob". The honor of being chosen could never outweigh the loss of face that might result if the team should fail in its allotted task.

Available facts revealed that the burglars had a well developed *modus operandi* that necessarily had to include the careful "casing of the job," familiarity with the patrol habits of the policeman on post, a waiting getaway car, and a lookout. It was clear that in order for the criminals to be so successful, they had to spend a considerable amount of time in the vicinity of the proposed crime. Acting upon this reasonable inference the officers systematically rode up and down every street in the sector. They "tossed" (police vernacular for "searched") every car that might conceivably be used by the burglars. Questionable loiterers were stopped and asked to explain their business in this locality. Many of those questioned had violated traffic regulations, some were guilty of other petty infractions. The patrolmen let some of these go about their business with a parting admonition, "We're giving you a break. If you hear of anything going on, let us know!" In this way several tips were received that led to good arrests. But the burglaries frequently were still occurring.

Gradually, as the radio car team grew familiar with the neighborhood, an interesting pattern was discovered. The criminal element seemed to congregate at two principal locations. One was at———Street and this was rumored to be the assembly point for the lower echelon of the Mafia. The other mobilization area was located one block south. An extraordinary number of young delinquents paid visits and conferred earnestly with the leaders of the Pirates, a gang whose headquarters was a stoop on this block. From police instinct and almost desperation, the two officers decided to concentrate on this spot as the point of greatest return in their search for the burglars.

The lords of———Street were the Pirates, a lower class delinquent gang of adolescents in their late teens. At any time of the day from eleven in the morning until one o'clock the next day, some member could be found on the favorite stoop observing the territory, ready to carry messages, give information to other members, warn them of danger, etc., etc. Although rarely did more than ten members congregate there at one time, there was reason to believe that they could mobilize seventy-five on short notice, especially since they could count on the support of the Corner Boys, an auxiliary gang of younger boys located one block west.

Patrolman C. descended on the Pirates like an avenging angel. He chased them, harassed them, "frisked them," embarrassed them, and when they were not respectful enough, he "flattened them." A former East Side gang boy himself, he "spoke their language" of force and terror. Lesser patrolmen, attempting a like campaign, had been challenged by the time honored formula, "Take off that uniform, and let us see how tough you really are!" But Patrolman C's personality, his gravel voice, his exploits, his reputation, his chest full of medals, and lastly, his fists, inspired such a healthy respect that no Pirate dared to confront him with this ultimatum. But this strategy resulted in a stalemate. The Pirates were being driven from their homeland, but the burglaries were continuing unabated and were no nearer a solution. From circumstantial evidence, conviction was strengthened that the Pirates were connected with the burglaries. For example, at three in the morning, several members of the gang were seen riding on Broadway and ——Street. They said they were coming home from a party although their clothes belied this. But next morning a report of a burglary on Broadway and——Street was received in the Precinct. About two weeks later the leaders of the Pirates approached the police officers in a conciliatory manner. In essence, they wanted to know what was wrong and why Patrolman C., in particular, was hounding them. The officer answered, "Because of the burglaries." And his partner added, "I suppose if the burglaries stopped, things might be different." No more was said at this time. But the offer was accepted without any formal acknowledgment. Like magic, the burglaries stopped when the crew was working. There resulted a *modus vivendi*, just between co-existence and cold war. The mission was accomplished, at least in part, because the burglaries ceased. Patrolman C's prestige and power rose to an even higher level. It was not uncommon for the new rookies in the station house to address him as "Sir."

For some time there was little friction between the radio car team and the Pirates. An informal, covert code of ethics was established and it was curious to see how deeply the gang's behavior was affected by that psychological pressure. Instinctively, the partners were aware that the tenuous bond between the gang and themselves was based on the gang's respect for them, both as policemen and as men beneath the facade of the uniform.

In time, it was realized that the Pirates gang was actually the central organizing committee, the party headquarters, for the youthful delinquents in the area. They held regular conferences with the delegates from outlying districts to outline strategy. A list of these accredited delegates would include: Cosmo, an all-around criminal who had been arrested for assaults, robberies, larcenies, and burglaries; Dunne, a slightly retarded youth; McHugh, who had an irresistible passion for taking late model automobiles; the Murphy brothers, dangerous in armed robberies, burglaries, and auto thefts; Butowski, a confirmed drug addict and auto thief.

A sophisticated lot, the Pirates did not build a body of ritual the way many other gangs do. Their concession to ceremony was the wearing of dark brown lumber jackets carrying the identifying name, Pirates, written across the back. But the younger Corner Boys who, by now, were trying to join with the older Pirates, more than made up for the older boys' cynical attitude. They sported the well known "zoot" suit. Every Corner Boy had his comb at hand with which he frequently set his "Ducktail" coiffure. At this time they were on a probationary status. They were tested and educated in the field. If they showed signs of promise, a couple of them were allowed to accompany the Pirates on tours of exploration to look over the terrain around the next "job."

Our main emphasis in this final section will be the pattern of leadership and the distribution of power within the Pirates gang, which is perhaps its most striking feature. There was no dictator over the Pirates. Power was not vested formally in one individual. Instead there was a very intelligent utilization of the talents of several members. By this arrangement they avoided the dangers of "the cult of personality" which, as recent events tell us, can wield a ruthless and destructive force. The junta or controlling group had the advantages of "collective leadership," that is, a system of separation of powers, and checks and balances.

In this manner, the same leaders remained in power for the period that they were in contact with the police; they maintained equilibrium in the face of shocks that would have overthrown a less flexible and stable system. There was no opposition or struggle for power within the gang because the controlling cell included the four personalities around whom revolutionaries might rally to seize power if one of them had been relegated to a lesser position. In addition, there was a very unusual psychological relation wherein one of the leaders, Blacky, was often placed in a position inferior even to ordinary members of the gang. In this way, the rank and file obtained a surrogate feeling of superiority over at least one of the leaders, so that potentially dangerous opposition was channeled into this harmless symbolic sense of mastery which deadened the urge to rebel.

CHAPTER XVI

LEADERSHIP AND THE POWER SITUATION

(1) Paulie

Paulie had real prestige in the gang. His was the final say in all important decisions. Older than the other members, by seven or eight years, he maintained a certain air of mystery. The younger Pirates might indulge in wild adolescent antics. Paulie remained aloof. He hated the police, perhaps from experience with them. He rarely spoke to them at all as a Pirate. He organized and "cut" crap games for older men and frequently engaged in serious conversation with the hardened professionals on——Street, two blocks from the Pirates' headquarters.

From talks with more garrulous members, it was later on learned that Paulie was the mastermind behind some of the gang's most impressive coups. From his contacts, information was obtained as to the most inviting location to burglarize. It was he who developed the strategy and outlined the major stages of each campaign of burglary or robbery. At the same time, he never jeopardized himself by physically taking part in these dangerous forays. He relied on the loyalty to the gang code to protect him in case any Pirate was caught. And his confidence was justified since he was never implicated directly. There is no doubt that he made a considerable profit from the criminal activities of the gang. Another vital duty which he performed was to get rid of the considerable loot, which might consist of jewelry, clothing, tools, or currency of large denominations. His contact with professional gangsters, fences, bookies, made him an ideal choice for this function.

(2) Lulu

Second in command was Lulu. (The feminine nickname is suggestive). Lulu was about twenty years old. From all reports he was married and had one child, although no one had ever seen his family with him. His life was dedicated to the gang. He was the tactician of the group and had a tremendous talent for anything connected with tools or electricity. Combined with a devil-may-care attitude, his abilities made him an outstanding burglar. While ostensibly working in an auto repair shop, it was discovered later, Lulu was repainting stolen automobiles, changing engine numbers, and selling them as his own. In fact, he "proved" ownership of his two automobiles by presenting forged registration certificates to the police. His proudest possession was a Cord automobile which had become a real collector's item. It turned out that the Cord, too, had been stolen. He had done such a clever job of disguising its identifying characteristics that, in spite of its rarity, he was able to avoid detection.

Lulu took care of the details of all the burglaries. He "cased the jobs"; looked over the wiring layout; learned the habits of the patrolman on the post; secreted burglars' tools in the building to be burglarized. Specific instances of his methods in planning a crime prove that he justified the gang's confidence in him. In an unguarded moment, he revealed that he had raced his car from the nearest Holmes Protective Service office to a jewelry store in order to time the period between an alarm set off by a broken window and the arrival of the Holmes' men at the scene. Consequently, he knew that it would give a thief three minutes and twenty seconds to clean out the window and make a getaway. That jewelry store had been burglarized in just such a fashion several months before. But continued success made Lulu too self-confident and careless. This finally led to his downfall.

(3) Solly, the Diplomat.

In view of the gang's frequent contacts with the police, a member with a personality suited to this new role responded. This was Solly, the diplomat. If there had not been constant police interrogation, Solly probably would have remained an undistinguished lesser light among the Pirates. Compared to the others, he was quiet and unassuming. A peculiar, neutral quality to his speech and behavior, the ability to listen quietly to a long harangue from an irate patrolman, and then by some noncommittal answer to pacify the speaker, taught the gang that they were better off when they let Solly do most of the talking in police encounters. With experience, he grew very adept at handling these matters which meant so much to the existence of the gang. Solly played the part of the decent fellow commiserating with the police over the bad habits of the other Pirates. He gave the impression that he was on the side of the law and eager to contribute any information that would be of value to the police in their search for burglars and other criminals. But all that he actually volunteered was hearsay reports of past activities about which nothing could be done. Never was there a shred to enable the recipients of the information to take positive preventive action.

However, in Solly's revelations about certain crimes, he inadvertently exposed the Pirates' connection to the burglaries in the sector. He strengthened to a conviction what had been conjecture and eliminated conclusively the possibility of coincidence in the cessation of crime in the area. It became increasingly more evident that the Pirates had been responsible for the wave of burglaries. The psychology of Solly's intermediate position was extremely complicated. It was a game of cat and mouse. The police were ready to pounce if he made a mistake and revealed too much, perhaps providing enough evidence to arrest and possibly convict a Pirate. Actually, it resembled closely the Ketman institution[1] which is an outgrowth of the psychological war between the Russian administrators and native intelligentsia of the occupied countries behind the "Iron Curtain." The adversaries act roles in a gruesome drama. Each side strictly conforms to a ritualistic code of speech and behavior, knowing full well that it is a masquerade, except that the penalty for removing the mask at the wrong time is death. This very element of danger makes the game so fascinating. Psychological subtleties of the highest order are attained in order to gain a victory within the straight and narrow limits of the rules, which become almost institutionalized through constant practice.

Solly, then, was employing "Ketman tactics" against the police. Although the officers were aware of it, there was little that could be done. Both sides were constrained by the psychodynamics of the social process. Solly did contribute information on the location of stolen cars which had been abandoned by thieves, who probably were Pirates in the first place. Their recovery enhanced the reputation of the patrolmen for good observation and alert police work. Believing that they had elicited from the gang a "hot tip" of a loft scheduled to be burglarized that night, the crew of the radio car covering Madison Avenue and————Street (the address of the supposed target) was ordered to give it plenty of attention in order to catch the burglars in action. Unfortunately, the ability to "handle" Solly was overtestmated. The burglary did take place, but it occurred at————Street and Avenue of the Americas in the flower market. Lulu (not Solly) had secreted himself in the building Friday afternoon and had spent a quiet weekend opening a well filled safe from which he took two thousand dollars. However, eventually the concentration on Solly paid off because he supplied the lead through which the case was finally broken.

(4) Blacky, Leader and Buffoon.

Blacky was the last and most peculiar of the group in power. Most of the time he played the clown, the butt of all the gang's earthy humor, which often took a brutal turn. In the rougher horseplay of the Pirates, Blacky was usually forced to run away to avoid a good drubbing. But Blacky was supreme in the domain of sex, the field where the others were sadly lacking. This may have been due to their lower class attitude toward girls and sex, which seems to be much more casual and matter-of-fact than that of the general middle class adolescent group. But casual or not, they looked to Blacky for leadership in matters relating to the opposite sex. For this special purpose he was the ruler and director. Therefore, in spite of his anomalous role in the other functions of the gang, he can be classified as a leader.

Girls hardly ever were allowed to stand around the headquarters stoop during the bull sessions, which took up so much time in the life of the gang. But when the gang broke up into twos and threes to leave headquarters, then girls became a normal and powerful interest. This was Blacky's province. He had a mistress and a "stable" of three or four girls who catered to him. He made these girls available to his special friends in the gang. In fact, he attempted to ingratiate himself with Patrolman C. by offering him a date with his girl friend. Where he hid this special "sex appeal" was a mystery. Rather dull and unprepossessing in appearance, he must have had some secret attraction that girls, but not policemen, could perceive. From talks with his associates, it was learned that Blacky was the "front man" who picked up girls at the week-end dances that they frequently attended. It was from this situation that a chain of events was set off which finally led to the demise of the Pirates. Strangely enough, each leader, except Paulie, played an unconscious part in the destruction of the gang.

Summary

The division of power allowed completely different personality types to function efficiently in the sphere of interest allotted to him. In this way, the clash of rivals was avoided because each had a measure of autonomy to satisfy him. Flexibility resulted from the variety of talents brought to bear on problem situations. Translating the theory of Pareto into gang terms, it was evident that the comparatively large number of positions open at the top levels permitted a circulation of the elite.

The arrows on the chart showing normal lines of communication indicate some reasons for the continued success and growth of the gang. They demonstrate that every one in the gang had some degree of power to prove to himself that he was a man. The leaders controlled the average rank and file member, but even the lowest member could lord it over the aspiring Corner Boys, who were willing to endure any amount of hazing as long as they were permitted to stay in the vicinity of the admired Pirates.

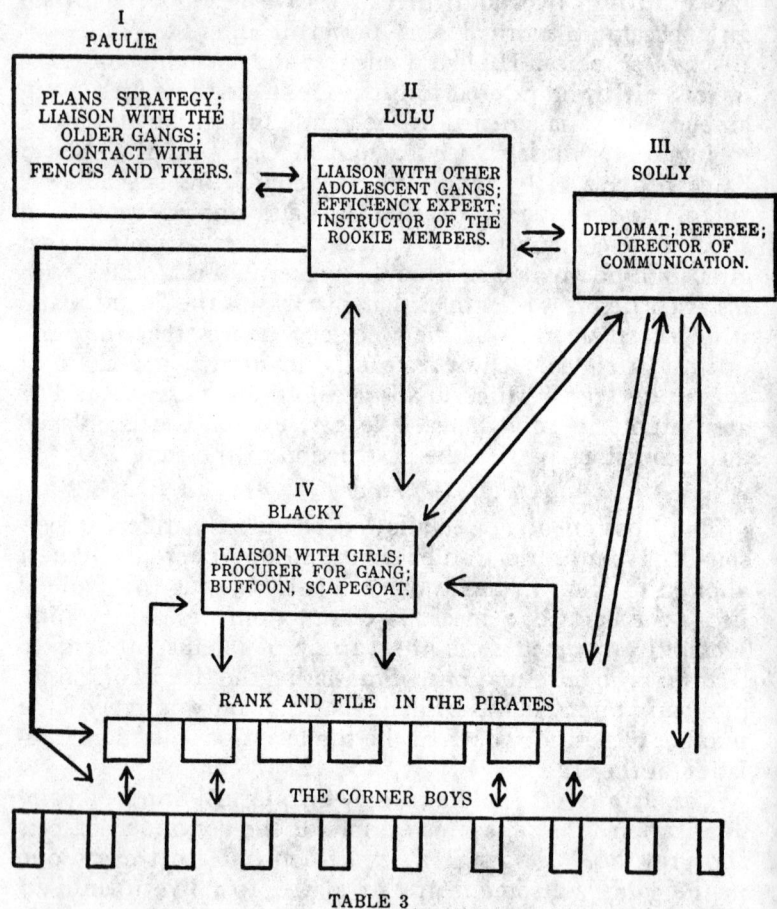

TABLE 3

DIAGRAM OF THE GANG POWER STRUCTURE

Two psychological and symbolic patterns are of deep interest to students of group dynamics. One has already been described; any member could assert his superiority over Blacky, one of the leaders. This short-circuited any dangerous potential lines of revolt, and made more secure the power of the other leaders. The second device, which served the dual purpose of establishing an hierarchy and manipulating the masses, was the established use of the headquarters' stoop by the power group. The leaders assembled on the higher steps; the ordinary members congregated on the sidewalk at a physically lower level. It was symbolic of their superior status for the leaders to stay on top. Blacky was never sure of his place there because someone would be certain to chase him off the steps, and down the block. When he returned he would find someone else in his place. The stoop gave them a psychological advantage in their dealings with representatives of other street gangs who came for conferences with them. When the radio car pulled up, the gang leaders finally had to come off the stoop to gather around the car. That is, all, except Paulie. He hated everything connected with the police, with good reason, because he had definitely cast his lot with those whose life would be spent warring against the police.

Are we justified in analyzing the complicated life style of a gang from the point of view of power? Such a view is reasonable. What are the driving forces of gang behavior? Thrasher terms it conflict; Lindner calls it mutiny. We propose that the guiding principle is the urge to prove manhood; Alfred Adler embraces the several points of view and would say that it is the desire to dominate and manipulate people and the environment. Stripped of non-essentials, these views suggest a struggle for power either against life and fate itself, or against more tangible and mundane entities.

Translation from Political Power to a Gang Power Situation

There is a rough correspondence between concepts of political power and the gang. A brief discussion of these relationships may help to clarify complexities which result from the attempt to apply general terminology to social processes that have acquired a special sociological dialect.

As a general rule a minority group, to seize and maintain power, must satisfy certain fundamental conditions. Its political force would possess, in the ideal case, the following:

(1) An apparatus;
(2) An ideology;
(3) A plan of action (strategy and tactics);
(4) A vanguard of professionals, including intellectuals;
(5) Possession of the instruments of power;
(6) A method of establishing legitimacy;
(7) Techniques of mass manipulation to help consolidate power;
(8) A plan and opportunity to institutionalize its power.

The weight of authority supports this combination and can be derived from such diverse experts on power as Feliks Gross, Guglielmo Ferrero and Adolph Berle Jr. Let us apply this framework to the Pirates.

Their apparatus was efficiently organized. Leadership was centralized with good channels of communication. The number of followers was sufficient without being unwieldy. No overt conflict disturbed the gang solidarity. Esprit de corps and morale were high.

Lower class gangs are neither eloquent nor literary. A gang ideology is never clearly stated in speech or writing. It is rather a summation of the overt and covert attitudes and values of the individual members. In the case of the Pirates the gang ideology might be paraphrased as follows: "Join and support the Pirates, and prove you are a man! If you help us to seize and establish power, you will gain protection, status, wealth, and power. Pirates receive the comfort of psychological support from the gang and supplant the anxiety and alienation of adolescent life. Instead of a humdrum toilworn existence, life is a series of thrilling adventures." Admittedly, it is a very attractive program.

Their plan of action was strategically contrived to gain power, wealth, and expansion of the gang's criminal activities (i.e., burglaries, robberies, larcenies). Paulie chose the targets and disposed of the loot at a profit; Lulu planned the tactics and details of procedure; Solly contributed diplomacy; Blacky provided recreation for their leisure. Perhaps unwittingly, they were using this scheme to establish legitimacy.

The four leaders were the vanguard that led the gang and the fellow travelers toward the seizure of power and fulfilled the dual role of elite and intellectual. Their advanced knowledge of techniques and theory of crime, their clever diplomacy, their pragmatic intelligence, their calculating avoidance of apprehension, demonstrated intellectuality in this specific situation.

In their possession were material instruments of power, including, it was dicovered later, an elaborate set of burglar's tools and several autos. Superior ability to that of rival gangs, and the interlocking role structure could be classified as non-material instruments of power.

Ordinarily, legitimacy is achieved by working for public approval. Here we find an extremely interesting variation on the theme, revealing the political acumen of the Pirates. For most gangs contact with the police is anathema. In middle class neighborhoods the boys feel that they are stigmatized as ruffians by constant attention from the police. In lower class sections the police are an enemy in perpetual war with the delinquent gangs. As we have shown, the Pirates rose above this deep-seated almost instinctive class prejudice and by the use of diplomacy made an attempt to turn a dangerous situation to their own advantage.

Again it was the class and ethnic distribution of that part of the city that made this plan feasible. In a middle class environment the Mayor and the Police Commissioner, as public servants, would soon be deluged with letters and telephone calls, demanding to know why the police were either constantly harassing a group of fine young men, or badgering a bunch of known hoodlums but making no arrests. The inconsistency of the two complaints is typical of middle class interpretations which depend on whether or not the boys are related to the complainants or whether the complainants' children are at odds with the gang in question.

In the lower class a similar situation calls forth an entirely different reaction. Even where the policeman may be hated, his power is respected. The symbolic authority of his uniform inculcates a respectful attitude at least among the older residents. The officer on the post is an important part of their daily life. He appears whenever one of the numerous ambulance calls is sent out; he settles the family fight; he gives the young wrongdoers another chance. Who delivers the baby in the absence of the doctor? Who carries home the drunken husband? To whom are they forced to turn for help and redress? The patrolman on post. Immigrants regard him with the eyes of the old world. Jewish and Italian elders often doff their hats when addressing the policeman. For the Puerto Ricans he is a major point of contact with the strange new world of New York. To the Irish who may have come from a village in which the priest and the constable were the two most important officials, the police officer is "one of their own kind." For all these reasons the policeman patrolling a beat on a lower class street has a lot more leeway and importance. There is no tradition in the neighborhood for making complaints about the police.

The masses that the leaders of the Pirates wished to manipulate were the rank and file of the gang, the Corner Boys, representatives of other gangs, and those boys on ——— Street who did not belong to the gangs. Subtle symbolic techniques were employed which imparted psychological significance to the spatial arrangements of the headquarters' stoop. Blacky's role as scapegoat for the gang provided a convenient safety valve to divert the latent hostility from the real leaders. The cumulative impact of these techniques of mass manipulation resulted in a show of power and success which tended to make other gangs submissive to the Pirates. As the Pirates held power in spite of occasional attempts to dislodge them, there was a gradual acceptance by rival groups of their hegemony. This change in attitude was the final corroboration that the Pirates had institutionalized their control over the delinquent youth in the area.

So much for the power structure of the gang. Its history,

viewed from any angle, probably would yield sociological insights that justify continuation of this analysis. We have seen how the Pirates flourished much to the consternation of Patrolman C. and his partner, who were eager to put an end to the gang's career. Rival gangs realized the strength of the Pirates' position and looked to them for leadership. This was most apparent in the case of "The Corner Boys" who were younger and less experienced in handling the various complications of delinquent group subculture. Directing his campaign against the Pirates to a more vulnerable point, Patrolman C. gave lots of attention to the Corner Boys, much to their discomfiture. Gradually, they moved into the protective shadow of the older gang and became an auxiliary to them. One day they all gathered at headquarters and at a prearranged signal, exhibited their wrists. Tattooed neatly in blue letters was the name "Corner Boys." Their pride was apparent. Now they were real men!

Lulu welcomed these new recruits and started to train them. Some mornings, at about three or four A. M., Lulu was spotted riding around with one or two Corner Boys. Although it was obvious that they were preparing to burglarize some loft, they could never be caught with enough evidence to justify an arrest.

Each tour of duty, Patrolman C., with his partner, visited ———Street to show the gang that they were on duty and to check street conditions. The Pirates had a lot of information about criminal activities in the neighborhood which sometimes alerted the radio car partners to problems demanding police action. The mysterious underground channels of communication in criminal circles deserve a serious study. It was amazing how fast they knew details of crimes before the cases had even been reported to the police.

On Sundays, the gang dressed up in "formal" attire and attended church. For most of them it was the large Catholic Church on———Street. But even the presence of this imposing house of worship located so near their headquarters did not ameliorate their delinquent attitudes toward life and society. An extraordinary feature of this close proximity to the church was that it served to reinforce the gang's tendency to interpret events from the point of view of power relations, manipulating others, and "fixing" a case. For example, their respect for religion and the clergy was expressed in such admiring terms as "Father R. is a swell guy. He's a real powerhouse. He can get anything he wants around here." In certain respects their attitude was justified by the facts of lower class life. Priests in such neighborhoods did exercise strong practical influence in everyday affairs. Sometimes, when called upon for help by a member of their parish, they might intercede with the police to gain another chance for some miscreant of "tender" years.

The large Boys' Club in the neighborhood should have been another socializing force for the adolescents in the community. But, here again, the boys defined the situation in terms of their own distorted values. Did the Club have a boxing ring? Fine! That meant fighting was approved. Only why confine it to the ring? They indulged in "free-for-alls" inside and outside the Club buildings, which necessitated frequent calls for police assistance to restore order. Were there regular meeting rooms? Good! The Pirates often met in the building for conferences; but they used the boiler room, not the meeting room, to hold their sessions.

The beginning of the end for the Pirates came, innocently enough, at a dance held at the——Church. Blacky, leading the way, in his special domain, danced with a very attractive girl. Her escort resented Blacky's attentions to her. A fight ensued which was quickly brought under control, but the damage had been done. To avenge Blacky, four or five carloads of Pirates set out the next night for Mulberry Street. They were unable to make contact with the enemy. Retaliation was swift. A few nights later an auto with lights off raced through——Street and sprayed the Pirates with bullets which fortunately did not hit anyone. They, in turn, with the "feel" possessed by most gang youths had "made" the car as it approached and had instinctively sought cover while mentally photographing the automobile. For days after this event, the Pirates systematically scoured the city, riding up and down the side streets in several automobiles searching for the assailants' vehicle. One day they came to Patrolman C. and reported that they were sure that they had spotted the car on———Street.

By some strange process of reasoning they had turned to the policemen, their deadly enemy, for help in coping with this crisis. The two patrolmen accompanied them on their time off to the street where the auto had been seen. Unfortunately, the car was gone. Upon checking the license number which the gang had noted, it was discovered that the car was not stolen and belonged to someone in Queens. This slight effort on their behalf made a deep impression on the gang and separated the partners from the general class of policemen in the gang's classification of external inimical forces.

Solly finally capitulated and disclosed the first definite information that could be used. In confidence and with requests to tell no one the source of knowledge, he intimated that Lulu had an arsenal of guns concealed somewhere. Lulu had rented these guns for twenty-five dollars to a gang who were robbing drug and liquor stores in Queens. Did Solly inform because he was grateful for the helping hand? Or was it a subtle device of power politics to eliminate a rival for control of the gang? Was there an undercover struggle for power in the gang of which the police were unaware? It was never discovered. But if this actually was the case, Solly miscalculated gravely the ultimate result of his action.

Events moved rapidly from this point on. Patrolman C. and his partner debated: (1) whether to search Lulu's autos to see if he had the guns concealed there, (2) whether to immediately inform the detectives, (3) whether to wait to see if this was another false trail as the others had been. Ultimately, the decision was made to investigate discreetly to see what they could turn up in the way of corroboration. The denouement was to come several days later. Patrolman C., this time with a rookie for a partner—his regular partner was off duty—had proceeded to———Street to check up on the Pirates. He observed Lulu walking east. As usual, Lulu sensed the presence of the police car even with his back turned to it. Equally acute, Patrolman C. saw that Lulu quickly put his hand inside his jacket and then sauntered on with exaggerated nonchalance. C., normally suspicious, but now doubly so, because of the recent disclosures about Lulu's activities, jumped to the conclusion that Lulu had just concealed a gun in his lumber jacket.

Lulu was "escorted" into the radio car. In response to the question of what he had concealed in his jacket, Lulu answered, "Nothing! You can search me if you want to." An immediate search revealed nothing. With his characteristic confidence, Patrolman C. refused to admit the possibility that Lulu was right and that his own intuition could be wrong. He immediately took command of the situation and ordered everyone out of the car. (Patrolman C. habitually ordered even other policemen who were his theoretical equals, and surprisingly enough, they usually followed his directions.) He then searched the street and the radio car thoroughly. Under the seat of the car he found a fully loaded revolver. Lulu, even under such pressure, watched carefully by two alert patrolmen next to him, had managed to conceal the gun under the seat as he entered.

In the station house, he at first conducted himself with his customary aplomb, until a detective of the old school decided that Lulu's breezy manner of answering questions insulted the hallowed dignity of the police department. As an impulsive reaction to the disrespect of a young hoodlum, the detective slapped Lulu once. An amazing thing then occurred, something that could never have been predicted. Lulu, on such slight provocation, broke down completely in the face of superior power. Gone was the pride, the panache, that had distinguished Lulu from the other Pirates. He confessed readily to approximately thirty burglaries, to lending and renting his guns to robbers who were later picked up, to systematically stealing cars including both his Cord and Chevrolet, and to forging the registrations.

Demoralized as he was, however, he still remained true to the gang code of loyalty. He refused to implicate any one in the immediate group. Sociologically, they were without doubt, as members of the same primary group, co-conspirators and accomplices, as well as accessories after the fact. Legally, it was another matter. The rest of the Pirates were not technically connected with this arrest. A glimpse of the real Lulu was revealed as he was being lodged in the cell by the arresting officer, Patrolman C. With deadly hatred, Lulu turned to him and said, "C., I had you in the sights of my rifle one hundred times, up there on the roof. Now I know I should have pulled the trigger."

Lulu was sentenced to prison for a term of three to five years, on charges which included unlawful possession of dangerous weapons, burglary, larceny, conspiracy. His enforced leave of absence was the death blow to the gang even though on previous occasions it had firmly withstood the arrests of minor members. Without Lulu, their general, the Pirates lost their cohesiveness and a powerful integrating figure. The gang's effectiveness appeared to diminish rapidly.

POSTSCRIPT

The postcript is of interest because it throws light on the fate of the Corner Boys. About a year after the events described above, a patrolman found a teen-ager wandering along Third Avenue after midnight. The officer stopped him, questioned him, and receiving unsatisfactory answers, ordered him to get home. This adolescent happened to be Van, a prominent member of the Corner Boys gang. Van walked slowly away with that peculiar gait of the experienced gang boy which flaunts his defiance of authority but stops just short of irritating the policeman to a point that might invite rougher handling. The police officer followed casually just to make sure that Van, whom he had sized up as a potential burglar, did not remain in the neighborhood. Suddenly, for no apparent reason, Van stopped, turned, and shouted in a belligerent manner, "You wouldn't be so tough without that nightstick. Take off the uniform and fight like a man!"

This abrupt metamorphosis from a craven young hoodlum to the contemptuous, arrogant brawler was stunning to the policeman. Before the officer could take any punitive action, Van ran over to an auto which had cautiously approached the scene of action; he entered and the car roared away. Other Corner Boys were in the car. They were in the vicinity for possible use as a getaway car in case Van had "pulled a job." The point to be stressed here is the psychology of the gang which forced Van, even in a desperate situation, to play the big shot, to prove he was a man, as soon as he realized that his behavior was being measured by the rest of his gang.

This incident added to other predatory forays of the Corner Boys which we have described earlier in the volume showed that the Pirates had lost their power to the "up and coming" Corner Boys. In terms of the theory of power it might be said that the Pirates had been defeated in war by the police. As a result the gang leadership had been dispersed and the members were demoralized. Theoretically, a revolutionary situation was thus created. A power vacuum ensued and the ambitious Corner Boys, still relatively untouched by the blow to the older group of Pirates, stepped in and took over without opposition.

---

1. Czelaw Milosz, The Captive Mind (New York: Alfred A. Knopf, 1953) pp. 54-81.

CONCLUSIONS

(1) Adolescent gangs may be profitably studied by using as a frame of reference the theory of power.

(2) The gang's attempt to gain status and power through the domination and manipulation of persons and events is a collective representation of the individual gang member's guiding fiction which is "to prove he is a man." In passing it is worthy of note that Alfred Adler's system of psychology is "tailor made" for the analysis of the gang since it is principally concerned with the struggle for power and the "masculine protest."

(3) The presence of the gang, real, constructive, or symbolic, gives the individual member ego support and courage. He gains a psychological sense of power and manhood which he does not possess at all when he is on his own.

(4) If single gangs can pose a threat to the peace and safety of the community—and they certainly do so—then the well meaning efforts to organize several gangs into a confederation may be a very grave error. Without significant changes in behavior and values on the part of such gangs, this maneuver may only multiply to extremely dangerous proportions the looming menace which even now we find extremely difficult to control. Exactly what these significant changes ought to be is a matter of intense concern to those who realize the gravity of the situation. The implications of our theoretical position lead to the following suggestions as a very minimum core of any feasible program.

(a) Formal and public recognition must be given to the social maturity of the younger generation and its readiness to assume a more equitable share of community responsibility.

(b) Adolescents ought to be given a voice and representation in government from the community level right on up.

It may well be that by helping to determine control, a sense of responsibility will be developed to observe the law.

While the Pirates were not outstanding for the wealth of ritual or ceremonial detail, it is instructive to see how they fit into the categories discussed earlier. The Corner Boys should prove even better examples.

Decoration—More evidence of the urge for self decoration can be found among the Corner Boys than among the Pirates. This can be explained logically enough in accordance with the theories presented by pointing out that since the Corner Boys were so eager to join the older group, they are, in effect, comparable to young novices undergoing the ceremonial preparatory to being inducted into the older men's group. In this connection we find tattooing of the wrists, special haircuts, zoot suits, motorcycle jackets and boots, which all correspond to expectation.

Age Grades—Paulie was the emissary of the men's gang whose duty it was to keep an eye on the Pirates. The Corner Boys were the youngest age group. Each was a distinct entity. Each member strove for admission into the next higher grade.

Education of the Novices—The Corner Boys were being trained and educated in the arts and sciences of the older group. Lulu was chairman of the department of criminology. As a part of his course, he led the boys on field trips after midnight to give them a baptism under fire. At the same time these dangerous sorties constituted the ordeal and trial which brought to light the latent propensities to "chicken out."

Profit for the Elders—Paulie stands out as a fine example of the gang Fagin. There is little doubt that the main source of his income was derived from the criminal operations of the Pirates.

Sexual Ambivalence—The carefully dressed coiffures of the Corner Boys, the feminine overtones in the leader's name, Lulu, point in this direction. The daily meetings at the stoop were reserved for men only.

We have offered a psychoanalytic explanation of these tendencies toward effeminacy. How can the swaggering young "he-man" rationalize to himself the impulse to behavior which negates all his efforts to flaunt his manhood? He does this by splitting the concept of manliness into two opposing yet complementary dimensions. One is exemplified by all those practices which we have described in rather lengthy detail and which are traditionally male activities. But this other sphere of manhood is the equally important task of being a "ladies' man." To succeed in this area, he has to make himself attractive to girls even if it involves the cultivation of a pompadour or the display of gay pastel colored garments.

Quality and Extent of Crime—The Pirates organized and directed such an impressive array of criminal activities that they may be justifiably presented as an example of the spreading menace of some of our delinquent gangs.

Anxiety and Alienation—The basic anxiety and insecurity of the most daring and resourceful member of the gang was dramatically revealed by Lulu's instantaneous demoralization when confronted by a type of authority which was impervious to his customary adjustive techniques. The facade of self confidence which had formerly been bolstered by his air of braggadocio collapsed completely and revealed the underlying weakness and anxiety. The alienation from people and society's traditional values dominates the picture of Lulu standing on the roof with his rifle pointing at Patrolman C., debating with himself whether or not to pull the trigger.

The analysis of the structure, function, and ideology of the Pirates again reveals those salient features which the authors observed repeatedly in their field investigations, and which as a result were made the basis for the theoretical system developed here. The evidence lends weight to the conclusion that this cross cultural comparison of modern gangs and primitive youth is more than an imaginative fantasy which attempts to draw parallels between two antithetical realms of existence. By this special path we have sought to unravel the hidden motivations and dynamics of the adolescent generation of our time.

SELECTED BIBLIOGRAPHY

Adler, Alfred, *The Practice and Theory of Individual Psychology* (New York: Harcourt Brace and Company, 1932).

Asbury, Herbert, *The Gangs of New York* (New York: Alfred A. Knopf, 1928).

Bateson, Gregory, "Some Systematic Approaches to the Study of Culture and Personality," *Character and Personality,* 11 (1942).

Bateson, Gregory, *Naven* (London: Cambridge University Press, 1936).

Bayley, N. and N. C. Jones, "Some Personality Characteristics of Boys with Retarded Skeletal Maturity," *Psychological Bulletin, 38* (1941).

Beals, Ralph L., and Harry Hoijer, *An Introduction to Anthropology* (New York: The Macmillan Company, 1953).

Benedict, Ruth, *Patterns of Culture* (New York: New American Library, 1934).

Bentley, W. H., *Pioneering on the Congo* (New York: Fleming H. Revell and Company), cited in W. I. Thomas, *Primitive Behavior* (New York, 1937).

Bettelheim, Bruno, *Symbolic Wounds* (Glencoe: The Free Press, 1954).

Bidney, David, *Theoretical Anthropology* (New York: Columbia University Press, 1953).

Bishop, Bernice P., *Museum Bulletin,* 61 (1924)

Bloch, Herbert A., *Disorganization: Personal and Social* (New York: Alfred A. Knopf, 1952).

Bloch, Herbert A., and Frank T. Flynn, *Delinquency: The Juvenile Offender In America Today* (New York: Random House, 1956).

Blumer, Herbert, "The Field of Collective Behavior," *Principles Of Sociology*, Alfred M. Lee, editor (New York: Barnes and Noble, 1951).

Blumer, Herbert, "Sociological Analysis and the Variable," *American Sociological Review*, 21 (December 1956).

Bogardus, Emory S., "Gangs of Mexican-American Youth," *Sociology and Social Research*, XXVIII (September-October 1943).

Bossard, James H. S., *The Sociology of Child Development* (New York: Harper and Brothers, 1948).

Bromberg, Walter, *Crime and the Mind: Outline of Psychiatric Criminology* (Philadelphia: J. B. Lippincott Company, 1948).

Bronowski, J., *The Face of Violence* (New York: George Braziller, 1955).

Brown, Lawrence G., *Social Pathology* (New York: F. S. Crofts and Company, 1945).

Cartwright, Dorwin, and Alvin Zander, *Group Dynamics Research Theory* (New York: Row, Peterson and Company, 1953).

Cassirer, Ernst, *The Myth of the State* (Garden City: Doubleday and Company, 1955).

Chambers, Bradford, "Juvenile Gangs of New York," *American Mercury*, LXII (April 1946).

Chapple, Eliot Dismore, and Carleton Stevens Coon, *Principles of Anthropology* (New York: Henry Holt and Company, 1942).

Chasan, Will, "Teen Age Gangs From the Inside," *New York Times Magazine* (March 21, 1954).

Cohen, Albert K., *Delinquent Boys: The Culture of the Gang* (Glencoe: The Free Press, 1955).

Cooley, Charles H., *Human Nature and the Social Order* (New York: Charles Scribner's Sons, 1922).

Crazzolara, P., "Die Gar-Ceremonie bei den Neuer," *Africa*, 5 (Resume), cited in W. I. Thomas, *Primitive Behavior* (New York: 1937).

Crawford, Paul, *Working With Teen-Age Gangs* (New York: The Welfare Council of New York, 1950).

Cuber, John F., and Robert A. Harper, *Problems of American Society—Values in Conflict* (New York: Henry Holt and Company, 1951).

Davie, Maurice R., "Pattern of Urban Growth," *Studies in The Science of Society*, George R. Murdock, editor (New Haven: Yale University Press, 1937).

Davis, Kingsley, "Adolescence and the Social Structure," *The Annals of the American Academy of Political and Social Science*, 236 (November 1944).

Davis, Kingsley, "The Sociology of Parent-Youth Conflict," *American Sociological Review*, X (August, 1940).

Dewey, John, *Human Nature and Conduct* (New York: Henry Holt and Company, 1923).

Eisenstadt, S. N., *From Generation to Generation: Age Groups and Social Structure* (Glencoe, Ill.: Free Press, 1956).

Erikson, Erik H., *Childhood and Society* (New York: Norton, 1950).

Ferrero, Guglielmo, *Pouvoir* (New York: Brentano's, 1942).

Fletcher, A. C. and F. La Flesche, "The Omaha Tribe," *Bureau of American Ethnology, Annual Report*, No. 27.

Frazer, James G., *The Golden Bough* (New York: The Macmillan Company, 1947).

Fromm, Erich, *The Sane Society* (New York: Rinehart and Company, Inc., 1955).

Furfey, Paul H., *The Gang Age* (New York: The Macmillan Company, 1928).

Gifford, E. W., "Tongan Society," *Bernice P. Bishop Museum Bulletin*, 61 (1924).

Glueck, Sheldon and Eleanor, *Delinquents in the Making* (New York: Harper and Brothers, 1952).

Glueck, Sheldon and Eleanor, *Unraveling Juvenile Delinquency* (New York: Commonwealth Fund, 1950).

Havighurst, Robert J., and Hilda Taba, *Adolescent Character and Personality* (New York: John Wiley and Sons, 1949).

Hollingshead, August, *Elmtown's Youth* (New York: John Wiley and Sons, 1945).

Hyman, Sidney, "The Issue of Presidential Disability," *New York Times Magazine* (February 26, 1956).

Inkeles, Alex, "Some Sociological Observations on Culture and Personality Studies," *Personality in Nature, Society, and Culture,* Clyde Kluckhohn, Henry A. Murray, and David Schneider, editors (New York: Alfred A. Knopf, 1954).

Kardiner, Abram, *Psychological Frontiers of Society* (New York: Columbia University Press, 1945).

Kinsey, Alfred C., Wardell B. Pomeroy, and Clyde E. Martin, *Sexual Behavior In the Human Male* (Philadelphia: W. B. Saunders Company, 1948).

Kramer, Dale and Madeline Karr, *Teen Age Gangs* (New York: Henry Holt and Company, 1953).

LaBarre, Weston, "The Cultural Basis of Emotions and Gestures," *Personal Character and Cultural Milieu,* Douglas A. Haring, editor (Syracuse: 1948).

Lander, Bernard, *Toward an Understanding of Juvenile Delinquency* (New York: Columbia University Press, 1954).

Landis, Carney, and M. Marjorie Bolles, *Textbook of Abnormal Psychology* (New York: Macmillan Company, 1948).

Lindesmith, Alfred R., *Opiate Addiction* (Bloomington, Ind.: 1947).

Lowie, Robert H., *An Introduction to Cultural Anthropology* (New York: Farrar and Rinehart, Inc., 1941).

Lynes, Russell, *A Surfeit of Honey* (New York: Harper and Brothers, 1957).

Malinowski, Bronislaw, *The Sexual Life of Savages* (New York: Eugenics Publishing Company, 1929).

Malinowski, Bronislaw, *The Dynamics of Culture Change: An Inquiry into Race Relations in Africa* (New Haven: Yale University Press, 1945).

Mannheim, Karl, *Ideology and Utopia* (New York: Harcourt Brace and Company, 1938).

Marcel, Gabriel, *Man Against Society* (Chicago: Henry Regnery Company, 1952).

May, Rollo, *The Meaning of Anxiety* (New York: Ronald Press Company, 1950).

Mead, George H., *Mind, Self, and Society* (Chicago: The University of Chicago Press, 1934).

Mead, Margaret, *From the South Seas* (New York: William Morrow and Company 1939).

Mead, Margaret, *Growing Up In New Guinea* (New York: William Morrow and Company, 1939).

Mead, Margaret, *New Lives for Old: Cultural Transformation-Manus, 1928-1953* (New York: William Morrow and Company, 1956).

Mead, Margaret, *Sex and Temperament in Three Primitive Societies* (New York: William Morrow and Company, 1935).

Mead, Margaret, *Male and Female* (New York: William Morrow and Company, 1949).

Miller, Nathan, "Secret Societies," *Encyclopedia of the Social Sciences*, XIII, 621-623 (New York: The Macmillan Co., 1942).

Milosz, Czeslaw, *The Captive Mind* (New York: Alfred A. Knopf, 1953).

Neumeyer, Martin H., *Juvenile Delinquency in Modern Society* (New York: D. Van Nostrand Company, Inc., 1949).

New York City Police Department, *Annual Report*, 1955.

New York City Police Dept. Report, *Spring* 3100, XXVII, No. 3 (March 1956).

New York City Youth Board News, VII (January, 1955).

Parsons, Talcott, *The Social System* (Glencoe, Ill: Free Press, 1951).

Parsons, Talcott, "Age and Sex in the Social Structure of the United States," *American Sociological Review*, VII (1942).

Porterfield, Austin L., *Youth in Trouble* (Fort Worth; Leo Potishman Foundation, 1946).

Radin, Paul, *The World of Primitive Man* (New York: Henry Schuman, 1953).

Redl, Fritz, "The Psychology of Gang Formation and the Treatment of Juvenile Delinquents," *The Psychoanalytic Study of the Child*, Anna Freud et al.; editors (New York, International Universities Press, 1945).

Riesman, David, *The Lonely Crowd* (New Haven: Yale University Press, 1950).

Riesman, David, *Faces in the Crowd* (New Haven: Yale University Press, 1952).

Rogers, Kenneth, *Street Gangs in Toronto* (Toronto: Ryerson Press, 1945).

Roscoe, J., *The Northern Bantu* (Cambridge University Press, 1915).

Sargent, S. S., *Social Psychology* (New York: The Ronald Press Company, 1950).

Slavson, S. R., *An Introduction to Group Therapy* (Commonwealth Fund, 1943).

Spaulding, Charles B., "Cliques, Gangs and Networks," *Sociology and Social Research*, XXXII (July- August, 1948).

Sullivan, Harry Stack, *The Interpersonal Theory of Psychiatry* (New York: W. W. Norton and Company, Inc., 1953).

Taft, Donald R., *Criminology* (New York: The Macmillan Company, 1950).

Tannenbaum, Frank, *Crime and the Community* (Boston: Ginn and Company, 1938).

Teeters, Negley K., and John Otto Reinemann, *The Challenge of Delinquency* (New York: Prentice Hall, Inc., 1950).

Thomas, William I., *Primitive Behavior* (New York: McGraw-Hill Book Co., Inc., 1937.)

Thrasher, Frederic, *The Gang* (Chicago: The University of Chicago Press, 1936).

Valentine, Alan, *The Age of Conformity* (Chicago: Henry Regnery Company, 1954).

Waller, Willard, *The Family: A Dynamic Interpretation* (New York: Dryden Press, 1938).

Wattenberg, William A., and James J. Balistrieri, "Automobile Theft: A 'Favored Group' Delinquency," *American Journal of Sociology*, LVII (May 1952).

Wattenberg, William A., and James J. Balistrieri, "Gang Membership and Juvenile Misconduct," *American Sociological Review*, XV (December 1950).

Webster, Hutton, *Primitive Secret Societies* (New York: The Macmillan Company, 1932).

Whyte, William F., *Street Corner Society* (Chicago: The University of Chicago Press, 1955).

Williams, Frankwood, *Adolescence: Studies in Mental Hygiene* (New York, 1930).

Wolfe, Thomas, *The Web and the Rock* (New York: Sun Dial Press, 1940).

Wylie, Philip, *Generation of Vipers* (New York: Farrar and Rinehart, 1942).

Znaniecki, Florian, *The Method of Sociology* (New York, Farrar and Rinehart, Inc., 1934).

INDEX OF NAMES

Adler, A., 155, 156, 163, 187, 207, 217
Asbury, H., 129
Atlas, C., 165
Auden, W. H., 145

Baldwin, J., 157
Balistrieri, J., 184
Barnett, L., 115
Bateson, G., 40, 89, 91
Beaser, H. W., 149
Beck, B., 166
Bender, L., 146
Benedict, R., XV, 24, 117, 126, 127
Berle, A., 208
Bettelheim, B., 86, 87, 89, 90, 105, 112, 116, 140
Bloch, H., 8, 13, 16, 37, 124, 135, 136
Blumer, H., 4, 186
Bogardus, E., 169
Bronowski, J., 158
Brown, L. G., 145
Burgess, E., 5

Chambers, B., 149
Chapple, E., 87, 88, 91, 93, 101
Chasan, W., 166
Clendener, R., 149
Cohen, A., XIV, 3, 15, 102, 175ff.
Cole, L., 37
Cooley, C. H., 157
Coon, C., 87, 88, 91, 93, 101
Crawford, P., 167

Darwin, C., 170
Davie, M., 5
Davis, K., 12, 108
Dewey, J., 157
Durkheim, E., 5

Einstein, A., 158
Eisenstadt, S., 74
Erikson, E., 159

Ferrero, G., 208
Fitzgerald, F. S. XIII
Frazer, J., 87, 93, 112, 131

Freud, S., 26
Fromm, E., 145, 155, 157, 172

Gillen, F., 60, 113
Gross, F., 208
Gumplowicz, L., 8, 170

Hall, G. S., 21
Hoijer, H., 91
Hemingway, E., XIII
Hightower, P., 130
Hollingshead, A., 130

Ibsen, H., 157
Inkeles, A., 24

James, W., 136, 157, 187

Kardiner, A., 135
Kennedy, S., 150
Kinsey, A., 103, 108, 110
Kvaraceus, W., 130

Lander, B., 5
Lewin, K., 119, 128, 157
Lindesmith, A., 16
Lindner, R., 69, 149, 154, 173, 207
Lowie, R., 87, 88
Lynd, R., 36
Lynes, R., 50

Malinowski, B., 101, 121, 122, 140, 144
Mannheim, K., 163, 172, 173
Marcel, G., 157, 158
Marquand, J., 37
Maslow, A., 144
May, R., 153, 154, 155
Mead, G. H. 157
Mead, M., XV, 71, 75, 86, 90, 92, 103, 105, 112, 124, 125
Miller, A., 68
Miller, N., 121, 128
Morgan, L., 22
Mursell, G., 130

O'Neill, E., 19

228

INDEX OF NAMES

Park, R., 5
Pareto, V., 205
Parsons, T., 12, 102, 103, 108
Porterfield, A., 8, 15

Radin, P., 112, 129
Ratzenhofer, G., 143
Redl, F., 14
Riesman, D., 145, 154, 162

Slavson, S. R., 187
Small, A., 143
Spencer, W. B., 60, 113
Sullivan, H. S., 157, 173

Taft, D., 171
Tannenbaum, F., 143, 161, 162
Tarkington, B., 19
Thomas, W. I., 61, 143, 144

Thrasher F., XIV, 3, 6, 102, 103, 175, 207
Twain, M., 19
Tylor, E., 22, 113, 122

Valentine, A., 145
Van Gennep, A., 101

Waller, W., 80
Wattenberg, W., 184
Webster, H., 86, 87, 88, 89, 90, 91, 92, 93, 126
Westermarck, E., 22
Whelan, R., 150
Wylie, P., 103
Whyte, W. F., 95
Williams, F., 11, 102
Wolfe, T., 166

Znaniecki, F., 16

SUBJECT INDEX

Adolescence: 9 ff., 19 ff.
  adverse conditions, 159
  ambivalence, 103 ff.
  comparison of primitive and modern, 116
  contradictions, 108
  prolongation, 12
  protest, 48
  subculture, 13, 14, 15
Age Grading, 42, 101
Alienation, 154
Ambivalence, 79
Anomie, 81
Anxiety, 153
Automobile, 131, 183 ff.

Bullroarer, 131

Children:
  deference, 41
  in colonial America, 41
  Omaha, 41
  Psychological forces, 46
  traditions, 43
Child Rearing Practices, 24
Churinga, 131
Conformity, 154
Culture and Personality School, 23

Delinquency:
  gradient, 4
  critique of theories, 175 ff.
Ecological Analysis, 193
Emotions, 44 ff.

Fraternities, 9, 59, 106, 136
Functional Interpretation, 25, 122, 140

Gang:
  code, 163
  conflict, 161
  criticism of theories, 4 ff., 164
  hangout, 100
  Harlem, 99, 106, 133
  ideology, 208
  leadership, 208
  lower class compared to middle class, 7ff., 15, 110, 167, 172, 174, 177, 179, 182, 204, 209
  Pachuco, 95, 106, 123
  philosophy, 161
  program, 208
  rituals, 25, 96
  routine, 177
  uniforms, 168
  war against world, 175
  weapons, 168

Hazing, 59, 106
Homosexuality, 103 ff.

Institutions:
  functional interpretation, 25
  related to personality, 23
Interstitial:
  area, 6
  period, 12
Inversion:
  dependent relationships, 49
  sexual, 74 ff., 81, 103 ff.

Ketman, 203, 204

Latent Functions, 26
Loss of Self, 157
Lower Class, 110, 167 ff., 174, 177, 179, 182

Manhood:
  symbols of, 164 ff.
Maturity, 44
Mensuren, 57
Middle Class, 15, 49, 110, 204, 209
Myths, 82

Needs, 143
Patterns:
  symmetrical vs. complementary, 41
Power:
  political, 208
  relations between age groups, 37, 48
  relations between sexes, 37, 50
Puberty Rites, 25 ff., 54, 86 ff.

SUBJECT INDEX

analytic chart, 86 ff.
circumcision, 60, 97, 124, 197
decoration, 55, 95
hazing, 59, 106
myth of rebirth, 82, 111
new language, 62, 99
new name, 61, 99
new personality, 63
scarification, 57 ff., 97
segregation, 67, 100
sexual ambivalence, 74, 103
Rites of Passage, 101, 139
Schools, 167
Sex Distinctions, 36

Societies:
for detailed analysis and complete listing see chart p. 86 ff.
African Chaga, 89
Amoxosa, 88
Andaman Islanders, 87, 101
Arapesh, 63, 71, 74
Arunta, 60, 87, 90, 92
Bagesu, 56
Bakitara, 59
Bakongo, 64, 84
Bechuana, 88
Bondei, 88
Bukaya, 93
Coast Murring, 92
Comanche, 120, 135
Crow, 44
Dukduk, 88
Euahlayi, 91
Fijians, 86, 87, 91
Iatmul, 91, 92
Ilpirra, 90
Jabim, 91
Kaffir, 88, 134
Kai, 93
Kakian, 93
Koombanggary, 91
Kurnai, 91
Kwakiutl, 93

Lower Murray Tribe, 92
Macquarrie, 91
Madagascar, 87
Maidu Indians, 88
Mandingoes, 88
Manus, 119, 134
Marquesan, 86
Masai, 86, 87, 116
Melanesian, 107
Mundugumor, 87, 116, 117, 119, 120, 133
Murngin, 92
Murrumbidgee, 92
Nandi, 61, 116
Neuer 58
New South Wales, 92
New Zealanders, 86
North American Indians, 91, 135
Northern New Guinea, 87
Omaha, 38, 39, 89
Omeo, 91
Ona, 91
Pawnee, 63, 65
Poro, 86, 91, 93, 117, 119
Samoa, 119, 124, 125
Solomon Islanders, 86
Sulka, 87
Susu, 88
Tahitians, 86
Tami, 93
Tchambuli, 86, 87
Tikopia, 116
Tonga, 60
Torres Straits, 91
Trobriand Islanders, 101
Tuscarora Indians, 91
Urrabuna, 92
Vey, 87
Yabim, 93
Symbols of Manhood, 163 ff.

Tamberan Cult, 74
Tattooing, 95, 96, 125
Truancy, 181